SONOMA VALLEY

ELIZABETH LINHART VENEMAN

Contents

SONOMA VALLEY

SOUTHERN SONOMA

Southern Sonoma is one of those places that doctors should send the hypertensive, because there's something about the place that makes your blood pressure drop despite having plenty of visitors. The Sonoma Valley and neighboring Carneros region are just so laid-back and slow-going that even finding parking is unnervingly easy, and sitting in what passes as rush-hour traffic here will barely get you tapping your fingers.

Apparently it has always been a pretty good, stress-free life in these parts. Mother Nature might mix things up a bit with the occasional fire or earthquake, but she also provides hot springs, redwood forests, burbling streams, fertile soils, and a friendly climate. In terms of climate, scenery, and growing conditions, the Sonoma Valley is a mini Napa Valley, but it

has been spared the same level of development by some favorable rolls of the historical dice.

In a sense, southern Sonoma is fairly close to paradise: a place where wine, history, scenery, and some of the best California produce combine in an area small enough to tour in a day or two. A visitor can spend the morning sipping splendid wine and be strolling through historic Victorian splendor by the afternoon, or might traverse a muddy mountain one hour and spend the next relaxing in a spa covered in therapeutic mud. There are few other parts of the Wine County as compact yet packed with opportunity.

Hundreds of years ago, these same natural attributes attracted numerous Native American tribes, who lived peacefully side by side without the turf battles common elsewhere. Even

© ELIZABETH LINHART VENEMAN

SOUTHERN SONOMA

HIGHLIGHTS

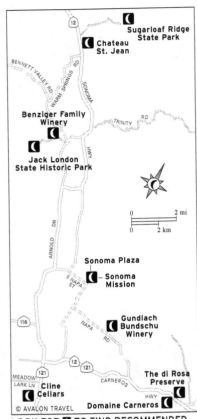

mer day at this historic winery's outdoor amphitheater (page 13).

(Sonoma Plaza: Spend an afternoon exploring the eclectic shops, tasting local boutique wine, and touring the historic sites (page 18).

(Sonoma Mission: The last California mission has been immaculately restored. Its museum sheds light on the important role it played in the region's history (page 18).

(Benziger Family Winery: See Benziger's biodynamic vineyards from a tractor-drawn tram, the most entertaining tour in the valley (page 38).

(Jack London State Historic Park: Scenic hiking trails surround the former residence of the valley's prolific author and adventurer, Jack London (page 40).

(Chateau St. Jean: Enjoy the reserve tasting and learn about wine while relaxing on the patio overlooking the valley (page 47).

(Sugarloaf Ridge State Park: Meander down the short nature trail or hike to the top of Bald Mountain for the best valley views (page 52).

(Cline Cellars: Enter an oasis of green at this historic winery next to a natural spring. You can also explore all of California's missions in miniature (page 59).

(Domaine Carneros: Take a private tour and learn how champagne is made, all with a glass of bubbly in hand (page 63).

(The di Rosa Preserve: Enter a wonderland of art and leave the Wine Country behind (page 66).

LOOK FOR (TO FIND RECOMMENDED SIGHTS, ACTIVITIES, DINING, AND LODGING.

(Gundlach Bundschu Winery: Witness Shakespeare or Mozart performed on a sum-

author Jack London sensed something intoxicating in the air. He relocated from Oakland to put down deep roots in the Sonoma Valley, transforming himself from working-class hero to gentleman farmer and landowner. The main characters in his 1913 novel *Valley of the Moon* spend months wandering up and down California in search of their nirvana, the Sonoma Valley.

The lucky locals have worked hard against the odds to keep their valley and flatlands so inviting. In the 1960s, they fought off a plan developed by car-crazed California to drive a freeway down the middle of Sonoma Valley. Instead it was built through the middle of Santa Rosa to the west. While fame and freeways brought the heaving masses to Napa and northern Sonoma, the valley became the land that development forgot.

By 1980 there was a grand total of two sets of traffic lights—and there aren't many more now. One of the busiest intersections in the valley, on the south side of Sonoma Plaza, is still very politely controlled by four simple stop signs. The valley's modern custodians are still a potent force, even defending a few local chickens in downtown Sonoma threatened with re-settlement. Such is the passion here to keep the "slow" in this place the locals call Slownoma.

Can the valley keep its identity amid modern population and development pressures? It's trying hard, but is swimming against the tide of tourism. Wineries and hotels are being mopped up by bigger and bigger conglomerates. The succulent local food is transforming into ever more expensive "cuisine." An average family home in the valley now costs more than $1.5 million. Visit quickly before Napa hops over the mountains, pushes up the prices, and ends the mellow fun.

In the long term, there's more hope for Carneros, simply because there is no "there" there. The vineyards that are slowly covering any remaining pastureland (that is, the land that's not already underwater) are effectively spiking future development. Chances are that nothing much will change here anytime soon—except perhaps that rush-hour traffic on the two-lane roads may worsen as more people visit or move to the Napa and Sonoma Valleys.

PLANNING YOUR TIME

The Sonoma Valley and Carneros are two of the easiest parts of Wine Country to visit, each having just one main road running its entire length. A visit to Carneros can be slightly harder to plan due to the lack of major towns, but it's easy enough to stop there for a few hours on the way to or from Sonoma and Napa.

Within the 17-mile-long Sonoma Valley,

the wineries, shops, and hotels are generally centered around the towns of **Glen Ellen** and neighboring **Kenwood,** and Sonoma itself. Without a well-planned strategy, it can be time-consuming to try to visit wineries at both the northern and southern ends of the valley, especially when the Sonoma Highway (Highway 12) slows down with northbound rush-hour traffic in the afternoon.

If you do find yourself traveling slower than you like on Highway 12, it's worth heading a few miles west at Glen Ellen or Boyes Hot Springs to pick up Arnold Drive, an alternative north-south route in the valley. It runs mainly through residential areas, but sticking to the 30 mph speed limit on this quiet road might be more relaxing than being tailgated on Highway 12. It runs right down to the junction with Highway 121 in **Carneros.**

It can easily take a full day to visit about five wineries around Sonoma and Kenwood, or in Carneros, and still have enough time for lunch without getting indigestion. An alternative strategy might be to pick four or five wineries that specialize in a particular wine. Or spend a full day exploring the shops and historic sights of Sonoma while tasting wine at several dedicated tasting rooms on the Sonoma Plaza. There are also four wineries just outside downtown.

If you do plan to visit wineries throughout the valley, get an early start. Their busiest times are mid-late afternoon, especially for the wineries around Kenwood, which most visitors only get to toward the end of the day. Most wineries open at 10am (a few at 11am) and close between 4:30pm and 6pm, depending on the season.

Wineries along the Carneros Highway (Highway 121) are generally clustered at the eastern and western ends of Carneros. Those at the western end include Viansa, Gloria Ferrer, and Cline, on the way from San Francisco to Sonoma. Those farther east are more spread out and generally lie between the road to Sonoma (Napa Road or Highway 12) and the city of Napa. They include Artesa, Bouchaine, and Michael Mondavi Family Winery.

For some reason very few wineries have any sizable trees in their parking lots, preferring instead to plant trees that either look stunted or have minimal leaf cover. Consequently there's usually no shade, and for the nine months of the year that the sun shines, parked cars quickly heat up to the temperature of an oven. Take a cooler if you plan a picnic or want to prevent that $100 bottle of wine from trying to become vinegar.

Compared to the Napa Valley, wine tasting in the Sonoma Valley is refreshingly cheap. Most wineries charge a tasting fee of either $5 or $10, perhaps more for tasting the more expensive reserve wines. It's a refreshing change from the Napa Valley, where $25 tasting experiences have become the norm. As in many other parts of the Wine Country, the tasting fee can sometimes be recouped when you buy one or more bottles of wine. Another way to curb expenses is to stop in at the **Sonoma Valley Visitors Bureau** (453 1st St. E., Sonoma, 866/996-1090, www.sonomavalley.com, 9am-5pm Mon.-Sat., 10am-5pm Sun.) and pick up free passes or "2 for 1" tasting specials dropped off by many nearby wineries.

GETTING THERE

A century ago there were more ways to get to Sonoma than there are today—by ferry, train, stagecoach, automobile, or plane. The train is long gone, ferries come nowhere near, the tiny local airports have no scheduled services, and there is no direct bus service to Sonoma, just some local connections to Santa Rosa and Petaluma—all of which leaves the car with a monopoly.

Getting there by car, however, is straightforward. From San Francisco the most traveled route is via **U.S. 101, Highway 37,** and **Highway 121,** which leads to the heart of Carneros and to the junction of **Highway 12** to Sonoma and the Sonoma Valley. The drive from the Golden Gate Bridge to Sonoma takes just under an hour, longer if you hit afternoon rush-hour traffic.

To avoid Sonoma and go straight to Glen Ellen, go straight on **Arnold Drive** at the junction and gas station about five miles after

joining Highway 121. It is a slower road but avoids heavy traffic and leads to the heart of Glen Ellen.

Other routes to the area from the north and east include Highway 12 east into the valley from U.S. Highway 101 at Santa Rosa, or Highway 37 west from I-80 at Vallejo to the junction of Highway 121. Be warned that Highways 37 and 121 through Carneros are infamous for nasty accidents due to the unexpected bends and dips, dawdling tourists, and high volume of commuter (in other words, speeding) traffic. One accident seemingly far away can clog all surrounding roads and highways for hours.

GETTING AROUND
By Car

The car is how most people get around Carneros and the Sonoma Valley. While navigating the area is fairly straightforward, keep in mind that the many local highways double as roads with their own names. This can be confusing, particularly when you stumble upon addresses written two different ways. While making your way around southern Sonoma, keep in mind that Highway 12 is also the Sonoma Highway from Santa Rosa to Sonoma, Broadway in the town of Sonoma, and the Carneros Highway when it joins Highway 121 and bends east toward Vallejo. Highway 121 also continues east until it T's with Arnold Drive, joining it south toward U.S. Highway 101. Along this stretch it is known both as Highway 121 and Arnold Drive. North of the T, Arnold Drive is also Highway 116, until the highway shoots off to the west toward Petaluma.

By Bus

If driving sounds too confusing, you can opt for public transit. **Sonoma County Transit** (707/576-7433, www.sctransit.com, $1.25-3.45) has several routes through the Sonoma Valley and to Santa Rosa, Guerneville, and other spots in the Russian River Valley as well.

By Bike

Biking is a great way to see the valley and

avoid the car-to-winery-to-car relay. To keep it fun instead of tiring, stick to the wineries around Sonoma and Glen Ellen and avoid long distances, summer heat, and tipsy drivers on major thoroughfares. Cruising around the empty flatlands of eastern Carneros on two wheels is a rewarding way to get off the beaten track and visit less-crowded wineries. Unfortunately, the western region is dominated by the busy (and narrow) thoroughfares, making for a white-knuckled cycling experience rather than a relaxing afternoon ride. The area around downtown Sonoma, however, is perfect for exploring by bike. The visitors bureau has a helpful map that gives the best bike routes, including one that hits all the historic downtown sites as well as the Ravenswood, Buena Vista, and Gundlach Bundschu wineries, which are within a mile or two of the plaza.

Some hotels and B&Bs have their own bicycles for rent. Otherwise, two shops rent bikes and supply tour maps. **Sonoma Valley Cyclery** (20091 Broadway, Sonoma, 707/935-3377, 10am-6pm Mon.-Sat., 10am-4pm Sun., $6-15/hour, $25-65/day) rents bikes, including mountain and tandem bikes, as well as bike trailers for kids. For an extra $25, you can have your bike delivered and picked up from your hotel, but maps and loads of advice come at no extra charge.

There is no physical address for the **Goodtime Touring Company** (707/938-0453 or 888/525-0453, www.goodtimetouring.com, $25-45/day), but it will deliver bikes to your hotel. It also rents basic bikes, road bikes, and tandems. The closest thing to biking luxury (short of having someone else pedal) is Goodtime's half-day guided tour of Sonoma-area or Kenwood-area wineries, which includes a gourmet lunch and wine-tasting fees. Those tours are $135, start at 10:30am, and conclude around 3:30pm.

Tours

The **Sonoma Valley Wine Trolley** (707/938-2600 or 877/946-3876, www.sonomavalley-winetrolley.com, 10:30am-4:30pm, $99) is another option. Departing from the Sonoma Plaza daily at 10:30am, the trolley (actually a four-wheeled replica of a San Francisco cable car) visits four wineries, where guests enjoy private tastings and the occasional tour. Along the way the driver points out sites of historical interest and around noon, lays out a gourmet picnic lunch supplied by **the girl & the fig** restaurant (110 W. Spain St., Sonoma, 707/938-3634, www.thegirlandthefig.com, 11:30am-10pm Sun.-Mon., 11:30am-11pm Fri.-Sat., $20).

You can also tour the wineries via Segway, albeit a little less leisurely and gracefully. **Sonoma Segway** (524 Broadway, Sonoma, 707/938-2080, www.sonomasegway.com, $99-129/tour, $40/hour rental) offers a 3.5-hour tour that includes a visit to a local winery, a stop at a local food-based business, and a full-fledged visit to historic Sonoma. You'll start off with a lesson on the Segway, and when you finish you'll get a complimentary bottle of wine (if you're of age, of course). If you'd prefer to traverse the Sonoma streets and paths on your own, rent a Segway—for just two hours or up to a month at a time.

Sonoma Valley

They must feed the ducks of Sonoma Plaza something special to make them stick around the car-choked plaza rather than flying a few miles north to the serenity of the valley. Getting out of Sonoma, as fascinating and historic as it is, is the only way to really get an idea of what valley residents are fighting to preserve.

The road north out of Sonoma passes fast-food outlets and a strip mall, about as close to urban sprawl as there is. In keeping with the valley's laid-back nature, it's a spaced-out, relaxed sort of sprawl linking Sonoma and three spring towns: Boyes Hot Springs, Fetters Hot Springs, and Agua Caliente, all of which look like they could do with a rejuvenating spa treatment themselves.

The towns end abruptly, and the serene valley lies ahead. Plum, walnut, and peach orchards once shared the valley with cows that must have thought they'd died and gone to heaven to be grazing here. Now the mighty vine has taken over the valley floor. There's really little else but green things along the Sonoma Highway, except the loose-knit community of **Kenwood** (with the valley's cheapest gas) and, at the border of Santa Rosa, the retirement community of Oakmont.

Slightly off the main road southeast of Kenwood, the town of **Glen Ellen** is a Wine Country town with plenty of fancy restaurants and inns hidden in the surrounding woods yet still with the valley's nice laid-back vibe. It's truly a one-street town, with a curious dogleg halfway down the main street that is the real center of it all—not that there's all that much happening. It has managed to remain quaint without succumbing to the fake frills that so many other old towns in the United States get wrapped in. One of the biggest buildings is an auto shop, a sign that real life still takes place in this part of the valley.

The Wines
The volcanic soils of the hot mountainsides and the rich alluvial plains of the valley floor make Sonoma an ideal place to grow a plethora of grape varietals, a fact the missionaries and immigrants of the 1800s quickly discovered. The valley doesn't have quite the number of different growing conditions and soils of the larger Napa Valley, but winemakers maintain that its wines can be just as good.

In many ways the Sonoma Valley and Napa Valley are more alike than different. Both have productive mountain growing regions, both are proportionally similar, face the same direction, and are affected by the same wind and rain patterns. The fact that Sonoma's early head start in winemaking in the mid-1800s petered out by the early 1900s seems to have had more to do with chance and bad business decisions by the early pioneers like Agoston Haraszthy. The larger Napa Valley wineries established in the late 1800s gained more commercial traction, perhaps due the greater availability of land. Once a critical mass of winemaking had been reached, there was no turning back.

Climate-wise, the Sonoma Valley has three distinct appellations. The **Sonoma Valley** AVA is the largest and includes some or all of the other two. It stretches from the top of the valley near Santa Rosa all the way down to the bay, bordered by 3,000-foot-high mountains on each side and encompassing 116,000 acres of land and about 13,000 acres of vineyards (compare that to the Napa Valley's 35,000 acres of vineyards).

The valley acts like a giant funnel, channeling cooler air (and sometimes fog) up from the bay, leaving the mountainsides to bask in warm sunshine. Zinfandel loves the higher, hotter elevations, while cabernet and merlot ripen well on hillsides and the warmer north end of the valley. Pinot noir, chardonnay, and other white varietals prefer the slightly cooler valley floor, especially farther south toward Carneros.

The 800 acres of vineyards in the cooler and rockier **Sonoma Mountain** appellation just up

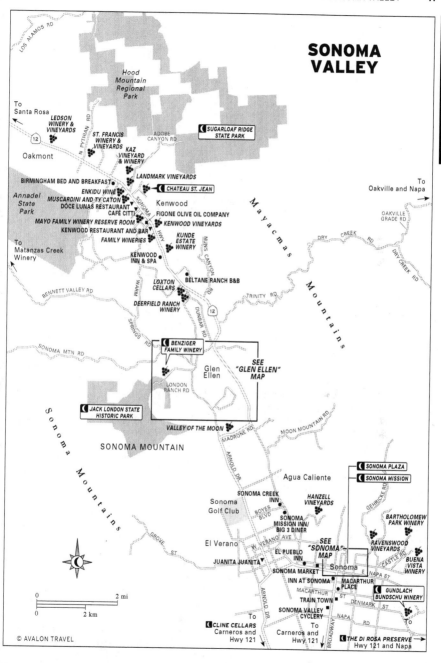

SONOMA VALLEY

To Santa Rosa

Hood Mountain Regional Park

LOS ALAMOS RD

LEDSON WINERY & VINEYARDS

ST. FRANCIS WINERY & VINEYARDS

KAZ VINEYARD & WINERY

Oakmont

N PYTHIAN RD

ADOBE CANYON RD

SUGARLOAF RIDGE STATE PARK

LANDMARK VINEYARDS

BIRMINGHAM BED AND BREAKFAST

ENKIDU WINE

MUSCARDINI AND TY CATON

DÓCE LUNAS RESTAURANT

CAFÉ CITTI

MAYO FAMILY WINERY RESERVE ROOM

KENWOOD RESTAURANT AND BAR

FAMILY WINERIES

Annadel State Park

CHATEAU ST. JEAN

Kenwood

FIGONE OLIVE OIL COMPANY

KENWOOD VINEYARDS

KUNDE ESTATE WINERY

SONOMA HWY

To Matanzas Creek Winery

KENWOOD INN & SPA

BELTANE RANCH B&B

LOXTON CELLARS

DEERFIELD RANCH WINERY

BENNETT VALLEY RD

WARM SPRINGS

NUNS CANYON RD

TRINITY RD

DUNBAR RD

SONOMA MTN RD

BENZIGER FAMILY WINERY

Glen Ellen

SEE "GLEN ELLEN" MAP

LONDON RANCH RD

JACK LONDON STATE HISTORIC PARK

VALLEY OF THE MOON

SONOMA MOUNTAIN

MADRONE RD

MOON MOUNTAIN RD

M a y a c m a s   M o u n t a i n s

To Oakville and Napa

OAKVILLE GRADE RD

DRY CREEK RD

S o n o m a   M o u n t a i n s

GROVE ST

ARNOLD DR

SONOMA PLAZA

SONOMA MISSION

Agua Caliente

SONOMA CREEK INN

HANZELL VINEYARDS

Sonoma Golf Club

BOYES BLVD

SONOMA MISSION INN/ BIG 3 DINER

SEE "SONOMA" MAP

El Verano

W VERANO AVE

EL PUEBLO INN

JUANITA JUANITA

SONOMA MARKET

INN AT SONOMA

Sonoma

MACARTHUR ST

TRAIN TOWN

SONOMA VALLEY CYCLERY

CLINE CELLARS

To Carneros and Hwy 121

ARNOLD DR

To Carneros and Hwy 121

GEHRICKE RD

BARTHOLOMEW PARK WINERY

RAVENSWOOD VINEYARDS

CASTLE RD

BUENA VISTA WINERY

E NAPA ST

MACARTHUR PLACE

DENMARK ST

GUNDLACH BUNDSCHU WINERY

BROADWAY

NAPA RD

THE DI ROSA PRESERVE

Hwy 121 and Napa

To

0   2 mi

0   2 km

© AVALON TRAVEL

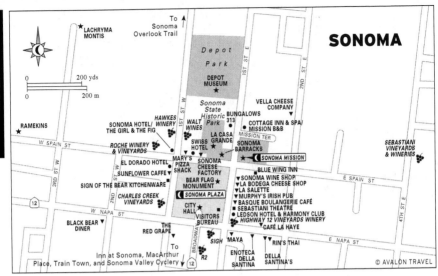

the hill from Glen Ellen vary widely depending on their exposure, but the region is known mostly for its cabernet, although chardonnay, pinot noir, and other white varietals are also grown here.

The newest appellation is **Bennett Valley,** created in 2003, which stretches northwest from the Sonoma Mountains toward Santa Rosa and only just overlaps with Sonoma Valley. Its 700 acres of vineyards are primarily planted with merlot and chardonnay and generally have rocky, volcanic-based soils. A gap in the low mountains west of the Bennett Valley lets ocean air and fog through and keeps growing conditions cool compared to the Sonoma Valley and the mountains.

SONOMA
Wineries
BARTHOLOMEW PARK WINERY

History is the big draw of **Bart Park** (1000 Vineyard Ln., Sonoma, 707/935-9511, www. bartpark.com, 11am-4:30pm daily, tasting $10), as it's known locally. Not only was it part of Sonoma wine pioneer Agoston Haraszthy's original estate, but the winery was also once home to a widower and her 200 Angora cats,

the site of a hospital, and an institution for "delinquent women." When the Bartholomew family bought the property in the 1940s, they returned it to its original purpose. For decades it was a family-owned winery until it was bought by the nearby Gundlach Bundschu Winery in 1994, and they still operate it today as a boutique sibling.

Bart Park's colorful history is detailed in a small but packed museum housed in the old hospital building, along with the small tasting room where you can taste the estate chardonnay, cabernet sauvignon, and merlot, as well as several wines from other vineyards around Sonoma. Only 4,000 cases are produced a year, though for such limited-production wines, they're not too expensive.

The real charm of Bart Park, however, has nothing to do with history or wine. The winery sits in some glorious open space, including what remains of the formal gardens of an old mansion that was burned down (reportedly by the delinquent women) and the small garden of the reproduction Haraszthy home. You can wander freely throughout as if it's your own private garden and find great shaded picnic spots with sweeping views of the valley. Miles of hiking trails start from the winery and wind up the nearby hillsides. Where they start is not obvious, however, so ask someone in the winery for directions. If you want a guided tour of the grounds and winemaking facilities, tours are $20 per person and take place at 11:30am and 2pm Friday and Saturday, and at 2pm on Sunday. Palladian Villa, a replica of Haraszthy's home, is open to the public free of charge noon-3pm Saturday and Sunday.

BUENA VISTA WINERY

Buena Vista (18000 Old Winery Rd., Sonoma, 800/926-1266, www.buenavistawinery.com, 10am-5pm, tasting $10) boasts that it was California's first premium winery, but the claim sounds more grandiose than it actually is. Today's Buena Vista sits on some of the land used by the original Buena Vista Winery, established by Agoston Haraszthy in 1858. Among the old winery structures that remain are the original hand-dug caves (now unsafe and closed), the original champagne cellar, and the old stone press house, which is today the visitors center and helps the site qualify as a California Historic Landmark.

Such status does not preclude Buena Vista from being a thoroughly commercial operation. Owned by the multinational conglomerate Ascentia Wine Estates, it produces half a million cases of wine a year from grapes grown in the Carneros area. The mid-priced Carneros estate wines include pinot noir, cabernet, merlot, chardonnay, and a newly released rosé and are all a pretty good value, costing $20-25. The flagship Ramal Vineyard wines are available only at the winery and include cabernet, pinot noir, chardonnay, syrah, and a port.

The winery attracts an estimated 120,000 visitors a year, and there is no doubt that the winery plays into its status as a tourist destination (there is even a 20-minute play about the founding of the winery). Still, the leafy complex of stone buildings is worth visiting for its historical importance. You can get inside the winery's caves with the Barrel Tour (11am and 2pm daily, $30, by appointment) and taste reserve wines as well as sample those still in the barrel. For a tasting geared more toward varietals than history, the Clonal Tasting ($25, by appointment) offers samples of multiple pinot noirs and chardonnays from different clones.

You can also explore the winery on your own. Like most other large wineries, the tasting room has an array of picnic food to be taken out to one of the plentiful hillside picnic tables. While well shaded, none of them offer much privacy on summer weekends when the winery tends to be swamped by busloads of visitors.

C GUNDLACH BUNDSCHU WINERY

Not many wineries in California can boast that they won awards for their wines almost 100 years ago, but **GunBun** (2000 Denmark St., Sonoma, 707/938-5277, www.gunbun.com, 11am-4:30pm daily, tasting $10), as it's known, is one of them. The 19 Gundlach Bundschu wines entered into the 1915 Panama-Pacific International Exhibition in San Francisco all won medals, and the winery today focuses on squeezing the highest quality wines possible out of its estate vineyards without buying grapes from anywhere else. The other aspect of the estate that makes this a winery worth visiting are the ample outdoor picnicking and entertainment opportunities in a peaceful part of the valley.

Today the 300 acres of Rhinefarm vineyards principally grow cabernet sauvignon, merlot, pinot noir, chardonnay, and gewürztraminer, together with some zinfandel, tempranillo, and a few other minor varietals. The winery's emphasis is on red Bordeaux- and burgundy-style wines, and the cabernets and merlots tend to have plenty of tannic backbone.

The tasting room is housed in one of the original stone winery buildings, which can feel cramped when full of visitors—but the fun atmosphere makes it more bearable. Browse the historical memorabilia, including old wine posters from the 1800s. A short walk away is the 430-foot-long hillside cave, which is often part of the seasonal tours offered once daily (2:30pm Thurs.-Mon., $20). The focus of the tours changes with the seasons, however, so check to see what you'll be seeing when you

HARASZTHY'S LEGACY

Although German and Italian families founded some of the oldest wineries still operating in this part of Sonoma, it was a Hungarian immigrant named **Agoston Haraszthy** who became the area's first big commercial winemaker, and in doing so helped change the face of the California wine industry.

Within a decade of arriving in the state, he had established the pioneering Buena Vista Winery in the Sonoma Valley and was producing some of the best wines in the United States. A decade later he was gone. While his contribution to California's wine industry was important, it was not quite as important as might be suggested by some of the accolades heaped upon him over the centuries.

Haraszthy is often called the Father of California Viticulture, for example, despite the fact that by the time he started bottling wine at Buena Vista the state was already producing about 240,000 gallons of the stuff. He is also sometimes credited with introducing the ubiquitous zinfandel grape to California, but there is some evidence that it arrived in the state even before he did.

One thing that is safe to say is that Haraszthy helped introduce European grapes and European-style commercial wine production to an industry still dependent on its missionary roots. He also had an entrepreneur's sense of self-promotion, which might explain his larger-than-life image.

His wine odyssey started in Wisconsin, of all places. He arrived there from Hungary and helped create what is now Sauk City, but the harsh Wisconsin winter quickly killed the vines he tried to cultivate. In 1849, like modern-day snowbirds, he headed west to the kinder, gentler climate of Southern California.

In San Diego, Haraszthy entered politics as a state legislator, and a combination of political and agricultural aspirations gradually drew him north. The 560-acre plot of land he bought in the Sonoma Valley in 1856 was quickly planted with many European grape varietals, and soon the Buena Vista Winery, with its hand-dug caves, boasted the largest vineyard in the United States and was producing award-winning wines.

He also reportedly helped plant vineyards for other Sonoma families that became (and still are) big names in the wine industry themselves, including Krug, Gundlach, and Bundschu.

By the 1860s, Haraszthy was combining his political and viticultural interests, promoting California wine across the country and getting state funding to travel around Europe to study winemaking techniques.

He returned in 1862 with thousands of vine cuttings collected in almost every European country, from Spain to Turkey. Among them are believed to be the cabernet sauvignon, pinot noir, sauvignon blanc, riesling, and semillon varieties that have become mainstays of the California wine industry.

Exactly what he brought back is open to debate, however, since cataloging and naming conventions in those days were unreliable. Some of those well-known grapes might also have stealthily arrived in California long before, and many others that he brought back never took hold.

Haraszthy's downfall was as sudden as his success. In 1863, facing financial problems, he sold his wine business to the Buena Vista Viticultural Society, a conglomerate in which he held almost half the shares, and took a management position. But within three years he was accused of mismanagement and Enron-style fraud in an attempt to create the biggest winemaker in California; in 1866 he quit.

What happened after this is still a bit of a mystery. Haraszthy left California in 1868 to run a sugar plantation in Nicaragua, but he disappeared in the rain forest and is believed to have been killed by a crocodile.

It's hard not to raise a glass to an immigrant who, in the space of 25 years, had been the co-founder of a Wisconsin town, a businessman, a politician, and a crocodile's meal. But as you raise that glass of mass-produced Sonoma Valley red wine, also consider that it might not taste quite the same (or be as cheap) if not for Agoston Haraszthy.

make a reservation. In winter it might be the cave, and in summer the winemaking facilities. In all cases, the price includes a sit-down tasting. During the summer months, on Friday or Saturday mornings, GunBun also offers a tour of the estate vineyards in a quirky former Swiss military vehicle called a Pinzgauer, followed by a tasting of some of the best estate wines.

GunBun also provides a shady patio, a picnicking area at the top of Towles' Hill overlooking the valley, and even a grassy amphitheater where you can see performances of Mozart during the summer. Overall it has one of the nicest outdoor spaces of any winery in the valley. Check the website for event schedules, or just pack a picnic before visiting.

SEBASTIANI VINEYARDS & WINERY

A visit to Sonoma would not be complete without a trip to the **Sebastiani Winery** (389 4th St. E., Sonoma, 707/933-3230 or 800/888-5532, ext. 3230, www.sebastiani.com, 11am-5pm daily, tasting $10-15), founded by one of the city's most important benefactors and philanthropists, Samuele Sebastiani. It's the only large winery within walking distance of the Sonoma Plaza and has both wines and a history worth exploring.

You may recognize the Sebastiani name from back in the 1970s when the winery pioneered the sale of cheap and cheerful half-gallon bottles of wine. Or from the Sebastiani Theater on the plaza, which the winery founder built along with other long-standing commercial and residential buildings around town. Regardless of the association, the Sebastiani Winery has been a key player in the Sonoma wine business since it was founded in 1904.

After many incarnations, the family sold the winery in 2008 to the Foley Family Wines, who reduced production to less than 200,000 cases of carefully crafted wine. The flagship wine is now the Cherryblock cabernet sauvignon, sourced from an old vineyard near the winery, but the best value is another proprietary wine called Secolo, a Bordeaux blend first made in 2001 to celebrate the winery's 100th anniversary. Both regularly garner 90-plus-point ratings from wine critics, but the Secolo is less than half the price of the $90 Cherryblock. Most of the other wines come from vineyards throughout Sonoma County and are reds, including merlot, pinot noir, zinfandel, and cabernet, together with a barbera that reflects Sebastiani's Italian heritage. Likewise, the winery has expanded its selections of white to now include viognier and roussanne besides just chardonnay. Several wines are available exclusively at the winery, including the Italian-style red blend Dolcino Rosso, and Eye of the Swan, a pinot noir-based wine with a pale pink color that reminded August Sebastiani (the successor to Samuele Sebastiani and an avid amateur ornithologist) of the eyes of a black swan.

The cool, vaulted visitors center is chock-full of Italian-themed gifts, but is on a scale that can feel slightly impersonal, with more of a corporate than a family atmosphere. For the $10 tasting fee, visitors can taste seven wines, and for another $5 they can sample two smaller-production, reserve selections. But really, it's worth taking one of the three daily historical tours of the cellars and old stone buildings to see some of the original winemaking equipment from the early 1900s and learn more about the history of the winery and its family. Complimentary tours are given at 11am, 1pm, and 3pm daily. Other tours and seminars are available by appointment. These generally cost around $20 and reservations should be made a week or so in advance.

RAVENSWOOD VINEYARDS

"To err is human but to zin is divine" is just one of the many droll mottos you'll find at the tasting room of this fun and friendly zinfandel specialist a few blocks north of downtown Sonoma. To use a wine industry pun, visiting here is a barrel of laughs; you're as likely to leave with a zin-inspired bumper sticker as a bottle of the jammy wine.

The vineyard-designate zins at **Ravenswood Vineyards** (18701 Gehricke Rd., 888/669-4679, www.ravenswoodwinery.com, 10am-4:30pm daily, tasting $10-15) exhibit the full range of flavors and styles that the humble zinfandel is capable of producing, from the full-throttle fruitiness of Dry Creek Valley and Amador County zins to the more subtle spiciness of cooler-climate versions from Mendocino and the Russian River Valley. In case none of those help you see the light, there's always the Zen of Zin, a zinfandel-dominated field blend that might help you on your journey of discovery.

Despite being known for zinfandel, Ravenswood also makes some remarkably good Rhône-style wines with the same rustic appeal as the zinfandels. The most expensive wines are the vineyard designates, which not only include plenty of zinfandels but also the flagship Pickberry meritage, a lush yet elegant blend of cabernet sauvignon, merlot, and malbec from the slopes of Sonoma Mountain, so named because the vineyard owner's kids used to pick blackberries there.

It's worth opting for the pricier tasting, which includes many of the best single-vineyard wines. If you're up early enough, the daily tour at 10:30am ($15) is an entertaining start to the day and usually includes tasting of barrel samples.

PLAZA TASTING ROOMS

With the exception of a few tasting rooms scattered among its cozy shops and inconspicuous eateries, downtown Sonoma gave very little indication that it was in the heart of one of the world's most celebrated wine countries. That changed between 2009 and 2012, when the number of tasting rooms blossomed from 6 to 22. Most are small family enterprises (5,000 cases or fewer) specializing in one or two varietals. The tasting rooms are likewise intimate. Generally only one or two people work the bar. While some offer the same white to red range found in many large wineries, most here specialize in only one or two varietals, sourcing their grapes from Oregon to Santa Barbara, creating an intriguingly diverse catalog of single varietals.

If starting with some bubbles, the recently opened **Sigh** (29 E. Napa St., Ste. C, Sonoma, 707/996-2444, www.sighsonoma.com, 11am-8pm Thurs.-Tues., $3-7/taste) in the retail courtyard of Sonoma Court Shops is a good place to begin. It is not affiliated with any winery and carries an assortment of bubbles, from cava to locally made sparkling wine to true champagnes from France. You won't find any Veuve Cliquot here, but instead only wine that has been hand selected by the proprietor, Jayme Powers.

Outstanding chardonnays, and a large cow sculpture made entirely of wine corks, are the specialties of **Charles Creek Vineyards** (483 1st St. W., Sonoma, 707/935-3848, www.charlescreek.com, 11am-6pm daily, tasting $5). One of the old-guard tasting rooms on the plaza and one of its larger wineries, Charles Creek makes about 12,000 cases of mainly chardonnay and cabernet sauvignon from vineyards across Sonoma and Napa. Fruit from both features strongly in many of the chardonnays, including the bright and tangy Las Patolitas ("little ducks") and the mellower La Sorpresa ("the surprise"). The several cabernets are also subtly different blends from famous-name vineyards all over Napa, many of them in mountain appellations that give the wines intensity and earthiness. The En Casa label of wines, which includes cabernet and syrah, offer the best values at under $25 a bottle, but none of the wines cost more than $40.

To move on to red, continue north on 1st Street to **Walt Wines** (380 1st. St. W., Sonoma, 707/933-4440, www.waltwines.com, 11am-6pm daily, tasting $10), where the focus is pinot noir. Sourcing their grapes from the Sonoma Coast, Anderson Valley, the Santa Rita Hills near Santa Barbara, and Oregon's Willamette Valley, Walt produces nearly a dozen distinctly unique pinot noirs. By buying fruit from such a large swath, the winemaker, Steve Leveque, formerly of Robert Mondavi Winery, is able to draw out the grape's delicate characteristics, each uniquely amplified in different appellations. For those in your party still content with whites, Walt offers two chardonnays, both from the Sonoma Coast. Bottles generally run about (and top off at) $60, but there are a few for $40. The price of a taste will get you sips of four pinot noirs and one chardonnay, but the service is warm and there is plenty of space to enjoy a bottle, if you take the plunge.

Cabernet rules across the street at **Hawkes Winery** (383 1st St. W., Sonoma, 707/938-7620, www.hawkeswine.com, tasting $10), but you're not going to find your typical bold Napa varietal here. Instead, Hawkes gets its fruit from the cooler Anderson Valley. The result is handcrafted cabernets that are balanced, lower in alcohol, and exceptionally food-friendly. The winery also offers a chardonnay and a merlot, just to shake things up. The chardonnay is particularly striking among California whites for lacking the oak-inducing malolactic fermentation, leaving a crisp, citrusy wine. It is also the best value at $20, while the rest hover around the $50 mark. The tasting room has a bright and airy feeling, and the vibrant red chairs and umbrellas outside offer a relaxed place to enjoy a nibble with your tastes.

For an all-in-one stop, the homey 1940s craftsman-style cottage just around the corner is home to the Carneros-based winery **Roche Winery & Vineyards** (122 W. Spain St., Sonoma, 707/935-7115, www.rochewinery.com, 11am-7pm Mon.-Sat., 11am-5:30pm Sun., free tasting), where you can taste chardonnays to pinots to merlots to a variety of dessert wines. All are sourced from the estate vineyards and cost no more than $33, quite a deal for tasting rooms in the area. Taste them indoors or outdoors on the sun-dappled patio, or buy a bottle to accompany the selections from the light tasting menu provided by the nearby **Sunflower Caffe** (421 1st St. W., Sonoma, 707/996-6645, 7am-5pm daily). If nothing on the menu is enticing, the laid-back winery also encourages patrons to bring along their own brown bags.

A bit of the Sonoma winemaking establishment can be found at the southeast corner of the plaza next to the Ledson Hotel. As the name implies, **Highway 12 Vineyards & Winery** (498 1st St. E., Sonoma, 707/939-1012, www.highway12winery.com, 10:30am-5:30pm daily, free tasting) makes wines from vineyards along the highway that runs through the Sonoma Valley and Carneros. Highlights include both the chardonnays, which are made in a plush, full-bodied style. Among the reds, the most interesting wines are the blends, from the traditional Bordeaux blend to the La Piazza blend of sangiovese, primitivo, and zinfandel. This should come as no surprise, as one of Highway 12 Winery's principal partners is Michael Sebastiani, member of Sonoma's famed Sebastiani winemaking clan and former winemaker at Viansa.

Strolling south of the plaza on Broadway, you'll come across the **R2** (654 Broadway, Sonoma, 707/933-1330, www.r2winecompany.com, 11am-6pm daily, tasting $10) tasting room. Pronounced "R-Squared" for the wine-veteran brothers Richard and Rodger Roessler, who opened this tasting room in 2011, the young winery specializes in pinot noir and Rhône-style blends. The cost of a tasting gets you five pours, including the above mentioned reds as well as a chardonnay, a bright rosé, and a lithe grenache blanc. Prices fall around the $30 mark, but you can find the rosé for $18 (a great bargain), while the bigger reds can go for as much as $60. If you are unsure of sipping on busy Broadway, the cool low-slung house with large doors that open onto a patio shaded by oversized umbrellas will surprise you by its charm, making the small trek worthwhile.

WINERIES BY APPOINTMENT

Many of the wineries open to the public in the Sonoma Valley are those of big producers that can attract big crowds. Some of the smaller vintners have opened tasting rooms on the plaza, but to actually see one of these boutique wineries, you'll need to call ahead and arrange a visit. The experience shares the more personal feel of the smaller plaza tasting rooms, but with the scenic perks that makes winery hopping so fun.

Hanzell Vineyards (18596 Lomita Ave., Sonoma, 707/996-3860, www.hanzell.com, 10am-3:30pm daily, tasting $45), just north of Sonoma, was established in 1948 by industrialist James D. Zellerbach and is today renowned for its luxury-priced but limited-production chardonnays and pinot noirs that regularly score over 90 points in reviews. The secret to its success is its very own Hanzell clones of both pinot and chardonnay. In fact, the pinot noir vineyard on the mountain slopes is said to be the oldest in California. The tour and tasting fee is pricey for Sonoma but buys a very personalized experience, including a jaunt into the vineyards, a tour of the winery and caves, and a sit-down tasting.

Sights

Sonoma is not the only Wine Country town with a rich history stretching back hundreds of years, but it holds the distinction of being ground zero both for the turbulent events that led to the creation of the state of California in the 1840s and for the beginnings of California's booming wine industry. Many of the most important buildings from that active period in the mid-1800s are still standing, making Sonoma one of the most historically alive Wine Country towns in Northern California.

◖ SONOMA PLAZA

Sonoma Plaza (Broadway or Highway 12 and Napa St.), the eight-acre square that over the past 180 years has seen religious uprisings, revolution, fires, and now large numbers of tourists is at the center of the region's history and is the heart and soul of the valley. Fascinating shops and boutiques selling everything from designer clothes to African handicrafts fill the streets around the plaza, along with galleries and some of the valley's best restaurants, many of them in historic buildings that date from the 1800s.

Sonoma Plaza was created in 1835 by General Vallejo for troop maneuvers, and for a long time was little more than a muddy patch of grazing land surrounded by a picket fence. It is now the largest town square in California, and despite being thoroughly gentrified and besieged by cars, still maintains a sense of grace that only somewhere with such a rich history can pull off.

An excellent self-guided walking tour of the plaza's many Victorian-era buildings is buried between the endless pages of advertisements in the free *Sonoma Valley Guide,* copies of which are usually in the **Sonoma Valley Visitors Bureau** (453 1st St. E., Sonoma, 866/996-1090, www.sonomavalley.com, 9am-5pm Mon.-Sat., 10am-5pm Sun.) on the plaza.

A few yards north of the visitors bureau is the **Bear Flag Monument,** a bronze statue that stands roughly where the flag was raised by settlers in 1846 heralding the eventual creation of the State of California and the demise of Mexican rule. Smack in the middle of the plaza is **Sonoma City Hall,** built from locally quarried stone with four identical sides—to give equal importance to traders on all four sides of the plaza, so the legend goes. Like most civil construction projects today, the building project came in late and way over its budgeted cost of $15,000, delayed by stonemason strikes and the ballooning price of materials following the 1906 San Francisco earthquake. It took five years to build and was finally completed in 1909.

◖ SONOMA MISSION

The north side of Sonoma Plaza was the first to be developed in the early days of Sonoma and is where the oldest buildings can be found, many now part of the Sonoma State Historic Park. **Mission San Francisco Solano de Sonoma** (114 E. Spain St., Sonoma, 707/938-9560, www.parks.ca.gov, 10am-5pm daily adults $3, children 6-17 $2, under 6 free), established in 1823, was the last of California's 21 missions but had a short religious life. Its land and buildings were seized by the Mexican government in 1834 along with all the other missions on the West Coast. By the end of the 1800s, Sonoma's once-proud mission had suffered the ignominy of being used as a hay barn and a winery, and of having a saloon built right in front of it.

Enter the unlikely figure of newspaper magnate William Randolph Hearst, who helped provide funding that enabled a preservation society to buy the mission in 1903 for $5,000. Restoration didn't start until 1911, however, by which time various collapses had left the building in ruins. The reconstructed building open

BATTLE OF THE CHICKENS

They are sometimes there, but officially they're not. The saga of the Sonoma Plaza chickens perfectly illustrates Sonoma's enduring small-town quirkiness in the face of the creeping invasion of expensive hotels, restaurants, and other newcomers.

At one point there were more than 100 chickens scratching out a living in the plaza, and they had plenty of local fans who appreciated the hick character they brought to the city. Letters to local newspapers told newcomers to "go home" if they didn't like the chickens. A city plan to cull the birds and keep their numbers to a more manageable 40 was met with squawks of protest from supporters.

"You'd see them crossing on the crosswalk. I think they learned from watching people," a reporter at the *Sonoma Index-Tribune* newspaper recalls. There was even one that regularly laid eggs in a plaza crafts store.

In 2000, however, the roosters were implicated in several pecking and scratching attacks on small children, marking the beginning of the end for the chicken population. In May that year, citing safety and liability issues, the city council voted to evict the chickens from the plaza and resettle them at local farms, a move that prompted a "roost-in" protest by 100 chicken lovers in front of city hall.

There was an attempt to reintroduce some friendlier breeds of chickens later that year, together with an "egg patrol" to ensure their numbers didn't get out of hand, but four of them quickly fell foul of local dogs, and the rest were rounded up and whisked off to safety.

Now there are officially no chickens, just the plaza's friendly duck population to occasionally hold up traffic. The Sonoma Ecology Center is keeping the town's pullet love alive with its annual **Tour de Coop** in which residents with backyard chickens open their homes, occasionally pouring wine and serving cookies, to other chicken enthusiasts.

---

to the public today has a large cross on the roof where an old bell tower used to be, but is otherwise largely the same as the original. In 1926 the mission was declared a historic landmark. For the $3 entrance fee (which also admits you into the other sights within the Sonoma State Historic Park) you can join a docent-led tour, which start every hour from 11am-2pm. You can also explore the mission on your own, checking out the tiny museum where displays and large watercolors depict life in the missions, or observe a moment of silence at the Native American mortuary monument situated in the dusty courtyard full of giant prickly pear cactus plants said to be as old as the mission itself. Just don't touch the cacti or you'll be pulling tiny hairlike spikes out of your hands for the rest of the day.

SONOMA STATE HISTORIC PARK

While the Sonoma Mission is a central part of this rambling historic park (363 3rd St. W.,

Sonoma, www.parks.ca.gov, 10am-5pm daily, adults $3, children 6-17 $2, under 6 free), the majority of the sights were built by or in the heyday of General Mariano Vallejo, the Mexican army commander who became a key figure in California's transition from a Mexican province to one of the 50 American states. A stroll through this well-maintained park is a window into California as it transformed from a wilderness to a cultural and political player.

Across 1st Street from the mission is the two-story adobe **Sonoma Barracks** building (707/939-9420, 10am-5pm daily), which was constructed in stages between 1834 and 1841 by Native American slaves captured by the same Mexican army it eventually housed. In 1860 it was converted to a winery by General Vallejo (many plaza buildings saw service as wine cellars or wineries over the years) and in the late 1800s became a store with an ornate Victorian facade tacked on the front. It was partly restored in the 1930s and was used

© ELIZABETH LINHART VENEMAN

Mission San Francisco Solano de Sonoma is part of Sonoma State Historic Park.

for private residences and offices until being bought by the state in 1958 and fully restored. The small museum housed there today contains artifacts from its military history. The courtyard was once the scene of grisly staged animal fights.

Next to the barracks is the old **Toscano Hotel,** which was built in the 1850s. Just across the small square behind the 1940s building that contains the Sonoma Cheese Factory is the site of Vallejo's first home, **La Casa Grande,** built in 1840 and where Vallejo was arrested by the Bear Flag party in 1846. The house itself burned down long ago, and just the two-story, adobe-brick servants quarters remain.

Vallejo's next home, built in 1850, reflected his new status as a state senator and is on 20 acres of parkland about a 10-minute walk west of the plaza on Spain Street at 3rd Street West. Vallejo called this new home **Lachryma Montis,** Latin for "tear of the mountain," the name given by Native Americans to a nearby spring that once supplied much of the town's water.

In a display of excess that would put many of today's movie stars to shame, Vallejo spent $150,000 (in 1850 dollars) to build and decorate the ornate Gothic-style Victorian house, construct numerous summer houses, and plant the huge 250-acre estate where he lived until his death in 1890. Even the wood-framed **Swiss Chalet** next to the house, originally used to store the estate's fruit (and, of course, used as a winery), was built from materials imported from Europe. Today it is a visitors center and museum (10am-5pm Tues.-Sun.). The house itself is open during museum hours and is still full of Vallejo's decadent marble fireplaces, rosewood furniture, chandeliers, and frilly lace. Tours for both Lachryma Montis and the Toscano Hotel are free with the park's $3 admission fee and are available 1pm-3pm Saturday and 1pm-4pm Sunday.

Back across the street from the mission entrance on Spain Street, the wobbly-looking adobe building with a long 1st-floor veranda is the **Blue Wing Inn,** a gold rush-era saloon and stagecoach stop that is thought to be one of the oldest unaltered buildings in the city and the oldest hotel north of San Francisco. While it is a part of the state park, it is not open to the public due to safety concerns. The park hopes to open the building once the required earthquake retrofitting has been completed; however, with the state park's budget as tight as it is, these plans are set in the very distant future.

DEPOT MUSEUM AND TRAIN TOWN
The scale-model trains that haul passengers around a 1.25-mile track at the Train Town amusement park in Sonoma are the only reminders of the once-thriving railroad that brought visitors to Sonoma Valley.

The first stretch of the original Sonoma Valley Railroad opened in 1879 and ran from Vineburg just south of Sonoma to Wingo, three miles south of present-day Schellville, where it connected with boats to San Francisco. It was soon extended down to San Pablo Bay and north to Sonoma Plaza. From the plaza it followed Spain Street and turned right on present-day Highway 12, running all the way up the valley to Glen Ellen.

Back in 1890, taking the ferry and train from San Francisco's Ferry Building to Sonoma took about two hours, not much longer than it takes by car now. But the rising popularity of cars in the early 1900s and the opening of the Golden Gate Bridge in 1937 eventually led to the demise of the region's railroads.

More about the history of the Sonoma railroads can be found at the small **Depot Museum** (270 1st St. W., Sonoma, 707/938-1762, www.vom.com/depot, 1pm-4:30pm Wed.-Sun., free), a block north of the plaza. The museum is an exact replica of the original railroad depot, which burned down in 1976, and is surrounded by Depot Park, popular with the city's drunks except on Friday when the farmers market takes over.

Riding the only trains left in town requires a visit to the brightly painted station of **Train Town** (20264 Broadway, Sonoma, 707/938-3912, www.traintown.com, 10am-5pm daily June-Aug., 10am-5pm Fri.-Sun. Sept.-May), a strange and often crowded combination of amusement park, model railway, and petting zoo. The train fare is $5.75 for all ages, but adults without children should be warned that the mandatory stop at the petting zoo at the halfway point can be a little tedious. The amusement park rides, which include a Ferris wheel and vintage carousel, each cost $2.75.

Entertainment
The Sonoma Valley is as much about olives as wine during the winter when the annual **Sonoma Valley Olive Festival** (www.olivefestival.com) is in full swing. The festival kicks off with the Blessing of the Olives at Sonoma's mission the beginning of December then runs through February. Check the website for a full list of the 30 or more events, including plenty of tastings and fun cooking demonstrations organized at wineries, restaurants, and outdoors to celebrate the oily fruit. There is even a cocktail departure from the wine world with Martini Madness, in which bartenders from all over the valley are challenged to stir (or shake) the best new martini. Many of the events are free, but the biggest usually require tickets, which are available through the event link on the festival's website.

Late May through June is lavender season in the Sonoma Valley, and the aromatic purple flower is celebrated with the annual **Lavender Festival** (8537 Hwy. 12, Sonoma, 707/523-4411, www.sonomalavender.com/festival.html, $5/person, under 12 free), usually the third weekend in June, at the Sonoma Lavender Barn next to the Chateau St. Jean winery in Kenwood. Learn about growing countless varieties of lavender, how to use the oil, and even how to cook with lavender. There's also a lavender festival held in early June at the **Matanzas Creek Winery** (6097 Bennett Valley Rd., Santa Rosa, 707/528-6464 or 800/590-6464, www.matanzascreek.com), near Glen Ellen.

Shakespeare in Sonoma celebrates the town's theatrical heritage and its great summer weather in August with weekend performances of Shakespeare's plays put on by the local Avalon Players group in the outdoor amphitheater at the **Buena Vista Winery** (18000

FIGHTING FIRE WITH WINE

On a breezy day in September 1911, a stove exploded in a cobbler's shop on the east side of Sonoma Plaza, setting off what the *Sonoma Index-Tribune* newspaper described as a "disasterous fire" that was eventually extinguished with the help of a quick-thinking wine merchant.

The town's fire truck and 100 firefighters were quickly on the scene of the original fire, but were soon overwhelmed when changing winds spread the flames to buildings up and down the street and, at one point, set fire to the grass on the plaza.

When the roof of Agostino Pinelli's wine cellars on Spain Street caught fire and he saw the fire truck was too far away to help, he and some firefighters connected a hose and pump to a 1,000-gallon tank of his wine and, as reported by the *Index-Tribune*, "A powerful stream of red wine was directed on the burning wine cellar."

Although the fire eventually destroyed most of the other buildings on 1st Street East, Pinelli's red wine was credited with helping firefighters prevent the fire from spreading to even more buildings on the south side of the plaza.

The Pinelli building is still standing today on 1st Street East near Spain Street. It was built in 1891 from local stone quarried by the Pinelli family, which also helped Samuele Sebastiani get his start in the quarrying business before he went on to establish the Sebastiani Winery. Today the building is home to offices and shops, including (rather appropriately) the **Sonoma Wine Shop** (412 1st St. E., Sonoma, 707/996-1230, 11am-6pm Wed.-Mon.).

Old Winery Rd., Sonoma, 800/926-1266, www.buenavistawinery.com). Tickets cost $25. For more information, contact the **Avalon Players** (707/996-3264, www.sonomashakespeare.com).

Among the big wine events in the valley during the year is the **Sonoma Valley Reserve**, usually held on the third weekend in May and October. Organized by the **Sonoma Valley Vintners & Growers Alliance** (707/935-0803, www.sonomavalleywine.com), the event is a two-day affair at which 40 wineries up and down the valley throw themed parties with free food, wine, and entertainment for those lucky enough to have a festival passport. One- or two-day tickets are available ($95 and $150, respectively) but they must be purchased in advance through the festival's website (www.reservesonoma.com)

THE SEBASTIANI THEATRE

Not only was California born in Sonoma, but so was California theater. What was believed to be California's first theatrical presentation, Benjamin Webster's *The Golden Farmer*, was put on by American soldiers in an old adobe storehouse converted to a theater in 1849.

Today, a theater of the silver screen era is one of the most prominent buildings on the plaza. **The Sebastiani Theatre** (476 1st St. E., Sonoma, 707/996-2020, www.sebastianitheatre.com, $8), built to replace the burned-down Don Theatre, was funded by Samuele Sebastiani, city benefactor and founder of the eponymous winery. It opened its doors in April 1934 with the film *Fugitive Lovers* starring Robert Montgomery. Today the theater still shows mainly art house movies with the occasional classic thrown in, like *Dr. Strangelove*, as part of its Vintage Film Series.

RAMEKINS SONOMA VALLEY CULINARY SCHOOL

The Napa Valley has the famous Culinary Institute of America, but the Sonoma Valley, not to be outdone, has its own renowned culinary school in **Ramekins** (450 W. Spain St., Sonoma, 707/933-0450, www.ramekins.com, $60-119), just four blocks from the plaza and voted 2005 Cooking School of the Year by the International Association of Culinary Professionals.

Ramekins has far more in the way of a hands-on cooking experience for casual visitors than the CIA over in St. Helena, including classes and demonstrations, sometimes by well-known chefs, that don't cost much more than a meal at many local restaurants, making the evening classes a fun alternative to eating a meal that someone else prepared. Check the website for a constantly updated schedule. Reservations are strongly suggested and can be made on the school's website or over the phone.

Shopping

Shopping is another major draw to this historic small town. Packed around the leafy plaza are countless shops. Many sit on the four main streets bordering the square, but most you have to hunt for in the nooks and crannies in remodeled historic buildings and tiny retail alleyways that penetrate each block. Some are throwbacks to the town's working-class and farm town past, and others are upscale boutiques banking on Sonoma's future as a Napa-esque Wine Country destination. Simply put, there is something for everyone.

Coming into town on Broadway you'll pass **Fat Pilgrim** (20820 Broadway, Sonoma, 707/721-1287, www.fatpilgrim.com, 10am-5:30pm Mon.-Sat., 11am-5:30pm Sun.). Billing itself as a "contemporary general store," this little roadside shop stocks eclectic and earthy housewares, jewelry, and garden supplies. You'll find quirky napkin rings, dime-store toys, and old-fashioned candies and preserves under the Fat Pilgrim label.

At the plaza, a good first stop for food lovers is **Sign of the Bear Kitchenware** (435 1st St. W., Sonoma, 707/996-3722, 10am-6pm daily). It is chock-full of kitchen gadgets, gleaming countertop appliances, Dansk and Le Creuset crockery, and everything you would need to set a gorgeous table. While the store carries big-name labels, look for the "Sonoma Grown" stickers that highlight local products.

Where Sign of the Bear is general, **Bram** (493 1st St. W., Sonoma, 707/935-3717, www.bramcookware.com, 10am-6pm Thurs.-Mon., 10am-5pm Tues.) is specific. Devoted entirely to clay pot cooking, the dark shelves are stocked with a beautiful selection of deep

skillets, stew pots, rondeauxs, open casseroles, tagines, rectangular bakers, brams, and roasters. In fact, most shoppers will be astounded by the range and diversity of clay pots available. If you are at a loss of how to use such a beautiful pot (indeed, they are all very lovely), stacks of cooking books fill the other side of the shop. Furthermore, the staff is extremely knowledgeable and eager to share their own experiences and prejudices.

Despite its name, **Large Leather** (481 1st St. W., Sonoma, 707/938-1042, www.largeleather.biz, 10am-6pm daily) is a pint-sized store filled to the brim with purses, backpacks, belts, wallets, and bracelets. In fact, anything you can think of that is or can be made out of leather, you can find here. All their items are hand-crafted and are designed by the two owners, Paul Terwilliger and Jessica Zoutendijk.

For more handcrafted artistry, but with a bit more polish, stroll just a few doors down to **Sonoma Silver Company** (491 1st St. W., Sonoma, 707/933-0999, www.sonomasilver.com, 11am-6pm daily), where the slender shop is awash in silver rings, pendants, bracelets, and earrings. Multiple local jewelers sell and showcase their work here, but many of the shiny trinkets are made in-house by the company's resident jeweler of 20 years.

More personal decadence is just around the corner at **PK Sonoma** (120 W. Napa St., Sonoma, 707/935-6767, www.pksonoma.com, 10am-6pm daily), where you can buy a spa treatment to take home with you. Made in small batches, PK Sonoma's skincare products like "Eye and Lip Silk" made with rose and German chamomile and "Goat's Milk Soap" are made from locally sourced herbs (lavender is a popular ingredient), giving the store a pleasant "farm to bathroom" sort of a feel. There are even herbal shampoos for your pet!

Bibliophiles can get their fix at two charming independent bookstores conveniently located across the street from each other on East Napa Street. **Readers' Books** (130 E. Napa St., Sonoma, 707/939-1779, http://readers.indiebound.com, 10am-7pm Mon.-Sat., 10am-6pm Sun.) is a well-stocked general-interest bookstore specializing in contemporary fiction. Looking for that first-edition Jack London to go with your travels in the Valley of the Moon? Jump across the street to **Chanticleer Books** (127 E. Napa St., Sonoma, 707/996-7613, www.chanticleerbooks.com, 11am-5:30pm Tues.-Sat.), where the small shop brims with used and rare books, mainly focused on Sonoma and the West.

Thirsty? Take a break from retail therapy and slip into **Proof'd** (19 W. Napa St., Sonoma, 707/938-2337, www.proofdspirits.com, 10:30am-9pm Sun.-Thurs., 10:30am-9:30pm Fri.-Sat.), Sonoma's only high-end liquor store. Forget shopping for vino. What you'll find here is an eclectic mix of hard-to-find Scotches, boutique tequilas, and unusual gins. But, true to Wine Country form, there is a tasting bar. You can pick from five beers on tap as well as a diverse and rotating selection of wines, of which you may taste, take a flight, or enjoy a full glass. Sadly, no highballs are poured, as permits for anything stiffer than wine are rare in these wine-soaked parts.

Recreation
SONOMA OVERLOOK TRAIL
Nowhere is the spirit of Slownoma better represented than in this three-mile trail just north of Sonoma Plaza that winds through woods and meadows to the top of Schocken Hill, with fine views over the town below. The site almost became home to another Wine Country resort in 1999, but residents banded together to ensure it was instead preserved as a city-owned open space.

Grab picnic supplies and head for the trailhead near the entrance to the Mountain Cemetery on West 1st Street about a half mile north of the plaza beyond Depot Park. Within an hour you'll feel like you're in the middle of nowhere. Dogs, bikes, and smoking are not allowed on the trail.

The **Sonoma Ecology Center** (707/996-0712, www.sonomaecologycenter.org) offers free docent-led weekend hikes along the trail during which guests learn more about the local ecosystem and the area's natural highlights.

Springtime is a big draw as the knowledgeable guides identify the abundant spring wildflowers and birds nesting in the area. Contact the center for more information.

GOLF
The grande dame of the valley golf scene is the **Fairmont Sonoma Mission Inn Golf Club** (17700 Arnold Dr., Sonoma, 707/996-0300), opened in 1928 and planned by the original investors to rival the famous Del Monte course in Monterey. The 18-hole, par-72 course is on 170 acres bordered by the Sonoma Mountains and vineyards. Only club members and guests at the neighboring **Fairmont Sonoma Mission Inn** (100 Boyes Blvd., Sonoma, 707/938-9000, www.fairmont.com/sonoma, $300-400) can play here, however.

On the other hand, the public **Los Arroyos Golf Club** (5000 Stage Gulch Rd., Sonoma, 707/938-8835) is open to all comers. Great for newer players, Los Arroyos offers nine holes, par 29, and good fun for everyone.

SPAS
Aware that local Native American tribes had long talked about the healing properties of Sonoma Valley's numerous hot springs, Captain Henry Boyes spent two years drilling all over his property at the southern end of the valley in search of them. In 1895 he hit what would turn out to be liquid gold—a 112°F gusher that ushered in decades of prosperity for the valley's hotel owners.

Within a few months, another source of the hot water had been tapped by the owner of the neighboring Agua Caliente Springs Hotel. By 1900 thousands of visitors were bathing in the new hot mineral baths every year, and developers saw the potential for mass tourism, especially with the increasing popularity of the new railroad that ran from San Pablo Bay to Sonoma and up to Glen Ellen.

Soon the Boyes Springs mineral baths and the Agua Caliente Springs Hotel were transformed into first-class resorts. By 1910 many other hotels and resorts had opened, including Fetters Hot Springs and Verano Springs, complete with vaudeville shows, dances, and concerts. The *Sonoma Index-Tribune* newspaper reported that 23,000 people came in on the railroads for the Fourth of July weekend in 1916, close to the peak of the resort boom. Just seven years earlier there had been no one to witness the annual Fourth of July parade except local residents.

Boyes Hot Springs Hotel (along with several other resorts) burned down in a huge valley fire in September 1923, and an exclusive new resort, the **Fairmont Sonoma Mission Inn & Spa** (100 Boyes Blvd., Sonoma, 707/938-9000, www.fairmont.com/sonoma, 7:30am-8pm daily), with its mission-style architectural touches, opened on the site in 1927.

Today, the inn is the only spa hotel in the valley with its own natural source of hot mineral water. Even if you're not a guest at the Fairmont-owned hotel, basic spa packages are available for $89-199, depending on how many extra salon pamperings are added on. The basic spa includes an exfoliating shower, warm and hot mineral baths, and herbal steam room and sauna, interspersed with various cold showers and baths (which include indoor and outdoor pools). There are yoga classes, and various add-on massages, stone treatments, and mud baths are also available to purify and relax you (until you see the bill).

Just south of the Sonoma Plaza, the **Garden Spa** (29 E. MacArthur St., Sonoma, 707/933-3193, www.macarthurplace.com/spa.php, 9am-8pm daily, $118-345) at the luxurious MacArthur Place inn is a good place for some luxury pampering, with a list of spa treatments that could cause you to tense up with indecision. All their signature treatments are made or inspired from the flowers, herbs, and fruit found in the garden. These are distilled into such luscious effusions as the pomegranate body polish, golden passionflower body wrap, peppermint foot soak, and the red wine grapeseed bath. The spa also offers a mud bath soak, a number of different types of massages, and facial and waxing treatments. Couples can get their treatments together, and all spa guests also have full use of the inn's tranquil outdoor pool and fitness center. It is encouraged to book whatever you choose to do here at least two weeks in advance, as space in this fragrant spa fills up.

Accommodations

Anyone expecting cheap and cheerful accommodation over the hills from the overpriced Napa Valley establishments will be sadly disappointed. The cheapest place to sleep in the valley is with Mother Nature in a campground. The second cheapest is more than $100 per night.

Like the wine made here, the Sonoma Valley is increasingly marketed as a luxury destination with luxury bells and whistles that command premium prices. The pressure to keep the small-town feel of Sonoma doesn't help either, ensuring that most hotels and inns stay small and planning hurdles remain high, thus limiting the number of rooms available. As in Napa, many places here sell a Wine Country lifestyle that mixes Mediterranean with Victorian influences, but there are some new options that throw a little more contemporary inspiration into the mix.

Apart from a few big resort or chain hotels, the accommodation scene in Sonoma Valley is one of small, usually independent establishments with a handful of rooms. The smaller the hotel or inn, the more likely there is to be a two-night minimum over weekends, especially during the busiest summer and early fall months. Cancellation policies might also be less than flexible. The peak hotel season is generally from the end of May through October, roughly corresponding to the best weather in the region.

The closest place for true bargain-priced accommodations is along the U.S. Highway 101 freeway corridor across the Sonoma Mountains, where most of the chain motels can be found. Stay around Petaluma or in the Rohnert Park and Santa Rosa areas, and it's only a 10-15-minute drive into the valley.

UNDER $150

The ◖ **Sonoma Hotel** (110 W. Spain St., Sonoma, 800/468-6016, www.sonomahotel.

com, $110-198) is one of the rare bargains in the valley, offering some of the cheapest rooms and a superb location in a historic building right on Sonoma Plaza next to the highly rated **girl & the fig** restaurant (110 W. Spain St., 707/938-3634, www.thegirlandthefig.com, 11:30am-10pm Sun.-Mon., 11:30am-11pm Fri.-Sat., $20). Even the four cheapest rooms have views of something worthwhile, but don't expect luxury. The rooms are small, dark, and sparsely furnished in the Victorian style of its heyday, but for this price in this location there's really nothing to complain about. More expensive rooms and junior suites get more light and floor space. In keeping with the price and the hotel's heritage (the building dates from 1880), there are few amenities, and you're likely to hear your neighbor's nighttime antics. Also be warned that the bathroom for one of the cheapest rooms (room 34), although private, is out in the hallway past the friendly ghost.

Most B&Bs in this area tend toward plenty of Victorian frills, but the **Sonoma Chalet** (18935 5th St. W., Sonoma, 707/938-3129 or 800/938-3129, www.sonomachalet.com, rooms $125-150, cottages $180-225) goes beyond the chintz to a fabulously over-the-top Swiss Family Robinson-meets-Wild West theme with its alpine murals, dark wood accents, antiques, and colorful fabrics. There are four individually decorated rooms in the main Swiss-style farmhouse: The two cheapest share a bathroom, while the larger of the other two has a fireplace and balcony. Several small cottages on the three acres of wooded grounds have claw-foot tubs and wood-burning stoves. These are also the only accommodations that accept small children. The leafy location on the edge of Sonoma is peaceful but a fairly long walk to most of Sonoma's shops and restaurants.

$150-250

A teddy bear slumbering on the bed greets everyone staying at the **Inn at Sonoma** (630 Broadway, Sonoma, 888/568-9818 or 707/939-1340, www.innatsonoma.com, $220-395). It is one of Sonoma's newest hotels, and what it lacks in historic charm it makes up for in

functionality and convenience, being only a few blocks from the plaza. The 19 guest rooms are furnished in slightly pastiche, flowery Wine Country style but have a full range of modern amenities, including fireplaces, DVD players, and luxury bathrooms. Some of the larger rooms have patios. The price, although not cheap, does include a hot breakfast, which for $10 more can be brought to your room, and an afternoon cocktail hour that includes a glass of wine, a selection of cheese, and house-made hors d'oeuvres.

El Pueblo Inn (896 W. Napa St., Sonoma, 707/996-3651 or 800/900-8844, www.elpuebloinn.com, $179-244) is actually more of an upscale motel but offers a lot of rooms for a modest price and is just a 10-minute walk from the plaza. It's also one of the few places with no weekend minimum-stay requirements. The cheapest here are the Adobe rooms, which have all the basic amenities, including free wireless Internet and a refrigerator—a handy asset when purchasing food and chilling wine is a key part of your vacation. Although they still hint at the 1950s motel rooms they once were, they now open onto a courtyard rather than a parking lot. The larger, more luxurious Sonoma and California rooms, added relatively recently, feel more hotel-like with DVD players, high ceilings, private patios, and the occasional fireplace. All rooms have access to the small outdoor pool and landscaped gardens.

A historic inn dating from 1843 is now home to the newly renovated **El Dorado Hotel** (405 1st St. W., Sonoma, 707/996-3030, www.eldoradosonoma.com, $165-225), offering stylish 21st-century accommodations for not much more money than a pricey Wine Country motel. The lobby exudes the style of a classy boutique hotel, but the luxurious spaciousness of the lounges doesn't quite make it upstairs to the 23 smallish guest rooms. They are instead decorated with simple modern furnishings and earth tones that give a nod to the hotel's mission-era history. A decent list of amenities includes CD players, flat-screen televisions, and wireless Internet access but doesn't stretch to bathtubs—only showers—or room service.

The courtyard swimming pool looks nice but is somewhat pointless unless you like to swim or sunbathe just yards away from diners spilling onto the patio from the hotel's bar and restaurant. Still, for the price and a location right on the plaza, it's hard to complain. All have a view of some sort from their small balconies—the best overlook the plaza, although they suffer from some associated street noise.

Kitty corner is the other historic hotel on the square. For almost the last 100 years, the **Swiss Hotel** (18 W. Spain St., Sonoma, 707/938-2884, www.swisshotelsonoma.com, $110-240) has offered a bed and a meal to travelers from near and far. With a renovation in the 1990s, the guest rooms have plenty of modern amenities, while the outside of the building and the public spaces retain the historic feel of the original adobe building. You'll find your room light, bright, and airy with fresh paint and pretty floral comforters. Downstairs, enjoy a meal at the restaurant or have a drink at the historic bar and take in the history.

Although located in the relative no-man's land of Boyes Hot Springs just north of Sonoma, the **Sonoma Creek Inn** (239 Boyes Blvd., Sonoma, 888/712-1289, www.sonomacreekinn.com, $145-199) is one of the cheapest non-chain hotels in the valley. At this price point it's more common to see IKEA furniture, but the furnishings here are delightfully quirky, and some look like spoils from local antique stores. The 15 rooms are small and laid out in motel style; all are clean and have air-conditioning and refrigerators, and some have tiny private patios.

OVER $250

MacArthur Place (29 E. MacArthur St., Sonoma, 707/938-2929 or 800/722-1866, www.macarthurplace.com, $450) is also doused in history; the original structure was built in 1850, but it has since been remade into a 21st-century, seven-acre exclusive spa resort. Nevertheless, the cookie-cutter faux-Victorian cottages and landscaped gardens that now fan out from the original Manor House provide 64 luxurious and spacious guest rooms, making it one of the larger hotels in Sonoma. All rooms are sumptuously furnished in a cottage style that makes it seem more like a luxurious B&B, and all have the usual modern conveniences for this price range. Other amenities include an outdoor pool, free DVD library, breakfast, evening cheese and wine, and the on-site steak house and martini bar, Saddles. Suites and cottages also come with a fireplace and decadent hydrotherapy tub. Try to avoid the rooms on the south side of the complex that overlook the neighboring high school or those bordering the street to the west.

The Chapel Suite with its vaulted ceilings and skylight above the bed is one of the more unusual rooms at the **Cottage Inn & Spa** (310 1st St. E., Sonoma, 707/996-0719, www.cottageinnandspa.com, $300), just a block north of Sonoma Plaza. This self-styled "micro resort" with its mission-style architectural flourishes is an oasis of calm and style. In general, the accommodations are all billed as suites, even those with only one room. Still, they are all luxurious and full of character with thick white walls, tile floors, and deep tubs ringed in cerulean blue tile. The pricier suites have private patios and fireplaces. The South Suite has a double-sided fireplace, the Vineyard View Suite is over 700 square feet with cathedral ceilings and panoramic views, and the three-room North Suite includes a full kitchen.

Just a bit farther up the street is the small **Bungalows 313** (313 1st St. E., Sonoma, 707/996-8091, www.bungalows313.com, $279-389). As the name implies, this is a cozy collection of five bungalows around a peaceful courtyard fountain. Each suite is decorated in Italian country style with modern luxuries like sumptuous linens, an LCD television, and a DVD player. All are spacious, with seating areas, a kitchen or kitchenette, and private patio, yet all are unique in some way. One has a fireplace, another a jetted tub, and the largest is 1,200 square feet. Like everywhere in Wine Country, prices vary due to time of year, but keep a lookout for specials on the website. Planning ahead will benefit you, but beware of the 14-day cancellation policy.

With all of its spot-on Victorian flare, it is hard to believe that when the **Ledson Hotel** (480 1st St. E., Sonoma, 707/996-9779, www. ledsonhotel.com, $395), a sibling to the **Ledson Winery** (7335 Sonoma Hwy., Kenwood, 707/537-3810, www.ledson.com, 10am-5pm daily, tasting $15-25) up the valley, was honored by *Condé Nast Traveler* magazine in 2004, it was for best *new* hotel. The Victorian-style brick building looks as old as the plaza itself. Three of the six rooms have balconies looking onto the plaza, and all include just about every luxury feature possible, from state-of-the-art entertainment systems and high-speed Internet access to marble bathrooms with whirlpool tubs. To complete the grandeur, recently renovated Centre du Vin downstairs pours not only Ledson wines but also a number of other local vintners along with an impressive selection of cocktails to accompany its French-inspired menu.

At the other end of the scale to the intimate Ledson Hotel is the 228-room **Fairmont Sonoma Mission Inn & Spa** (100 Boyes Blvd., Sonoma, 707/938-9000, www.fairmont.com/sonoma, $300-400), which dates from 1927 and is now owned by Fairmont Hotels. It is luxurious, even by Fairmont standards. The well-heeled are drawn to the 40,000-square-foot full-service spa, use of the exclusive Sonoma golf club (17700 Arnold Dr., Sonoma, 707/996-0300) next door, and one of the best (and most expensive) restaurants in the valley, the Michelin-starred Santé. Many of the rooms have tiled floors and plantation-style wooden shutters to complement their colonial-style furnishings, and some have fireplaces. Despite the exclusivity, the in-room amenities are typical of a chain hotel, albeit a high-end one.

Food

Sonoma's food scene has gradually been transformed over the years from rustic to more stylish, but the change has not been nearly so dramatic and universal as in some other Wine Country towns. Some high-profile chefs have been sent packing in recent years after their restaurants flopped. A foie gras eatery didn't last

long, and even the Viansa Winery's once-successful Sonoma Plaza outpost, Cucina Viansa, eventually closed. Many of the most successful establishments are small and relaxed, retaining a degree of intimacy that some of their cousins in the Napa Valley seem to have lost. The key to a restaurant's longevity here seems to be honesty, modesty, and reasonable prices.

There's a strong European theme to food in the valley, but ingredients will likely be fresh and local, representing the giant produce basket that is Sonoma County. Expect to see menus change throughout the year as vegetables, fish, and meats come in and out of season.

Also expect to see that local produce in a cocktail glass. That's right. Sonoma has caught the mixology bug. Bartenders are throwing fresh basil, cucumber, ginger, and peaches in with their rye whiskeys, boutique gins, and antique bitters and liqueurs to create libations dangerously complex and tasty. The all-important wine list is not the only drink menu you must pore over now; cocktail menus also compete for clout and diners' palettes in most of the valley's notable restaurants.

CALIFORNIA CUISINE

Café La Haye (140 E. Napa St., Sonoma, 707/935-5994, dinner Tues.-Sat., entrées $19-30) is a trusted and well-loved restaurant. Local ingredients are the backbone of simple yet polished dishes like beef carpaccio, pan-seared steelhead trout, and a daily risotto, while the wine list is dominated by smaller wineries from all over Sonoma and farther afield. The uncluttered, split-level dining room is small, so either book well in advance or be prepared to sit at the bar in front of the tiny kitchen. The café is part of La Haye Art Center, which contains studios and the work of several local artists.

◀ **the girl & the fig** (110 W. Spain St., Sonoma, 707/938-3634, www.thegirlandthefig.com, 11:30am-10pm Sun.-Thurs., 11:30am-11pm Fri.-Sat., brunch 10am-3pm Sun., $20) is somewhat of a valley institution, having moved to the Sonoma Hotel on the plaza from its previous home in Glen Ellen, spawning a cookbook and also a wine bar in its old Glen Ellen digs. The French country menu includes main courses like free-range chicken and duck confit, Sonoma rabbit and *steak frites,* an excellent cheese menu, and delicious salads, including the signature arugula, goat cheese, pancetta, and grilled fig salad. The Thursday evening Plat du Jour menu is a bargain at $34 for three courses. To match the Provençal cuisine, the wine list focuses on Rhône varietals, with many from local Sonoma producers. There's not a cabernet to be seen. But thirsty patrons can also opt for a shot of Pernod or an aperitif of absinthe. The restaurant usually closes at 10pm, but a smaller brasserie menu is offered until 11pm on Friday and Saturday.

With the sleek makeover of the historic **El Dorado Hotel** (405 1st St. W., Sonoma, 707/996-3030, www.eldoradosonoma.com, $165-225) came the overhaul of its restaurant, **El Dorado Kitchen** (405 1st St. W., Sonoma, 707/996-3030, breakfast 8am-11am daily, lunch 11:30am-2:30pm daily, dinner 5:30pm-9:30pm Sun.-Thurs., 5:30pm-10pm Fri.-Sat.,

$20-30). Not only did it get the same modern treatment as the namesake hotel, but it also joined the farm-to-table movement that has been the hallmark of big-name Wine Country restaurants for the past 10 years. Several Thomas Keller alums have been at the helm, giving the restaurant the notoriety it deserves. Under the tutelage of the current chef, Armando Navarro, the menu has a regional comfort-food bent with entrées of roasted pork shoulder, corn ravioli, and steamed clams with chickpeas and chorizo. Inside the restaurant is all cool dark wood and slate minimalism, while outside by the pool the casual dining scene is more Miami than Sonoma. There is a pared-down bar menu for those in just for a nibble, or a chance to taste one of their original cocktail creations.

FRENCH

It's not the best place for a relaxed dinner, but for wine, light evening food, and outstanding people-watching opportunities, the **Ledson**

© ELIZABETH LINHART VENEMAN

sidewalk dining at the Ledson Hotel

Hotel & Centre du Vin (480 1st St. E., Sonoma, 707/996-9779, www.ledsonhotel.com, 11am-9:30pm daily, $20) on the plaza can't be beat, with a beautifully detailed and ornate (but faux) Victorian-style dining room that spills out onto the sidewalk. The small but tight menu offers American-style French cuisine that can be happily washed down with Ledson wines that are available only here and at the winery itself. You may also opt for a flight of white or red wine accompanied by appropriately flavored appetizers ($20), or even beer or a house-styled cocktail.

ITALIAN

Ask any of the valley's winemakers where they like to eat and the list will likely include the family-owned Italian trattoria **Della Santina's** (133 E. Napa St., Sonoma, 707/935-0576, www.dellasantinas.com, lunch 11:30am-3pm and dinner 5pm-9:30pm daily, $20). The big outdoor patio and the simple Italian country food garner consistently good reviews, so reservations are usually essential despite the casual atmosphere. As you would expect, the restaurant excels at pastas, fish, and spit-roasted meats. If the excellent local and Italian wine list does not satisfy, there's a $12 corkage fee, lower than the $20 charged by many other restaurants. Right next door to the restaurant is the wine bar and wine shop **Enoteca Della Santina** (127 E. Napa St., Sonoma, 707/938-4200, www.enotecanextdoor.com, 4pm-10pm Sun. and Tues., 2pm-10pm Wed.-Thurs., 2pm-11pm Fri.-Sat.), which serves 30 California and international wines by the glass accompanied by appetizers at its copper-topped bar. It's a great place for a pre-dinner drink while you wait for your table at a nearby restaurant, or for a late glass of port to end your day.

Sonoma's Italian heritage is not only represented by fancy trattorias. **Mary's Pizza Shack** (www.maryspizzashack.com), founded by Italian New Yorker Mary Fazio in 1959, has been around longer than many other Sonoma restaurants and now has 19 branches throughout the North Bay. It might now be a chain, but you will at least be eating in the town where it all started. The traditional or build-your-own pizzas (starting at $13 for a medium) are consistently good, and there's a big selection of traditional pasta dishes ($11-18), including spaghetti with baseball-sized meatballs. Local branches are on the plaza (8 W. Spain St., Sonoma, 707/938-8300, 11am-11pm Sun.-Thurs., 11am-midnight Fri.-Sat.) and in Boyes Hot Springs (18636 Sonoma Hwy., Sonoma, 707/938-3600, 11am-10pm Sun.-Thurs., 11am-11pm Fri.-Sat.).

Some inventive thin-crust red (with tomato sauce) and white (no tomato sauce) pizzas at **The Red Grape** (529 1st St. W., Sonoma, 707/996-4103, http://theredgrape.com, 11:30am-9pm daily, $14) include a bacon, caramelized onion, and crème fraîche pizza, and another with marinated flank steak and cheddar cheese. There are plenty of less inspiring, but cheap, pizza and pasta options, and it's worth looking for a seat on the patio. The restaurant is named after a type of particularly sweet tomato and surely is a nod to its home in Wine Country. And befitting any Wine Country eatery, The Red Grape has an impressive wine menu with over 30 mostly local wines, of which you can order by the glass or by the bottle. Both, however, are a bit pricey for a casual pizza joint.

MEXICAN

Tired of looking at wine menus? Want something with a little more, um, bite? Pull up a bar stool at **Maya** (101 Napa St. E., Sonoma, 707/935-3500, www.mayarestaurant.com, 11:45am-3pm and 5pm-9pm Mon.-Thurs., 11:45am-11pm Fri.-Sat., 11:45am-9pm Sun., $12-18), at the corner of 1st and Napa Streets, and pick from one of the 60-plus tequilas on the menu. You can opt for a cool margarita on the rocks, or take it straight with lime and salt. Either way, the food, especially the addictive spicy roasted pumpkin seeds, will help wash it down. Influenced by the cuisine of the Yucatan Peninsula, the menu relies heavily on fresh fish and locally grown fruits and vegetables. Ceviche, fish tacos, and carnitas slow-roasted in banana leaves sit alongside taquitos, nachos, and enchiladas. Like the food and the tequila, the atmosphere is both casual and sophisticated with a decor of worn wood, exposed brick wall, and colorful peasant paintings à la Diego Rivera.

If a monster burrito is what you crave, particularly to soak up excess wine or to refuel after a long bike ride, try the roadside Mexican diner **Juanita Juanita** (19114 Arnold Dr., Sonoma, 707/935-3981, www.juanitajuanita.com, 11am-8pm Wed.-Mon., $8-16, cash only), on the west side of Arnold Drive just north of Sonoma. Although it isn't the cheapest taqueria food in Sonoma, it has come to be known as some of the best in this part of Sonoma County, and the ramshackle building with a patio is as colorful as the food. Choose one of the favorites listed on the menu, like the Jerk in a Blanket chicken, and you can't go wrong. Some of the food can be mind-blowingly spicy. Indeed, the menu warns: "Food isn't properly seasoned unless it's painful to eat."

PORTUGUESE

Hearty Portuguese food in rustic, Mediterranean-inspired surroundings are the hallmarks of **La Salette** (452 1st St. E., Ste. H, Sonoma, 707/938-1927, www.lasalette-restaurant.com, 11:30am-2:30pm and 5pm-9pm daily, $17-24), just off the plaza. The menu reflects Portugal's seafaring colonial history with traditional dishes such as the Portuguese national soup, *caldo verde,* complementing international influences like pan-roasted Mozambique prawns and the filling Brazilian stew *feijoada completa.* The wine list includes a wide range of both local and Portuguese wines, plus a dozen madeiras and 19 ports.

THAI

If a table is hard to come by at popular Della Santina's or you simply fancy some Thai food, right next door—with an equally nice outdoor patio space—is the popular **Rin's Thai** (139 E. Napa St., Sonoma, 707/938-1462, www. rinsthai.com, 11:30am-9pm Sun. and Tues.-Thurs., 11:30am-9:30pm Fri.-Sat., $18). Fresh local ingredients feature strongly in the classic Thai dishes that include curries, noodles, and Thai-style barbequed meats, and the elegant Zen interior of the old Victorian house and the pretty patio are far from the usual hole-in-the-wall atmosphere of Thai restaurants. Rin's also offers takeout and delivery (minimum $35) for those craving some gang dang (spicy red curry) or tom yum (spicy and sour soup) in their hotel rooms.

CAFÉS

If you just want a cup of coffee or a quick pastry, swing by the **Basque Boulangerie Café** (460 1st St. E., Sonoma, 707/935-7687, http:// basqueboulangerie.com, 7am-6pm daily); only pay attention after ordering as customer names are only called once when food is ready. The line to order often snakes out the door on weekend mornings and at lunchtime throughout the week, but it usually moves fast. The wide selection of soups, salads, and sandwiches can also be bought to go, which is handy because table space inside and out is usually scarce.

There are more seating options at the colorful **Sunflower Caffe** (421 1st St. W., Sonoma, 707/996-6645, 7am-5pm daily) across the plaza, but the line, and the wait, can be just as long. It sells a fairly basic selection of cheap beverages and sandwiches, but the real gem is a big patio hidden down the side passageway of the El Dorado Hotel. It is an oasis of greenery with plenty of tables. Later in the day, you can swap your espresso for a beer or a glass of wine, which are only $2 and $5, respectively, during the café's daily happy hour 3pm-4pm.

BREAKFAST

Need a hearty breakfast or down-home lunch before you get going on a full day of wine tasting? Stop in at the **Big 3 Diner** (18140 Hwy. 12, Sonoma, 707/939-2410, www.fairmont.com/ sonoma, 7am-9pm daily, $8-20). The restaurant is part of the Fairmont Sonoma Mission Inn property, which explains both the tip-top prices and the upscale diner cuisine. But it's good stuff—the kitchen uses high-quality (often organic and local) ingredients to create its fancy Benedicts and sandwiches. Even the locals approve, coming in to be greeted by name by the friendly and efficient service staff.

If staying at the **Fairmont Sonoma Mission Inn** (100 Boyes Blvd., Sonoma, 707/938-9000, www.fairmont.com/sonoma, $300-400), order room service from Big 3 or walk over to the large friendly dining room, sparkling with wooden chairs and tables and a pleasant casual atmosphere.

PUBS

With no microbreweries in this part of Sonoma, the next best place to find beer is **Murphy's Irish Pub** (464 1st St., Sonoma, 707/935-0660, www.sonomapub.com, 11am-10pm Sun.-Thurs., 11am-11pm Fri.-Sat., $15) just off the plaza behind the Basque Boulangerie. It's one of the few places in the valley where beer trumps wine, and live music, usually of the Irish variety, gets people dancing four nights a week. The food includes pub standards like fish-and-chips, shepherd's pie, and Irish stew, as well as sandwiches and a kids' menu. Unfortunately, the pub also stays true to its Irish roots with its beer selection, which includes international favorites but little in the way of Northern California brews. But the upshot is that there is a healthy selection of whiskeys: Irish and Scotch, single malt, blended, and bourbons. There is even a Welsh whiskey. And this being Wine Country, you can taste a flight for $23 or $44.

PICNIC SUPPLIES

The Sonoma Valley is like one giant picnic ground. Many of the wineries have large open spaces or picnic tables, and the more adventurous can drive or hike into one of the many parks in the valley, such as the outlook above Sonoma, Jack London State Park, or up into the western hills in Sugarloaf State Park.

Many wineries now offer a limited selection of deli-style food in their visitors centers or gift stores, but some offer more than most, including **Bartholomew Park Winery** (1000 Vineyard Ln., Sonoma, 707/935-9511, www.bartpark. com, 11am-4:30pm daily), with its selection of Sonoma Valley cheeses, and **Buena Vista Winery** (18000 Old Winery Rd., Sonoma, 800/926-1266, www.buenavistawinery.com,

10am-5pm). Still, you may want to take advantage of the excellent (and cheaper) offerings in town.

Good bread can usually be found at most delis, though many places run out by lunchtime. Two bakeries supply most of the valley's bread, both centrally located. The **Basque Boulangerie Café** (460 1st St. E., Sonoma, 707/935-7687, http://basqueboulangerie.com, 7am-6pm daily) on the plaza sells not only sandwiches and salads to go but also freshly baked breads. It is one of the leading suppliers of bread to grocery stores in the area. The other big local bread supplier is **Artisan Bakers** (750 W. Napa St., Sonoma, 707/939-1765, www.artisanbakers.com, 6:30am-3pm Mon.-Sat., 7am-2pm Sun.), in a nondescript building about half a mile from the plaza. It also sells a picnic-worthy selection of sandwiches, salads, and pizza.

Three good cheese shops are around the plaza. On the north side is the **Sonoma Cheese Factory** (2 Spain St., Sonoma, 800/535-2855, www.sonomacheesefactory.com, 8:30am-5:30pm daily), which is easy to spot: Just look for the ugliest building, a brutal 1940s edifice that stands in stark contrast to the Victorian character of the rest of the plaza. It is the home of Sonoma Jack cheese and also sells other strangely flavored cheeses (which, thankfully, you can usually taste first) as well as a limited selection of salads and fancy sandwiches. A less crowded place to buy cheese is the historic **Vella Cheese Company** (315 2nd St. E., Sonoma, 707/938-3232 or 800/848-0505, www.vella-cheese.com, 9:30am-6pm Mon.-Sat.), a block north of the plaza in a former brewery building. It's the latest incarnation of the cheese store opened in the 1930s by Thomas Vella. Some of the best cheese in Northern California can be found directly on the plaza at the **La Bodega Cheese Shop** (412 1st St. E., Sonoma, 707/996-1230, http://sonomawineshop.com, 11am-6pm Thurs.-Mon.). The small shop also serves lunch with homemade pastas, soups, and salads, all so fresh that it is like eating in someone's personal kitchen. The deli case in the front offers a small but very select assortment of cheeses, but for $9 or $15 you can order a cheese plate and delay your picnic for an hour while you munch at one of their sidewalk tables.

Perhaps the easiest option for getting everything in one place is to visit one of the valley's excellent general grocery stores. The **Sonoma Market** (500 W. Napa St., Sonoma, 707/996-3411, 6am-9pm daily), is not far from the plaza. Here you can find a surprisingly great selection of lunch options, some hot, some gourmet, as well as local wine and good cheese. Another option is the **Vineburg Deli & Grocery** (997 Napa Rd., Sonoma, 707/938-3306, 6am-6pm daily), just south of Sonoma not far from the Gundlach Bundschu Winery. Perhaps not as upscale as the Sonoma Market, this smaller grocery caters more to the local blue-collar set, selling hearty lunches that lean more toward the picnics of your childhood.

FARMERS MARKETS

One way to soak up the atmosphere while picking up supplies is to visit one of Sonoma's **farmers markets.** The valley's prolific farmers congregate in Depot Park, a block north of the plaza on 1st Street West, 9am-12:30pm every Friday year-round, and in front of city hall, 5:30pm-dusk on Tuesday May-October. At either event you can browse local produce as well as cheese, meat, and bread in addition to the odd art or craft.

Information and Services

First stop for visitors to the Sonoma Valley should be the **Sonoma Valley Visitors Bureau** (453 1st St. E., Sonoma, 866/996-1090, www.sonomavalley.com, 9am-5pm Mon.-Sat., 10am-5pm Sun.) in the Carnegie Library building in the middle of the plaza right next to city hall and across from the Sebastiani Theatre. It publishes a free valley guide, and its staff is happy to dispense all sorts of local information, answer any questions, and offer advice for nothing more than an entry in the visitors book. Furthermore, don't be shy to ask for any complimentary tasting passes often dropped off here by neighboring wineries, or for a "I Heart Sonoma" sticker, which when worn will frequently get you discounts

and other perks at certain tasting rooms. There's a branch of the visitors bureau at the **Cornerstone Sonoma** (23570 Arnold Dr., Sonoma, 707/933-3010, www.cornerstonegardens.com, 10am-5pm daily, gardens 1pm-4pm daily) in Carneros.

If you're staying in the valley, be sure to pick up a copy of the **Sonoma Index-Tribune** newspaper (www.sonomanews.com), which has been published for more than 100 years and now comes out twice a week. It is full of local news, gossip, event information, and reviews. Up in Kenwood the **Kenwood Press** is the local rag and is published twice a month. Either in their print or online edition (www.kenwoodpress.com), you can find out about local events and get a flavor for the town.

For wine-related information, including events at individual wineries, check the website of the **Sonoma County Wineries Association** (www.sonomawine.com), which represents all of Sonoma's wineries, including those in the valley. The **Heart of Sonoma Valley Association** (www.heartofthevalley.com) represents only those wineries around Glen Ellen and Kenwood and organizes plenty of local events throughout the year.

Services are concentrated in the town of Sonoma. Plan on getting any cash you may need here before venturing up to Glen Ellen or Kenwood. There is a **Bank of America** at 35 West Napa Street and a **Wells Fargo** just down the street at 480 West Napa Street. The town's main **post office** is located at 617 Broadway. If you are faced with a medical emergency, head for the **Sonoma Valley Hospital** (347 Andrieux St., Sonoma, 707/935-5000, www.svh.com), which has a full-service emergency room.

Getting There and Around

The town of Sonoma lies over the mountains west of the Napa Valley. The main route through the valley is Highway 12, also called the Sonoma Highway. From Napa, drive south on Highway 29, turning west onto Highway 12/121. Turn north on Highway 12 to reach downtown Sonoma.

If driving from the Bay Area, take U.S.

Highway 101 north, then Highway 37 east. Highway 37 becomes Highway 121, then Highway 116 as it winds into the city of Sonoma. If you're driving south on U.S. Highway 101, you can turn off onto Highway 12 south in Santa Rosa and take a scenic journey down into the Sonoma-Carneros wine region.

Parking in downtown Sonoma is easy in the off-season and tougher in the high season (summer and fall). Expect to hunt hard for a spot during any local events, and prepare to walk several blocks. Most wineries provide ample free parking on their grounds.

For your public transit needs, use the buses run by **Sonoma County Transit** (707/576-7433, www.sctransit.com, $1.25-3.45). Several routes service the Sonoma Valley on both weekdays and weekends. You can use SCT to get from the Sonoma Valley to Santa Rosa,

Guerneville, and other spots in the Russian River Valley as well.

GLEN ELLEN

Only six miles up Highway 12 from Sonoma, but tucked away in the leafy glen of Sonoma Creek, Glen Ellen gives very little sign of being a part of "Wine Country." The sleepy town hugs Arnold Drive, which parallels Highway 12. Its population is just 784, and on the main drag through town there are only two grocery stores, a handful of good, but casual restaurants, a hardware store, and a couple of tasting rooms. Even in the height of summer, this town, cool under its shady oak canopy, can feel deserted.

But Glen Ellen has always been a popular draw, particularly with the literary set. Hunter Thompson even made his home here in the mid-1960s. But its most famous writer

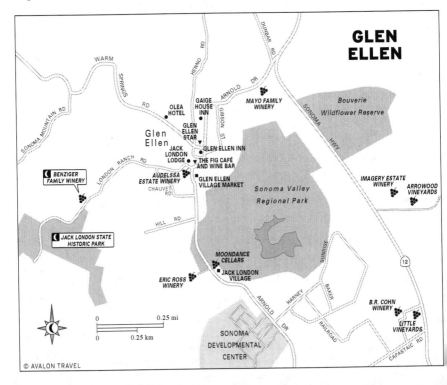

© AVALON TRAVEL

© ELIZABETH LINHART VENEMAN

Glen Ellen was home to both Jack London and Hunter S. Thompson.

in residence was Jack London, whose presence can be felt throughout the area, from his haunt up on Sonoma Mountain, now Jack London State Park, to the redbrick Jack London Saloon, which first opened its doors in 1905, to the tranquil, if slightly eerie, Sonoma Development Center where London set his 1914 story, "Told in the Drooling Ward."

As for wine, Glen Ellen is home to the Sonoma Mountain appellation, which produces unique cabernets from its rocky soils and cooler temperatures. Within the diverse microclimates also can be found chardonnay, pinot noir, sauvignon blanc, Semillon, and zinfandel.

Wineries

VALLEY OF THE MOON

At **Valley of the Moon** (777 Madrone Rd., Glen Ellen, 707/939-4510, www.valleyofthemoonwinery.com, 10am-4:30pm daily, tasting $5-10), 150 years of history juxtaposes with the highest winemaking technology California has to offer. Since the Civil War era, this Sonoma institution has passed through many hands and

produced hundreds of wines. The circa-1860s stone buildings house late-model stainless-steel fermentation tanks as well as classic oak barrels. In the tasting room, you'll find a small list of boutique wines, from an unusual sangiovese rosé to a classic California cabernet. Valley of the Moon takes pride in its awards, and you'll find that almost every wine you taste has its own list of medals. Check the website for a list of upcoming wine events that show off this great Sonoma landmark at its best.

LITTLE VINEYARDS

Step back in time to Sonoma in the 1980s at **Little Vineyards Family Winery** (15188 Sonoma Hwy, Glen Ellen, 707/996-2750, www.littlevineyards.com, 11am-4:30pm Thurs.-Mon., tasting $10). Just past B. R. Cohn, this is an unpretentious must for aficionados of big reds and seekers of the laid-back, bohemian attitude that Sonoma is known for. The century-old farmhouse vineyard, planted with 17 acres of grapes, is the dream creation of Joan and Rich Little for the production of premium reds. Little Vineyards is nestled in the Valley of the Moon between the rocky, sun-drenched slopes of the Mayacamas and Sonoma Mountain ranges and has a down-home, old-school valley feel. Zinfandel, syrah, and cabernet sauvignon are the primary varietals here, as well as a small block of cabernet franc, malbec, petite sirah, and merlot. The tasting room walls, lined with guitars, reflect another of Rich Little's passions—music. Taste a fusion of both in the acclaimed Band Blend. A true boutique winery, Little produces only 2,200 cases a year.

B. R. COHN WINERY

If you're a cabernet lover, then you have something in common with Bruce Cohn, founder and owner of **B. R. Cohn Winery** (15000 Sonoma Hwy., Glen Ellen, 800/330-4064, www.brcohn.com, 10am-5pm daily, tours by appointment, tasting $10). He is so fond of cabernet that he has planted all 100 acres on a former dairy with cabernet sauvignon. His Olive Hill vineyard has its own microclimate warmed by an underground geothermal aquifer (the same one that feeds the valley's hot springs) and shielded from cool air by Sonoma Mountain.

The olive trees surrounding the buildings and lining the driveway give the vineyard not only its name but also some award-winning olive oil that is also available in the tasting room. The French picholine olive trees are relatively young by olive standards—only 140 years old—and the eight acres around the winery form the largest picholine orchard in the valley. The estate oil is 100 percent picholine, and various blended oils are also available, together with some unusual vinegars, such as raspberry champagne vinegar and cabernet vinegar. Many can be tasted at the winery.

As you walk from the parking lot up to the tasting room, you might also hear Doobie Brothers songs wafting over the patio, giving away Bruce Cohn's other profession as the manager of the Doobies since the early 1970s and some other bands in the 1980s, including Bruce

Hornsby and Night Ranger. The music connection continues to this day—the winery hosts an annual fall music festival charity event featuring members of the Doobies plus countless other rock and country musicians.

ARROWOOD VINEYARDS & WINERY

The professional vibe and pricey tasting fees at picturesque **Arrowood Vineyards & Winery** (1437 Sonoma Hwy, Glen Ellen, 800/938-5170, www.arrowoodvineyards.com, 10am-4pm daily, tasting $15-25) are more in line with Napa's Silverado Trail than Sonoma's Valley of the Moon. That said, the wines here are exceptional. Founder Richard Arrowood's philosophy is simple—produce world-class wines with as little intervention as possible using grapes grown exclusively in Sonoma County's diverse microclimates that showcase the area's diverse soils. Current winemaker Heidi von der Mehden continues to execute Arrowood's vision. Located in a New England-style farmhouse with a wraparound veranda, the airy tasting room overlooks well-manicured vineyards and commands lovely views of the Sonoma Valley from its place on the eastern hillside. Arrowood is known for sublime cabernet sauvignons, so be sure to taste one (or more) of the award-winning single-estate reserve cabs when you visit. Then relax on the veranda and soak in the magnificent vistas.

IMAGERY ESTATE WINERY

The world's largest collection of wine-label art by some well-known contemporary artists (including Sol LeWitt and Terry Winters) is one reason to visit **Imagery Estate Winery** (14335 Sonoma Hwy., Glen Ellen, 707/935-4515 or 877/550-4278, www.imagerywinery.com, 10am-4:30pm Mon.-Fri., 10am-5:30pm Sat.-Sun., tasting $10). Another is the wide variety of small-lot wines that are available only at the winery itself. Imagery was established as a boutique offshoot of the **Benziger Family Winery** (1883 London Ranch Rd., Glen Ellen, 888/490-2739, www.benziger.com, 10am-5pm daily, regular tasting $10, reserve and estate wines $20) in the 1980s when art labels were catching on. Thirty years later, visitors can view much of the artwork in Imagery's gallery/tasting room.

Benziger focuses on creating unusual wines from vineyards on the 20-acre estate and other vineyards throughout Sonoma, including Ash Creek, which is the highest-altitude vineyard in Sonoma County. Imagery produces fewer than 8,000 cases of wine per year, which include sangiovese, barbera, malbec, petite sirah, viognier, grenache, and tempranillo. Most are priced $20-40.

MOONDANCE CELLARS

Located in a charming historic complex of buildings called Jack London Village, **Moondance Cellars** (14301 Arnold Dr., Glen Ellen 707/938-7550, www.moondancecellars.com, 11am-5pm daily, tasting $10) is the warm and welcoming tasting room belonging to charismatic owner and winemaker David Cohen and his wife, Priscilla. The buildings are some of the oldest in Sonoma County, dating back to the mid-19th century, and were the site of a sawmill owned by General Vallejo. Over the years, the buildings have been home to a gristmill, a distillery, and a winery, among other businesses.

Moondance currently shares the small storefront with **Sonoma Valley Portworks** (http://portworks.com), so visitors can sample Moondance's selection of award-winning sauvignon blanc, pinot noir, merlot, and cabernet sauvignon alongside Portworks' muscat, sherry, and port. Other goodies available in the tiny tasting room are Moondance's grapeseed oils and mustards. The ramshackle, clapboard buildings are also home to funky little shops and restaurants including **Wine Country Chocolates** (www.winecountry-chocolates.com). And, according to local lore, Jack London Village is not only haunted, but also housed a recording studio and crash pad used by Janis Joplin and Van Morrison. Look for Cohen's souped-up 1965 red Corvette out front, and drop in for a taste and some lively conversation.

ERIC ROSS WINERY

You can almost imagine author Jack London himself relaxing with a book in the cozy tasting room of the **Eric Ross Winery** (14300 Arnold Dr., Glen Ellen, 707/939-8525, www.ericross.com, 11am-5pm daily, tasting $10), across the street from the Jack London Village complex. The bright red-painted rustic building throngs with visitors on summer weekends, but during the week you'll likely have the comfy leather sofa inside to yourself. On winter days the fireplace makes it all the more homey; just imagine a few artfully crammed bookcases, and this could be Jack London's living room.

The metal-topped corner tasting bar almost seems like an afterthought, but it's where all the action is to be found. The winery itself is located in Marin, but this is the winery's only tasting room and the place to sample the range of pinot noirs, zinfandels, syrahs, tempranillo, and other wines, sourced from Russian River Valley, Sonoma, Dry Creek, Mendocino, and Lodi.

The pinots in particular are worth trying, and there are usually two or three available to taste, each from a different vineyard and each with a distinct character featuring classic Russian River complexity and smoothness. The syrah and zinfandel also offer some of the same cool-climate elegance and a refreshing alternative to more exuberant examples from the warmer Sonoma Valley found at other wineries. One of the more unique offerings is the white Rhône-style marsanne-roussanne, a full-bodied white that balances wonderful aromatics with a refreshing acidity. All the wines are made in limited quantities; total production at Eric Ross is only about 3,000 cases per year.

AUDELSSA ESTATE WINERY

The small downtown tasting room of **Audelssa Estate Winery** (13750 Arnold Dr., Glen Ellen, 707/933-8514, www.audelssa.com, 11am-5pm daily, tasting $15) resembles more of an upscale café, with neat rows of tables and even a sofa.

This is a small family-run operation started in the late 1990s that now makes a modest 3,000 cases of wine per year, sourced

Learn about biodynamic farming on Benziger's Biodynamic Discovery Trail.

predominantly from its highly regarded mountain vineyards on the other side of the Sonoma Valley. The result has been an impressive collection of accolades from national wine critics for its cabernet sauvignon, syrah-based blends, and a Bordeaux blend called Summit, all exhibiting the intensity that's unique to mountain-grown fruit.

You can choose from the standard tasting menu or opt to take advantage of the café atmosphere and splurge on the wine and cheese pairing for a breathtaking $40. While the tasting fee may be on the high side for this part of the valley, the intimate atmosphere and outstanding wines make it a worthwhile stop.

◖ BENZIGER FAMILY WINERY

With vines poking out from the hillside grass, free-range cockerels crowing, and its collection of rustic wooden buildings hidden among the trees, the mountainside **Benziger Family Winery** (1883 London Ranch Rd., Glen Ellen, 888/490-2739, www.benziger.com, 10am-5pm daily, regular tasting $10, reserve and estate wines $20) seems like an old family farm rather than a commercial wine business. In some ways it is. The Benziger family came from New York in the 1980s to this former hippie ranch and transformed it into the valley's only biodynamic winery while managing to keep three generations of Benzigers happy on its 800 acres. Some 30 Benziger folk now call this land their home, many of them working in the winery.

Biodynamic farming principles go beyond organic and attempt to re-create the natural interactions between all elements of the environment. To get a better understanding of this complex style of land stewardship, hop aboard one of their 45-minute tractor-drawn wine tram tours. You'll wind through the gorgeous and slightly wild-looking estate while learning about biodynamic principles, the natural environment, and, of course, the vines, the vintages, and winemaking in general. The tour concludes with stops at the winemaking facility and hillside storage cave, and a special tasting of biodynamic wines. It's the best tour in the valley for the money (only $20) and culminates with a basic tasting back at the winery. Tours are offered every half hour 11am-3:30pm daily, but the tram isn't big, so in the summer you should buy a ticket as far in advance as possible. Call the winery for the seasonal schedule, or book a reservation on their website. If you miss the tour, check out the Biodynamic Discovery Trail just off the parking lot. The short walking tour guides you through the basics of biodynamics, while also providing a lovely place to sit in the shade and take in the scenery. There is also an instructive map and exhibit on the way to the tasting room that not only details the farm's history but also illustrates what grapes grow where on the property.

Once you're in the tasting room, you'll be reminded that this is a large-scale operation. The long bar pours a mix of organic and biodynamic Bordeaux blends, cabernet, zinfandel, and sauvignon blanc, all grown on the property. Other vintages on the tasting menu are grown in Los Carneros and elsewhere in Sonoma and Northern California. Prices are reasonable, starting at $25 and hovering around $45 per bottle.

The tasting room is also filled with wine-related gifts and the standard cheese and salami fare, made more exciting with beautiful, handcrafted pickled veggies. Once you have selected your wine and snacks, head out to one of the many picnic options. Nibbling on food purchased elsewhere is also fine, and some of the shady spots even have Wi-Fi.

MATANZAS CREEK WINERY

It's worth the 10-minute drive up scenic Bennett Valley Road (off Warm Springs Rd.) from Glen Ellen to visit **Matanzas Creek Winery** (6097 Bennett Valley Rd., Santa Rosa, 707/528-6464 or 800/590-6464, www.matanzascreek.com, 10am-4:30pm daily, tasting $5-10), especially in May and June when the lavender is in full bloom and is quite a sight (and smell) to behold. The winery is in Sonoma's newest appellation, Bennett Valley AVA, and is nestled

at the foot of the hills surrounded by woods, flower-filled gardens, and the largest planting of lavender in California. Like the fields outside, the tasting room is filled with the scent of lavender in the form of soaps, oils, cut stems, and all sorts of other aromatic products for pampering and cooking. You'll also find wine, of course, including syrah and sauvignon blanc. But the winery is particularly well known for its chardonnays and limited-production merlots.

An estate tour and tasting ($10) begins at 10:30am daily, but for an additional $25 and some advanced planning (i.e., by appointment) you can taste the winery's limited-release vintages paired with cheese. If neither option appeals to you, printed guides to the surrounding flower and lavender gardens are available in the tasting room. Although no food is sold at the winery, this is a great place for a picnic accompanied by a bottle of chardonnay or sauvignon blanc. The lavender is harvested each year right before the winery holds its annual Wine & Lavender event, usually at the end of June. Tickets for the wine, food, and lavender party are $75 and should be booked in advance.

MAYO FAMILY WINERY

The **Mayo Family Winery** (13101 Arnold Dr. at Hwy. 12, Glen Ellen, 707/938-9401, www.mayofamilywinery.com, 10:30am-6:30pm daily, $6-12) breaks from the chard-cab-merlot juggernaut of Sonoma, producing an array of interesting Italian varietals. Here you might taste your first smoky rich carignane or barbera, enjoy a fruity white viognier, or savor the chianti-based sangiovese. Mayo Family boasts a big presence in the region, with an at-the-winery tasting room and the prized reserve tasting room up north in Kenwood (9200 Sonoma Hwy., 707/833-5504, Thurs.-Mon. 10:30am-6:30pm, reservations recommended, $10). At the reserve tasting room, your experience includes seven tasting pours of Mayo's very best wines, each paired with a small bite of gourmet California cuisine created by on-site chefs. Bon appétit!

LOXTON CELLARS

Although it's officially an appointment-only winery, visiting **Loxton Cellars** (11466 Dunbar Rd., Glen Ellen, 707/935-7221, www.loxton-cellars.com, 11am-5pm daily, free tasting) is usually as easy as checking to see if the sign is out on the road at the end of the driveway. If it is, then someone's home to pour some wines on the makeshift tasting bar set up in the corner of the spotless, warehouse-style barrel room. Visiting here is as unpretentious an experience as you can have in a valley that is already pretty laid-back.

Owner and winemaker Chris Loxton used to be assistant winemaker at neighboring Wellington Vineyards and had plenty of experience before that in his native Australia, so he knows Sonoma well and knows how to make distinctive red wines. He focuses mainly on syrah and zinfandel made from both Sonoma Valley and Russian River Valley grapes, including a shiraz from Australian vine clones, an earthy syrah from hillside fruit, a robust syrah port, and a dry rosé syrah. More recently he added cabernet sauvignon and a cabernet-shiraz blend—a sure sign that there's an Aussie at work.

Loxton owns no vineyards, instead working through lease agreements with established growers and helping them manage their vineyards. With just 2,000 cases made each year, the small-lot wines from quality vineyards offer outstanding value for the money, with most costing $20-30 a bottle. Call ahead and arrange a personal tour ($15) of the vineyards and winery from Chris himself to gain more insight into the wines and his winemaking style.

Recreation

Nothing screams picnic quite like Glen Ellen's shaded glens, oak-studded grasslands, and gently rolling hills. Thankfully this little hamlet has plenty of open space to spread a picnic blanket or stretch your legs after an afternoon of touring. Wedged between Highway 12 and Arnold Drive is the **Sonoma Valley Regional Park** (13630 Sonoma Hwy., 707/565-2041, www.sonoma-county.org/parks, sunrise-sunset daily, parking $7). A favorite with locals, the 162-acre park has paved and unpaved trails that wind through open oak woodland on the valley floor. Horseback riders, mountain bikers, and hikers are all welcome here, as are dogs, especially at the park's one-acre, fenced-in dog park. Picnic tables can be found along the paved multiuse trail that bisects the park.

If you want to take full advantage of the beauty of the valley, it is worth it to plan ahead and book a guided tour at the nearby **Bouverie Preserve** (13935 Hwy. 12, 707/938-4554, www.egret.org/visit_bouverie). Home to 130 species of birds, 350 species of flowering plants, and diverse ecosystems that range from chaparral to mixed evergreen forest, the 535-acre preserve is accessible only on docent-led tours. Despite the lost spontaneity, a guided tour through this beautiful spot gives visitors a window into the natural world that gives the valley such beauty and produces such great wine.

◖ JACK LONDON STATE HISTORIC PARK

The big dog in all of Glen Ellen's open space is the 800-acre **Jack London State Historic Park** (2400 London Ranch Rd., Glen Ellen, 707/938-5216, 9:30am-5pm Thurs.-Mon., $8/car). It is a short distance past the Benziger Family Winery and offers a unique combination of scenic hiking and self-guided history tours around the buildings that once belonged to one of the valley's, and indeed California's, best-known authors.

From the entrance kiosk, turn left to visit the **House of Happy Walls** (10am-5pm Thurs.-Mon.), the former residence of Jack London's widow, Charmian, and now a museum about the author's life. From there it's only a half-mile walk on a paved trail to London's grave and the ruins of the spectacular **Wolf House,** his 17,000-square-foot dream home that burned down accidentally just before it was completed in 1913. There was speculation that it was arson, but modern-day investigators conducted a forensic arson investigation and concluded the fire was probably caused by spontaneous

the House of Happy Walls at Jack London State Historic Park

combustion of rags soaked in highly flammable turpentine and linseed oil used during construction. Today, only the monumentally thick stone walls remain in the dappled shade of the surrounding redwoods, but in the House of Happy Walls there's a model of just how impressive the house would have looked had it not met such a fiery fate.

The parking lot for the miles of **hiking** trails is to the right after the entrance. From there, the Beauty Ranch Trail winds around the buildings on London's former ranch, including the **cottage** (noon-4pm Thurs.-Mon., fee) where he wrote many of his later books and died at a youthful 40 years old. Many of the other buildings once belonged to the 19th-century Kohler and Frohling winery, including a barn, an old distillery building, and the ruins of the winery itself. Others, like the piggery known as the Pig Palace, were built by London himself.

From the Beauty Ranch Trail, the Lake Trail goes uphill past the vineyards and through the redwoods for about half a mile to the forest-fringed lake created by London, where there are picnic spots and restrooms.

From there, explore the oak woods and meadows on a series of looping trails, or take the long Mountain Trail to the park summit next to Sonoma Mountain. That hike is about seven miles round-trip but can be lengthened by taking loops off the main trail. Another long hike is the Sonoma Ridge Trail, which leaves the Mountain Trail and twists through forests and clearings with sweeping views before reaching the connecting Vineyard Trail via Orchard Trail leading back to the lake.

Mountain biking is allowed on all the trails in the park except the Cowan Meadow, Fallen Bridge, and Lake Trails, plus the Mountain Spur Trail leading up to the park summit (2,370 feet). You might see a member of the Benziger family from the winery down the road hurtling by, but be aware that all trails are shared with hikers and some with horses. The Sonoma Ridge Trail loop is recommended over the Mountain Trail to the summit, which is a steep uphill and perilously rocky downhill.

Accommodations

UNDER $150

Attached to the redbrick Jack London Saloon and the board and batten Wolf Restaurant, the **Jack London Lodge** (13740 Arnold Dr., Glen Ellen, 707/938-8510, www.jacklondonlodge. com, $95-185) anchors this section of downtown and provides a less expensive lodging than others along Arnold Drive. While the two other structures harken back to Jack London's time, the 22-room lodge is more modern, with a broad patio, a kidney-shaped pool, and clipped lawns that are reminiscent of the 1960s instead of the 1860s. Inside, the inn goes for the latter Victorian feel with dark wood furniture, rich floral linens, and low lighting, but the age of the building shines through. The vines draping the balcony are a nice touch, as is the hot tub, and the creek running through the back of the property.

$150-250

To stay in authentic historic lodgings, book a room, suite, or cottage at the 🄲 **Olea Hotel** (5131 Warm Springs Rd., Glen Ellen, 707/996-5131, www.oleahotel.com, $170-375), a B&B tucked away behind Glen Ellen. Built at the turn of the 20th century to accommodate railroad travelers, it has been receiving guests for over a hundred years. In 2011, the property changed hands and the once-quaint and slightly funky accommodations got a sleek makeover. Today, spare and modern furnishings grace the rooms, which are all equipped with flat-screen TVs and Internet access. Some rooms come with a stone fireplace, while others boast an expansive porch overlooking the charming and well-maintained grounds. For more privacy, 300-square-foot cottages dot the property. All guests receive a hot two-course breakfast, and are encouraged to end their day with a soak in the outdoor communal hot tub and the complimentary dessert and dessert-wine tasting in the lobby. The revamped hotel also offers massage services ($110-210)

and accommodations for your pooch (an extra $25) that include his/her own welcome basket full of treats, doggie bags, bowls, and towels.

A little less polished but loaded with charm is the **Glen Ellen Inn** (13670 Arnold Dr., Glen Ellen, 707/996-1174, http://glenelleninn.com, $140-240), right in the center of town. Billed as cottages, the seven rooms are more like 1940s-style bungalows that each open out to a shared overgrown courtyard with a hot tub overlooking the creek. Like the restaurant only feet away in a separate building, the rooms are decorated in bold earth tones with overstuffed beds and chairs. The interiors feel a little dated and heavy-handed, but they are still exceptionally cozy, surrounded by the lush greenery of the glen with the creek bubbling outside. Each room is outfitted with a deep whirlpool tub and a gas fireplace. Many have mini-fridges.

Just outside of Glen Ellen, the **Beltane Ranch B&B** (11775 Sonoma Hwy., Glen Ellen, 707/996-6501, www.beltaneranch.com, $150-240) looks like a little piece of the Deep South landed in the vineyards. The Victorian-era house with its New Orleans-style wraparound veranda and lush gardens sits in the middle of the valley at the end of a long driveway, far from the madding crowds of Highway 12. The five tastefully furnished, white-paneled rooms evoke a bygone era without going over the top, and all open onto the veranda. The ranch is actually 1,600 acres of vineyards, pasture, and woods at the bottom of the Mayacamas Mountains, with miles of hiking trails and a tennis court for guests.

OVER $250

An alternative to the big-name luxury resorts in the valley is the lavishly appointed and fantastically Zen **Gaige House Inn** (13540 Arnold Dr., Glen Ellen, 800/935-0237, www. gaige.com, $300-450), where the serene setting is complemented by contemporary Asian-inspired furnishings, gourmet breakfasts, a big outdoor pool, and indulgent spa treatments to help soften the financial blow. The cheapest of the 23 rooms and suites in the main Victorian house start at $275 midweek and $315 weekends during the summer, and as the price increases the features include fireplaces and small private Japanese Zen gardens. The more expensive suites include fireplaces and truly indulgent bathrooms, while the Creekside rooms add a private patio overlooking Calabazas Creek to the package. Vaulting into the next price category are stunning, Asian-minimalist spa suites, each with its own freestanding granite soaking tub, sliding glass walls, and contemporary furnishings. They start at $445 per night. In 2012 the Gaige House came under the management of the Four Sisters Inns, a group known for unique, high-quality accommodations. The inn itself has changed very little under the new management, except their website now offers special deals and discounts, so be sure to check it out before booking your stay.

Food

CALIFORNIA CUISINE

Some of the most reasonably priced food in the valley, together with free corkage all the time, can be found in the heart of Glen Ellen at **The Fig Café and Wine Bar** (13690 Arnold Dr., Glen Ellen, 707/938-2130, 5:30pm-close daily, brunch 10am-3pm Sat.-Sun., $13-20). It is the North Valley offshoot of the popular **the girl & the fig** restaurant in Sonoma (110 W. Spain St., Sonoma, 707/938-3634, www.thegirlandthefig.com, 11:30am-10pm Sun.-Mon., 11:30am-11pm Fri.-Sat., $20) and serves up some of the same French bistro fare, although slightly scaled down. The menu leans more toward comfort food with grilled sandwiches, thin-crust pizzas, and main courses like braised pot roast. The warm interior and weekend brunch make it a sure bet. The Sonoma-dominated wine list is also more compact, but markups are modest enough that you might not even decide to take advantage of the free corkage—a generous policy, but one that's slightly curious for a wine bar.

Down the road is the yellow-ochre **Glen Ellen Inn** (13670 Arnold Dr., Glen Ellen, 707/996-6409, www.glenelleninn.com, 5pm-9pm Wed., 11:30am-9pm Thurs.-Tues., $17).

With low ceilings, warm lighting, and lush earth tones interior, the restaurant of the Glen Ellen Inn can either feel like a cool retreat from a hot valley afternoon, or a cozy hideaway on a cold wintry night. The restaurant seats 80, but thanks to patio seating, tables on both a covered and an open-air deck, and more tucked throughout the old building, it feels like a much smaller operation. A well-stocked bar sits just off the main entrance, encouraging a quiet cocktail in a romantic atmosphere. The serving staff is friendly and knowledgeable about the expansive wine menu and the tasty and unpretentious California-style food once you are seated. The menu boasts heavy hitters such as steak and lamb shank, but for a lower price point the lamb burger is perfectly executed, and the seasonal salads such as the grilled peach and baked Brie are nicely conceived and reach all the right notes. Desserts here are something to behold though bordering on a little too fussy.

The newest kid in town is the **⟨ Glen Ellen Star** (13648 Arnold Dr., Glen Ellen, 707/343-1384, www.glenellenstar.com, 5:30pm-9pm Sun.-Thurs., 5:30pm-9:30pm Fri.-Sat., $18). Representing the newest wave of California and also Wine Country cuisine, the Glen Ellen Star serves locally sourced, wood oven-fired fare (i.e., pizzas, roasted meats, vegetables, and iron skillet quickbreads) that leans heavily toward comfort food with a slightly urban sensibility. The interior is spare, with brushed metal chairs, light walls, and a gleaming, stainless steel kitchen. Reservations are encouraged, but the patio and bar seating remain open to walk-ins.

PICNIC SUPPLIES

Glen Ellen not only has top-notch places to picnic, but also a great local grocery to pick up supplies, the **Glen Ellen Market** (13751 Arnold Dr., Glen Ellen, 707/996-6728, www.sonoma-glenellenmkt.com, 6am-9pm daily). Owned by the same partners as the Sonoma Market, this full-service grocery is stocked with all the essentials in addition to an outstanding deli that serves upscale treats like asparagus wrapped in proscuitto and golden beet and goat

© ELIZABETH LINHART VENEMAN

the Glen Ellen Star

cheese salads, along with down-home favorites like fried chicken. There is even a whole deli case devoted to specialty cheeses, and one of the best and most diverse olive bars around. If you're looking for a bottle to take on your picnic, there is a whole aisle of just local vintages (many of which cannot be found at most grocery stores) at exceptionally good prices.

While only open seasonally May-December, the **Red Barn Store** (15101 Sonoma Hwy., Glen Ellen, 707/996-6643, 9am-6pm Thurs.-Sun. Apr.-Christmas) sells produce from the organic Oak Hill Farm, and some fabulous freshly cut flowers, as well as handmade wreaths, making it worth a stop. You can find this little gem of a store off Highway 12 just north of Madrone Road near Glen Ellen.

FARMERS MARKET

The place to go for the valley's freshest fruits and vegetables is the **farmer's market** (14301 Arnold Dr., Glen Ellen, 415/999-5635, 10am-2pm Sun. May 15-Oct. 30) at the Jack London Village. In addition to luscious tomatoes and juicy stone fruit, you can also find eggs, cheese, sweet treats, locally crafted oils and vinegars, art, and even music.

Information and Services

The small town of Glen Ellen does not have a visitors center, so stock up on your maps and tips before you leave Sonoma. The **Sonoma Valley Visitors Bureau** (453 1st St. E., Sonoma, 866/996-1090, www.sonomavalley.com, 9am-5pm Mon.-Sat., 10am-5pm Sun.) will have information for Glen Ellen. Some of the local inns and hotels will have some visitor information, however.

Likewise, don't expect to find much in the way of wireless Internet access or reliable cell phone reception. But if you do need to communicate the old-fashioned way, there is a **post office** located at 13720 Arnold Drive, next to Jack London Lodge.

Getting There and Around

The heart of Glen Ellen is located just off Highway 12 over seven miles north of Sonoma.

Arnold Drive is the main street through town and actually runs all the way to Sonoma. To get there from Santa Rosa, take Highway 12 east, through Kenwood, for 15.7 miles.

KENWOOD

Kenwood is the last town in the Sonoma Valley before you hit Santa Rosa to the north. Here the valley fans out and the Mayacamas Mountains to the east grow wilder and more rugged. Thankfully, this translates to three large state and regional parks for picnicking, hiking, mountain biking, horseback riding, and even stargazing. Unlike the towns of Sonoma and Glen Ellen, Kenwood is loosely arranged on Highway 12 and lacks a traditional main street. Instead, the center of town sits in the Kenwood Village Plaza, with its post office, two tasting rooms, and a popular restaurant.

Firmly planted in the Sonoma Valley AVA, Kenwood is home to a number of large castle-like wineries, in addition to smaller, mostly independent operations. In Kenwood you will also find the most renowned and luxurious spa in the valley, but that does not mean that the funky town has been minted in Napa's up-scale image. The food options here are modest, and there are plenty of goofy roadside stands and shops to browse local art, pottery, and knick-knacks for your garden back home.

Wineries
KUNDE ESTATE WINERY

The **Kunde Estate Winery** (9825 Sonoma Hwy., Kenwood, 707/833-5501, www.kunde. com, 10:30am-5pm daily, tasting $10-20) sprawls across 2,000 acres of valley land, making it the largest family-owned winery in the West and providing enough space for a whopping 800 acres of estate vineyards where 20 varietals of grapes are grown from the valley floor up to elevations of 1,000 feet on the terraced hillsides. In fact, the winery has enough vineyards, and varied enough growing conditions, to make only estate wines and still have enough fruit left to sell to neighboring wineries.

Grapes have been grown here by the Kunde family since 1904, and today it is best known for its zinfandel, cabernet sauvignon, and vineyard-designate chardonnays. It also makes a few unusual wines among its bargain-priced Tasting Room series, available only at the winery, including a fruity gewürztraminer, a strawberry-laced grenache rosé (both perfect picnic wines), and an intriguing blend of cabernet and zinfandel called Bob's Red. There are plenty of good picnic wines to complement an alfresco lunch in the shady lakeside picnic area.

The spacious tasting room rarely seems crowded, but if you want to escape it, the winery offers a variety of tasting (and touring) options. The best tasting option is in the Kinneybrook Room, where you can taste ($10) the more expensive Grand Estate reserve wines while relaxing in one of the leather club chairs. Free tours of the aging caves stretching half a mile under the hillside behind the winery occur almost daily, just ask. Other tours (also read hikes) are led up the mountain every Saturday and require a reservation. For the $30 you will also explore the caves, the vineyards, and learn about the winery's sustainable practices. The tour ends with a tasting at the mountaintop tasting room 1,400 feet above the valley floor. If you want to skip the perspiration, pay another $10 and jump aboard one of the winery's passenger vans to the mountaintop tasting room (reservations must be made two days in advance).

DEERFIELD RANCH WINERY

Tasting at **Deerfield Ranch Winery** (10200 Sonoma Hwy., Kenwood, 707/833-5212, http://deerfieldranch.com, 10:30am-4:30pm daily, tasting $10-25), you won't get any sweeping vistas, sipping wine through dappled sunlight, or wafts of fresh lavender sweeping up from the valley because all tastings, despite the beauty of the ranch, take place inside the cave. Sounds cool, right? Well, it is, and not in that musty cold cave kind of way. The winery is set off from the highway, deep in the Sonoma countryside. As you approach it, you'll see two life-size rusted metal giraffes standing by the lake. The winery itself looks both quaint and industrial. This feeling follows as you pass the crush pad, the fermenting tanks, and barrels of wine on the way to the cave. Once there, you'll be amazed at how warm and cozy the wineglass-shaped cave really is. Filled with plush couches and overstuffed chairs instead of the standard tasting bar, the room makes you feel like you have paid a premium for a VIP or reserve tasting. But the price is only $10. To add to the bargain, you are likely to get a seasoned employee or partner who knows their wine. Deerfield utilizes 26 vineyards to produce 12 different varietals, which are carefully crafted without the use of sulfites due to an allergy by the winemaker. This added complexity really shows, particularly with Cove Cuvee, a Bordeaux-style blend.

FAMILY WINERIES

Perhaps the cheapest wine-induced buzz in the Sonoma Valley can be had at **Family Wineries** (9380 Sonoma Hwy., Kenwood, 888/433-6555, www.familywines.com, 10:30am-5pm daily, tasting $5), a cooperative tasting room on a busy Kenwood corner. Five wineries are featured, and there are usually plenty of tastes for the regular tasting fee, including an especially varied selection of pinot noirs and chardonnays. All the wineries represented are small family-owned affairs, and on weekends some of the winemakers themselves often do the pouring.

David Noyes Wines (707/935-7741, http://davidnoyeswines.com) is a producer of mainly pinot noir, chardonnay, and zinfandel sourced from some well-known vineyards in the Dry Creek and Russian River Valleys and made using spare production capacity at some equally well-known wineries. In some respects it's a virtual winery, except David clearly knows his vines and wines, having started his winemaking career at Ridge Vineyards and having helped the Kunde family establish the Kunde Estate Winery in the late 1980s. He started his own label in 2001 and now also works as part of the winemaking team at nearby Wellington Vineyards.

The **Macrae Family Winery** (707/888-0238, http://macraewinery.com) also specializes in Russian River Valley pinot noir and chardonnay, but also has some full-throttle reds in its portfolio, including merlot and cabernet sauvignon. **S. L. Cellars** (707/833-5070, www.slcellars.com) is a small producer of pinot noir and chardonnay sourced from the Carneros and Russian River Valley regions, but it also makes a syrah from Dry Creek Valley, as well as three flavors of sparkling wine: brut, almondine, and framboise. **Collier Falls Vineyards** (707/433-7373, www.collierfalls.com) is based in the Dry Creek Valley and produces a few thousand cases a year of zinfandel, cabernet sauvignon, primitivo, and petite sirah from its estate vineyards. Rounding out the tasting menu is **Wine Tree Farm** (209/470-7617, http://winetreefarm.com), which produces Rhône varietals from the Lake Amador region. The small winery makes unusual blends, featuring largely grenache, syrah, and mourvèdre.

Tasting at the large U-shaped bar is a low-key affair, and pourers are happy to jump from winery to winery. There are light snacks available, urging you to take a bottle (prices rarely rise above the $35 mark) to the broad, shaded patios in either the front or the back of the converted old farmhouse.

MUSCARDINI AND TY CATON

These two tiny wineries maintain a cosponsored tasting room in a stylish strip mall in the village of Kenwood. As you drive down the highway it's easy to miss the tiny bar, which would be a crime for any true oenophile. **Muscardini** and **Ty Caton** (8910 Hwy. 12, Kenwood, 707/938-3224, www.muscardini-cellars.com, www.tycaton.com, 11am-6pm daily, tasting $10) pour some of the best wines in all of Sonoma. Planting his first grapes in 2000, Michael Muscardini proved himself a quick study, making wines that six years later were winning awards, most notably for his organic sangiovese. Focusing on Italian varietals, Muscardini grows many of his own grapes while sourcing the rest from growers inside the Sonoma Valley. As such, the tasting room is chock-full of barbera, tesoro, syrah, and, of course, sangiovese. A real treat is the dry and crisp Rosato di Sangiovese, a rosé recently given 91 points by *Wine Enthusiast*.

Also started at the millennium, Ty Caton has become a favorite in the valley, known for producing excellent wine at extremely affordable prices. Ty Caton makes vintages of what you would expect here with bold cabernets, big syrahs, and zesty zinfandels. The award-winning Tytanium is a blend of five varietals that includes cabernet sauvignon, syrah, petite syrah, merlot, and malbec, but its price point is $80, putting it out of range of many wine enthusiasts. Instead, for a terrific value, look for Ty's Red, another blend that, while not taking home the gold, is, for $34, one of the best deals in the valley.

For $10 you'll get to taste six of any of the Ty Caton or Muscardini vintages available. But beware: If you seem interested in the wines you're sipping, the tasting room staff will not only give you the long story about each vintage they pour, they'll also start opening and pouring everything they've got in the shop. If you're visiting on an off-season weekday, you may find yourself alone in the shop, discussing the wine regions of California and various varietals for more than an hour. Even in-season, this small tasting room preserves the kind of wine-tasting experience that wine lovers have been coming to Sonoma for decades to enjoy.

ENKIDU WINE

Located next door to Muscadini and Ty Caton is the spare tasting room of **Enkidu Wine** (8910 Hwy 12, Kenwood, 707/833-6100, www.enkiduwines.com, noon–6pm daily, tasting $10). Even more of a recent upstart than its neighbors, Enkidu began making wine in 2003 and opened its tasting room doors in 2009. The owner and winemaker, Phillip Staehle, is a native to the area and began honing his craft in the mid-1980s. While Enkidu has no vineyards of its own, Staehle spends much of his time roaming the Sonoma and Russian River Valleys for fruit, seeking out the perfect soil, right climate, and unique varietals (some of which are heritage, hailing from the oldest vineyards in the valley) to produce his unusual brand of wine. Like other vintners in the area, Enkidu produces a sauvignon blanc, chardonnay, syrah rosé, pinot noir, zinfandel, petit sirah, cabernet, and their most popular—a big Rhône blend. But each vintage is delivered with an unusual twist. Staehle says he is making wine in the "European Tradition," but it is a bit more than that. The Bedrock Zinfandel has a shocking, but tasty finish of earthy cola, the Fazekas Petite Syrah is lightened by a touch of white chocolate, and the Syrah Rosé is delightfully creamy with dual notes of strawberry and grapefruit. Some of the bold tweaks can be a little bit of a miss, but there is no doubt that Enkidu produces some of the best and most unusual wines (very affordable, too, at $25-45 a bottle) in the valley.

Adding to the experience is the fact that it is a small operation. Producing only 4,000 cases per year and keeping just five employees, Enkidu feels to be a labor of love. Likewise, the tasting room staff is knowledgeable, fun, friendly, and big admirers of what they are pouring. Open until 6pm daily, Enkidu is great place to stop after the big wineries have closed.

◀ CHATEAU ST. JEAN

If you were to build your own personal château in the Sonoma Valley, you couldn't pick a much better location than this. A long driveway through the vineyards leads up to **Chateau St. Jean** (8555 Sonoma Hwy., Kenwood, 707/833-4134, www.chateaustjean.com, 10am–5pm daily, tasting $15–25), a white turreted mansion at the foot of the mountains. The walk from the parking lot to the tasting rooms leads through a manicured formal garden, and on the other side of the reserve tasting room is a patio and expanse of lawn overlooking the valley and its vineyards.

Although St. Jean is best known for its white wines (which include multiple chardonnays, pinot blanc, riesling, and fumé blanc), it also has its share of big reds, including Cinq Cepages, a Bordeaux-style red blend of five varietals—some grown in a tiny vineyard perched on a steep slope above the winery—that is always rated highly by critics. Other red wines are Sonoma County cabernet sauvignon, merlot, syrah, and pinot noir, as well as some powerhouse reserve and estate versions priced $50-200. Some, like the riesling, fumé blanc, and several pinot noirs are available only at the winery.

The spacious main tasting room has a small deli and countless Wine Country gifts, but it's worth spending a little extra to taste wines in the more comfortable and intimate reserve tasting room. Upstairs from the reserve tasting room, there's a small gallery featuring the work of local artists. St. Jean also offers VIP reserve tasting in a private room and an hour-long sensory analysis class—just some of the additional educational courses and tours offered. Prices for these vary between $35-75, but for $45 you can get a tour of the winery, an education in history and *terroir*, along with a gourmet boxed lunch.

LANDMARK VINEYARDS

Landmark Vineyards (101 Adobe Canyon Rd., Kenwood, 707/833-0218, www.landmarkwine. com, 10am-4:30pm daily, tasting $5-15) was one of the first California wineries to make only chardonnay, though it has since expanded to include pinot noir, syrah, grenache, and most recently rosé, all made using grapes from the 11 acres of estate vineyards and others sourced from all over California.

Chardonnay still accounts for the majority of the 25,000-case production, and the wines range in price from the $25 Overlook chardonnay up to the most expensive $40 Damaris Reserve. But the rosé is a lovely picnic wine at $20, and the reds, also very reasonably priced, are generally well liked by critics.

A large mural behind the tasting bar livens up an otherwise drab room, but the best aspects of the Spanish-style buildings are outside. The large shady courtyard outside the tasting room leads to a fountain and gardens with a view straight over the vineyards to Sugarloaf Mountain in the distance. On Saturday afternoons you may hop aboard the horse-drawn carriage for a tour of the vineyards for no additional charge or reservation required, or arrange for the private Estate Tour that includes

a tasting at the end. You may also just take advantage of the few picnic tables where you can snack on the selection of cheese and charcuterie offered inside. There is also a free bocce ball court to test how straight you can throw after a few glasses of wine.

KAZ VINEYARD & WINERY

This is the one winery in the valley where it's guaranteed that the owner will be pouring the wine in the tasting room. Kaz (a.k.a. Richard Kasmier) is also as close as you'll get to a renegade winemaker, producing just 1,000 cases per year of bizarrely named wine blends and ports, some dominated by relatively rare grapes for California, such as the red alicante bouschet and lenoir, which is a varietal more commonly found in Texas or in tiny amounts in some California blends. The wines will not be to everyone's taste, but it's unlikely that you won't find at least one that tickles your fancy.

Kaz also grows syrah, cabernet franc, chardonnay, and dechaunac in his 2.5-acre organic vineyard (he once grew an unimaginable 15 varietals on five acres) and buys other grapes from neighboring wineries. A winery motto, "No harm in experimenting," ensures that many blends will change each year, though some are pretty much constant, including the ZAM (zinfandel, alicante, and mourvèdre), Sangiofranc (sangiovese and cabernet franc), and Mainliner (100 percent lenoir). For added interest, all the wine labels are vintage photos hand-colored by Kaz's wife, Sandi.

Kaz Vineyard & Winery (233 Adobe Canyon Rd., Kenwood, 877/833-2536, www.kazwinery.com, 11am-5pm Fri.-Mon. or by appointment, tasting $5) is four driveways up the road from Landmark Vineyards, on the left (drive slowly because it's easy to miss). The tiny tasting room doubles as a barrel storage area, and it doesn't take many people to fill it up, but Kaz keeps the crowd entertained and you'll quickly get to know everyone around you. The unmarked door at the back of the tasting room opens onto a small garden with just enough room for a private picnic.

© ELIZABETH LINHART VENEMAN

A tasting at St. Francis Winery & Vineyards comes with beautiful views.

ST. FRANCIS WINERY & VINEYARDS

Named to honor the Franciscan monks who are widely credited with planting California's first wine grapes, **St. Francis Winery** (100 Pythian Rd., Kenwood, 888/675-9463, www. stfranciswine.com, 10am-5pm daily, tasting $10) is a place for red-wine lovers, and particularly merlot fans. Merlot grapes have been grown here since the winery was established in 1971, and St. Francis was one of the first California wineries to bottle merlot as a standalone wine rather than as part of a Bordeaux-style blend.

The spacious tasting room is one of the best-designed in the valley. Windows running the length of the room look out onto the vineyards and mountains, and you can easily escape into the garden if it gets too crowded.

Picnickers are welcome on the sun-drenched patio across the lawn from the tasting room, while the tables just outside the large picture windows are reserved for those indulging in the charcuterie and wine pairing (11am-4pm daily May-Oct., no reservation required, $25), which includes a selection of local cheeses, charcuterie, and house-made rillettes, and either a flight of reserve wines or a full pour of your selection. Want to make it into a lunch? For $38, you can get five courses that highlight the diversity of the wine selection and include a Banh Mi sandwich and slow-roasted lamb. Call or check the website for the current seating schedule and to make a reservation, which is strongly encouraged.

LEDSON WINERY & VINEYARDS

At the top of the valley, the "Castle," as it's known to locals—a description that at first was meant more in a derogatory sense but has now been embraced by the **Ledson Winery** (7335 Sonoma Hwy., Kenwood, 707/537-3810, www. ledson.com, 10am-5pm daily, tasting $15-25) is about as ostentatious as Sonoma gets, and it's still a far cry from the palaces (and actual castles) in the Napa Valley.

Enter through the grand front door, pass the sweeping staircase, polished oak accents, and marble fireplaces, and you almost feel

© ELIZABETH LINHART VENEMAN

Ledson Winery is one of the most opulent in the Sonoma Valley.

like you're walking onto the set of some Wine Country soap opera. There are no fewer than six tasting bars in various rooms, together with a small marketplace stocked with wines, mustards, vinegars, a selection of cheeses, sandwiches, and other not-too-exciting picnic supplies including macaroni and potato salad. You can picnic on the grounds in the shade of a giant oak tree, although there's limited space and you can only eat food bought at the winery itself.

Almost every grape varietal is represented in the portfolio, including the estate merlot; cabernet sauvignon from northern Sonoma; chardonnay, pinot grigio, and pinot noir from the Russian River Valley; Rhône varietals from Sonoma and Mendocino; and the unusual orange muscat from the Monterey area that's worth tasting. It's a case of pick your poison—there's bound to be a wine to please everyone—but the highlights include the estate merlot, both the Russian River and Carneros chardonnays, and the red meritage blends.

Shopping

There is not much in the way of shopping in Kenwood, but a few shops stand out and deserve a stop. The wacky **Swede's Feeds Pet Garden Gifts** (9140 Sonoma Hwy., Kenwood, 707/833-5050, www.swedesfeedskenwood. com, 10am-6pm Mon. and Wed.-Fri., 10am-5pm Sat., 11am-4pm Sun.) is technically a country feed store, but it carries everything from chicken feed to decorative pots to unusual succulents, outside fireplaces, garden sculptures, and even bright pinwheels. Even if you don't have a garden, this is a great place to stop and spend some time browsing. Quality gifts can also be found across the highway at the **Kenwood Farmhouse** (9255 Sonoma Hwy., Kenwood, 707/833-1212, 11am-5:30pm Wed.-Fri., 11am-5pm Sat.-Sun.). A cute little red farmhouse, it showcases local artisans and has a selection of fair-trade clothing and various household, garden, and kitchen wares.

A little farther down is the **Figone Olive Oil Company** (9580 Sonoma Hwy.,

garden supplies at Swede's Feeds Pet Garden Gifts

Kenwood, 707/282-9092, www.figoneoliveoil.com, 10:30am-5:30pm daily). A well-known California oil producer with ties to the Sonoma Valley, Figone has been in the family olive oil business since the early 1990s and has become well known in the state's burgeoning olive oil industry. Figone makes its own oils from olive groves in the Central Valley and Sonoma Valley and also presses oil for some other well-known oil suppliers, including winemaker Bruce Cohen here in the Sonoma Valley. The B. R. Cohen oils are sold in the tasting room along with Figone's own oils, some in hand-marked bottles. There are usually several oils and vinegars to taste (for free) against a backdrop of the shiny equipment (some of it hand-me-downs from the Figone's Italian cousins) in the glass-walled olive press room. The variety can be both dizzying to the imagination and the taste buds. Taking home selections like Persian Lime and Blood Orange olive oils and the 20-year-old aged balsamic vinegar will breathe new life in any old homemade salad.

Recreation

ANNADEL STATE PARK

Redwoods, oaks, meadows, and a large well-stocked lake make **Annadel State Park** (6201 Channel Dr., Santa Rosa, 707/539-3911, 9am-6pm daily, $6/car) one of the most diverse of Sonoma Valley's parks. It's easily accessible from both Santa Rosa and Kenwood. Most trails start from Channel Drive, which is reached by driving north from Kenwood on Highway 12; just before the road becomes four lanes, turn left on Melita Road, then left on Montgomery Drive, and left on Channel Drive.

The rocky trails that make Annadel a bone-jarring ride for mountain bikers today also give away its previous life as an important source of obsidian for Native American tools and rock for cobblestones for cities up and down the West Coast in the early 1900s. There's still some evidence of quarrying on many of the trails, including the aptly named Cobblestone Trail, which used to be the route of a tramway carrying rock down the hill to the railroad.

Mountain bikers love the fact that most of

the trails are either single-track or double-track and strewn with rocks for a bit of added fear. This is probably not the best place for novice bikers to find their wheels, but it offers some of the best midlevel mountain biking in the Bay Area, with plenty of technical trails and an elevation gain and drop of about 1,000 feet for most loops.

Popular downhills include the Lawndale Trail from Ledson Marsh, a smooth, fast single-track through the forest; the Marsh Trail loop; and the rockier Orchard and Cobblestone Trails (including the Orchard Loop). Lake Ilsanjo is pretty much the center of the park and a good start and end point for many biking loops, although it can be relatively crowded on summer weekends. The best way to reach it from the main parking lot is to ride up the Warren Richardson fire road, saving the single-track for going downhill.

An alternate entrance that avoids the entrance fee and is popular with mountain bikers is on Lawndale Road. From Highway 12, take a left just north of the Landmark Winery; the unmarked dirt parking lot is on the right about a mile down the road. Farther up Lawndale Road, forking off to the right, is Schultz Road, leading to the Schultz Trailhead. It's better to bike up the Schultz Trail and come down Lawndale, but you will have to bike up to the Shultz Trailhead as there is no parking there.

The best time to go **hiking** in Annadel is spring or early summer when the wildflowers are in full bloom in the meadows around Lake Ilsanjo, named after two former landowners, Ilsa and Joe Coney. The two-mile trek from the parking lot up the Warren Richardson Trail to the lake gives a good cross section of the park's flora, starting in a forest of redwoods and Douglas fir and climbing up through oaks to the relatively flat area around the lake where miles of other trails converge.

Steve's "S" Trail, which branches off and then rejoins the Richardson Trail, is one of the few trails off-limits to bikes and therefore worth taking if you'd prefer to avoid speeding bikers. Allow about four hours to make the round-trip and explore the lake area.

The Cobblestone Trail to Rough Go Trail is an alternate but rockier and longer ascent to the lake, and one on which you're more likely to meet bikers hurtling down the hill or some of the park's wild turkeys ambling across your path. At the lake are picnic areas and restrooms, plus access to the rest of the trail network.

Fishing at the lake is also popular, with largemouth bass and bluegill the most common catch. The Park Service suggests the purple plastic worm as the best bait for bass, and garden worms or grubs are favored by bluegills. Anyone over age 16 must have a California fishing license.

◖ SUGARLOAF RIDGE STATE PARK

Sugarloaf Ridge State Park (2605 Adobe Canyon Rd., Kenwood, 707/833-5712, $8) is perfect for either a quick fix of shady redwood forests or for hikes to some of the best views, both terrestrial and extraterrestrial, in the valley. It's about a 10-minute drive up Adobe Canyon Road from the Landmark and Kaz wineries, putting it within easy reach of the valley floor for picnics and short day hikes. The park is open from sunrise until about two hours after sunset. It also has the only campground in the valley, which is now operated by Team Sugarloaf, a local nonprofit that stepped in to run the park when the state threatened to close it over budget issues.

The somewhat barren hillside near the entrance is deceiving. From winter to early summer, a 25-foot waterfall tumbles just a few hundred yards from the parking lot along the Canyon Trail, and the 0.75-mile-long shady Creekside Nature Trail runs from the picnic area.

The big **hiking** draw is the seven-mile round-trip slog up to the summit of 2,729-foot Bald Mountain, rewarded by spectacular 360-degree views of the North Bay. It starts off on paved fire roads, but the paving soon ends as the trail climbs 1,500 feet in about three miles with no shade at all, so take a hat and plenty of water in the summer. From the summit, the Grey Pine Trail offers an alternate route downhill, and on the way up there's a short detour to the peak of neighboring Red Mountain, which sits, technically on private property.

To get 12 inches closer to the sun, there's an equally long and hot hike from the parking lot to the 2,730-foot summit of Hood Mountain, which actually lies in neighboring Hood Mountain Regional Park. The dirt parking lot for the Goodspeed Trailhead is on the left of Adobe Canyon Road next to a stand of redwood trees just before the road starts climbing steeply.

From the lot, the Nattkemper-Goodspeed Trail crosses and follows Bear Creek through the forest, eventually crossing the creek again and steepening for the next three miles into exposed grass and scrubland. Eventually it reaches a ridge where you can bear left for the sweeping views west from the Gunsight Rock Overlook, or turn right and trek the remaining half mile up to the Hood Mountain summit. Allow at least five hours round-trip. During fire season (June-Oct.) the trail is occasionally closed about halfway up but is still a good place to go for a picnic.

Sugarloaf is also home to the **Robert Ferguson Observatory** (707/833-6979, www.rfo.org, $3 for night viewing, under age 18 free, daytime solar viewing free), the largest observatory open to the general public on the West Coast. It's just a short walk from the main parking lot ($8 parking fee). Check the website or call for a schedule of daytime solar viewing and regular stargazing through 8-, 14-, and 24-inch telescopes. There are usually one or two public day- and night-viewing sessions per month, plus regular astronomy classes throughout the year ($23 for one class, $75 for a series of six). Ask about the huge 40-inch refractor telescope (as of this printing, the observatory is still in the process of being built).

MOUNT HOOD REGIONAL PARK

Just to the north of Sugarloaf Ridge State Park is **Mount Hood Regional Park** (1450 Pythian Rd., Santa Rosa, 707/565-2041, 8am-sunset daily, $7/car). It also sits not too far up the road from the valley's tasting rooms (the closest being St. Francis Winery), but with less of a big-name reputation the picnic tables, situated beneath bay laurels, oaks, and redwoods just off the trailhead parking lot, are more likely to be empty.

From there, the Lower Johnson Ridge Trail hugs Hood Creek, switchbacking up 2,000 feet through riparian woodland to the exposed higher elevations of the park. The Pond and the Valley Loop Trails veer off the main trail to the right, and true to their names offer excellent valley vistas and picnic sites around Merganser and Blue Heron Ponds. This area is also abundant in natural springs. If you are eager to summit the valley's highest peak, Hood Mountain (2,730 feet), Lower Johnson Ridge Trail turns into Panorama Ranch Trail, which leads to the Orchard Meadow Trail (from which you can take a shortcut) and the Hood Mountain Trail. Hood Mountain is less than a mile from where its namesake trail departs from Panorama Ranch Trail, but it is a steep, dusty climb. Gunsight Rock Overlook is less than half a mile away and showcases the occasional glimpse of the Golden Gate Bridge in addition to its peregrine falcon resident in the spring and summer.

While the Johnson Ridge Trail is hiking only, the Hood Mountain and Panorama Ranch Trails are both mixed-use, funneling in mountain bikers from the Los Alamos Road trailhead in Santa Rosa If you are looking for a quiet backcountry experience, take the hiking-only Summit Trail as an alternative to Hood Mountain. An added benefit is that the trail slices through the pygmy forest that sits in the saddle of Hood Mountain's northeastern slope. Mostly made up of Sargent cypress, the forest is roughly 10-15 feet high and extends for nearly a quarter mile. Despite the riparian and forested reprieves, the majority of the park is exposed chaparral and home to wonderful rock outcroppings, poison oak, and in the summer, rattlesnakes and blistering temperatures. Bring plenty of water and sunscreen.

HORSEBACK RIDING

Rides of 1-3 hours, together with more expensive private rides that include lunch, are available in Sugarloaf Ridge State Park through the **Triple Creek Horse Outfit** (707/887-8700, www.triplecreekhorseoutfit.com). Rates start from $60 for one hour, and groups don't usually exceed six riders. Reservations must be made in advance, and rides are limited to those over eight years old and weighing less than 220 pounds. Wear appropriate footwear, and arrive at the stable (located at the end of the main parking lot) about a half hour before your date with the horse. Rides in Sugarloaf Ridge State Park are offered year-round, and on the half dozen nights during the summer when the moon is full there are two-hour rides offered at dusk for $90. If you want to turn it into a more epicurean outing, picnic lunch tours are popular, as is the Mountain Top Tasting/Ride Combo that features a visit to the Kunde Estate Winery.

THE KENWOOD SPA

If you are looking for some famous Wine Country pampering after all that wine tasting and dusty exploring of the area's regional parks, make an appointment at **The Kenwood Spa** (10400 Sonoma Hwy., Kenwood, 800/353-6966, www.kenwoodinn.com/spa.php). It might not have its own source of mineral water like its cousins down in Sonoma, but the spa makes full use of the surrounding vineyards and has been declared one of the top resort spas in the United States by *Condé Nast Traveler* every year 2007-2012. The wraps, baths, and other treatments use vine and grape-seed extracts to purify body and mind. If you are looking to purify your body *of* wine after days of wine tasting, you can choose from other edible treatments like Ultimate Chocolate Mint Body Truffle ($140 for 50 minutes) or the Spicy Mud Slimming Wrap ($165 for 75 minutes). For treatments that don't sound like you're ordering something at a restaurant, the spa also has an array of clinical facials, Hollywood-esque oxygen treatments, and plain old massages. You can purchase all these separately (the cheapest being an aromatic Jacuzzi soak for 20 minutes at $55), or you can select from one of

their spa packages, which last from 1.5-5 hours and cost $265-585. Some treatments include lunch or a bottle of sparkling wine, and the staff is often accommodating if you want to swap out one treatment for another. There is a package for couples (80 minutes for $390), and for all non-hotel guests there's a $50 day-use fee on top of the regular fees. Regardless of what extravagance you opt for, reservations are a must.

Accommodations
$100-200

If an extravagant inn and spa is not within your budget, consider staying at the **C Birmingham Bed and Breakfast** (8790 Hwy. 12, Kenwood, 800/819-1388, www.birminghambb.com, $175-205). Built in 1915 and now a registered National Historic Landmark, this five-room B&B exudes all the charm you could hope for. Each room is decorated in different colors with plenty of antiques and Craftsman touches. Guests enjoy a two-course hot breakfast served on china and crystal, wireless Internet, and a complimentary wine-tasting card for free wine tasting at 30 wineries in the Sonoma Valley. Children not welcome in the main house, but the Monroe Cottage, attached to the old water tower and with a full kitchen and living room, accommodates kids 6-12. Pets are also welcome in the Monroe Cottage for $10 extra per night.

OVER $200

To make your stay in Kenwood a fabulous wine-and-spa retreat away, stay at the **Kenwood Inn & Spa** (10400 Hwy. 12, Kenwood, 707/833-1293, www.kenwoodinn.com, $250-400, no children under 18, no pets). The Tuscan-style villa has 29 posh guest rooms attached to its world-renowned spa. Guests are also encouraged to indulge in the inn's rustic-yet-elegant Italian restaurant where dishes such as pancetta-rolled pork tenderloin, Sonoma-raised lamb, and house-made pastas compete for excellence with the carefully selected wine menu. The only problem with the Kenwood Inn is that you may have trouble prying yourself away long enough to go wine tasting. Expect to pay premium room prices during the summer and fall high season.

CAMPING

With cheap rooms at a premium in the valley and not a drop of rain falling for about five months of the year, camping starts to look attractive, especially when the campground also happens to be just 10 minutes from many wineries and a stone's throw from some of the best hiking trails in the area.

The year-round **Sugarloaf Ridge State Park** campground (2605 Adobe Canyon Rd., Kenwood) is the only one in the valley and has a lot going for it if you can stand the summer heat (it does get cooler at night). It's a somewhat typical state park campground, with a small ring road serving the 49 mostly shady sites for tents and small RVs (up to 27 feet), drinking water, restrooms, fire pits, and picnic tables. Be sure to bring quarters for the recently renovated showers.

Sites 1-11 and 26-28 back onto a small creek, across which is the start of a popular hiking trail. Most of the rest of the sites are at the foot of a hill and get the most shade, although none can be described as truly secluded. Year-round reservations can be made through www.reserveamerica.com or by calling 800/444-7275. You can also call the camp manager at 707/833-6084 to learn more about availability and potential closures. Fees are $35 year-round, but only include one car per campsite; every car is an additional fee.

Food

CALIFORNIA CUISINE

Aside from the upscale dining at the Kenwood Inn & Spa, Kenwood is slim on the type of chic eats found elsewhere in Wine Country. A favorite, however, is the quirky ◖**Dóce Lunas Restaurant** (8910 Sonoma Hwy., Kenwood, 707/833-4000, www.docelunasrestaurant.com, 11:30am-2:30pm and 5pm-8:30pm Wed.-Sat., 10am-2:30pm and 5pm-8:30pm Sun., $17-20), located in the quasi-strip mall that serves as the center of town. The small menu is farm-fresh California and all over

the map, representing the heritage and globe-trotting culinary career of chef and co-owner Alex Purroy and his wife, Jackie. Expect short ribs, kalua pork, and schnitzel with the typical Wine Country flair that includes specialty salts, truffle oil, and a carefully selected wine list. Once you've finished your meal, best completed with their Sticky Toffee Pudding, wander upstairs to ramble through the Dóce Lunas antique store. Adding to the eclectic atmosphere are the random plates on display as homage to the places all over the world where Alex has cooked. The four tables outside on the peaceful patio are perfect for summer evening dining.

Eating outdoors right next to the vineyards is one of the attractions of the **Kenwood Restaurant and Bar** (9900 Sonoma Hwy., Kenwood, 707/833-6326, noon-8:30pm Wed.-Sat., noon-8pm Sun., $18-28). The simple country decor inside is pleasant enough, but the outdoor patio that's open during the summer is one of the most idyllic places to eat in this part of the valley, overlooking vineyards and surrounded by flowers. The small plates and main courses are simple and unpretentious combinations of local ingredients that appeal to a wide range of diners. You'll find shrimp "louis" along with duck spring rolls and steak tartare for starters, and steamed mussels, pork tenderloin, and mushroom ravioli on the main course menu. The wine list is also dominated by locals and includes wines from almost every valley winery as well as the rest of Sonoma, plus a few bottles from Napa, France, and Italy for good measure.

ITALIAN

Café Citti (9049 Sonoma Hwy., Kenwood, 707/833-2690, www.cafecitti.com, lunch 11am-3:30pm daily, dinner 5pm-8:30pm Sun.-Thurs., 5pm-9pm Fri.-Sat., $12) is a roadside cottage known for its rustic northern Italian food, particularly the moderately priced rotisserie chicken dishes and risottos. The tasty focaccia sandwiches and pizzas also make it a popular lunch stop for winery workers in the area. Buy food for a picnic, or hang out on the patio with a tumbler of the cheap and tasty house wine.

Information and Services

Like Glen Ellen, Kenwood is shy of visitor services, but many of the hotels and wineries are accustomed to directing visitors to the best places to see. The **Kenwood Press** is the local rag and is published twice a month. Either in their print or online edition (www. kenwoodpress.com), you can find out about local events and get a flavor for the town. Cell phone reception is better here than in Glen Ellen, due to its proximity to Santa Rosa, but don't count on finding reliable wireless Internet access everywhere.

Getting There and Around

Kenwood is located on Highway 12, 11 miles east of downtown Santa Rosa and 4 miles north of Glen Ellen.

Los Carneros

Replace the vineyards with grass, throw in a few more cows, and the Carneros area would probably look a lot like it did 100 years ago. *Carneros* is Spanish for sheep or ram, and grazing was the mainstay of the region for hundreds of years. In fact, it has more of a Wild West feel to it than most of the Wine Country and was home to the annual Sonoma Rodeo until 1950. These days it's car and bike racing at the Infineon Raceway that draws adrenaline addicts, but even here the area's bovine history is celebrated by the snarling supercharged cow that sits atop the giant raceway billboard.

In addition to the grazing land that used to dominate the Carneros area, there were also fruit orchards growing every type of soft fruit. The first vineyards were thought to have been planted in the 1830s, and by the end of the 1800s the advent of the ferries and railroad had made Carneros a veritable fruit and wine basket.

Phylloxera and Prohibition wiped out the small wine industry in Carneros in the early 1900s, and it didn't get back on its feet again until the 1960s. By then the fruit growers had moved elsewhere, and the march of the vineyards across the pastureland began.

Today, the western part of Carneros primarily resembles grazing land, and huge marshes still merge at the edge of the bay with the low-lying flatlands. Drive east and the low-rolling hills are now covered with vineyards as far as the eye can see, a sign that cows will probably not return anytime soon.

The Wines

The 39,000-acre Los Carneros appellation borders San Pablo Bay and straddles the county line dividing Napa and Sonoma Counties, though the majority of its vineyards are actually on the Sonoma side of that line. Hence it's included in this chapter and not in the Napa Valley chapter, although both regions claim it as their own. The cool winds that blow off the bay and the murky cloud cover that often takes half the morning to burn off in the summer help make this one of the coolest appellations in California, ideal for growing pinot noir, chardonnay, and other grapes with a flavor profile that makes crisp, aromatic, and well-balanced wines.

Not surprisingly, those two varietals fill 85 percent of the vineyards, but more winemakers are now discovering that very distinctive wines can be made from syrah and merlot grapes grown here. Carneros is about as cool as it can be for merlot to ripen completely, and the resulting wines have a greater structure and subtlety than their hot-climate cousins.

Despite its cool, damp appearance, Carneros actually gets less annual rainfall than any other part of Napa or Sonoma County. In addition, the fertile-looking topsoil is usually only a few feet deep and sits on top of a layer of dense

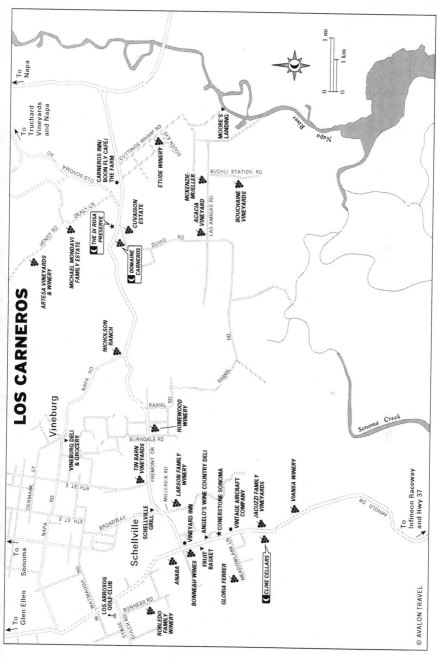

LOS CARNEROS

CHAMPAGNE CENTRAL

The French fiercely guard the word *Champagne*, and over the last few decades they have forced much of the rest of the world to accept that a sparkling wine can only be called Champagne if it comes from the Champagne region of France, just east of Paris. Their hardest won battle was with the United States, and it wasn't until 2006 that the U.S. government agreed to prevent American wineries from using traditional French regional names like Burgundy and Champagne on their labels.

The agreement was part of broader trade talks, but there was a small catch for the French: American wineries already using the term *Champagne* on their labels could continue to use it. Most California wineries, however, have long stuck to the term *sparkling wine* to describe their bubbly and *méthode champenoise* to describe how it's made.

Champagne-style wines have popped up all over the world over the centuries, from the sophisticated cava wines of Spain that have been made for hundreds of years to the more recent rise of sparkling wines in California, where Carneros is the center of it all.

In the 1980s and 1990s, the world's top producers of cava and champagne saw the potential of Carneros to produce world-class sparkling wines, and many set up shop in the area. The two biggest cava makers in Spain, Freixenet and Codorníu, are represented by the Carneros wineries **Gloria Ferrer** and **Artesa**, while **Domain Carneros** is the American outpost of champagne house Taittinger.

The local wineries of many other big French champagne houses, including Mumm, Krug, and Moët & Chandon, might be located in the nearby Napa Valley, but all grow a large proportion of their champagne grapes in Carneros.

The cool climate of Carneros is ideally suited for growing the two most important champagne grape varietals, chardonnay and pinot noir. Brisk winds and overcast summer mornings might not be the best conditions for touring with the top down, but a taste of some crisp local champagne more than makes up for the morning chill.

---

cold clay that is unforgiving to vines and forces them to put more energy into producing fruit than leaves.

There are far fewer wineries in the Carneros region than its size might suggest. Its prized cool growing conditions mean that most of the vineyards seen from the road are either owned by, or sell their grapes to, wineries based outside the area. Those that are open range from international champagne houses to tiny family-owned businesses where you're more likely to experience informative (and occasionally free) tasting sessions that used to be the norm in Napa and Sonoma but are, alas, no more.

Finding some of the wineries can be a test, best taken when sober. Plenty of big white signs mark the vineyard owners, but they're of absolutely no help in actually finding a winery, so a sharp eye is needed to spot the tiny signs tied to trees and posts. Most of the bigger wineries are fairly obvious from the main road, however, and there are only a few back roads on which to get lost.

WINERIES
Western Carneros
VIANSA WINERY & ITALIAN MARKETPLACE

The **Viansa Winery** (25200 Arnold Dr. Sonoma, 707/935-4726, www.viansa.com 10am-5pm daily, tasting $5-10) and its pretty gardens are perched on a windswept knoll overlooking the wetlands of Carneros, and the Italian heritage of its founders, Sam and Vicki Sebastiani of the famed Sonoma family, is obvious from the Tuscan-style architecture of the terra-cotta-roofed villa.

But the real smoking gun is the Italian varietals filling the tasting menu. Of course there are the usual Carneros characters like cabernet sauvignon, merlot, pinot noir, and chardonnay, but largely you'll find red Italian varietals like sangiovese, barbera, dolcetto, nebbiolo, and freisa, and whites including pinot grigio, arneis, and vernaccia. If you've never heard of most of those grapes, the $5 tasting of four wines will be a good introduction. For $5 more, you can opt for the premier tasting of the winery's reserve wines.

Either way, the crisp, food-friendly reds and whites will get your mouth watering for some antipasti. Luckily, Viansa is geared heavily toward food, which it sees as a natural pairing to its wines. In the ample tasting room, there is plenty of deli-style food available such as soups, sandwiches, salads, and even wood-fired pizzas in the summer. Many of the wines are also a perfect accompaniment (and price) for a picnic, and you can buy most by the glass from the tasting bar, but in the summer months, you might end up feeling more like a Mediterranean sardine yourself, as it is such a popular destination for busloads of visitors.

The neighboring 90-acre wetlands restored by Viansa with the bay in the distance make a fine view from the numerous picnic tables on the long terrace, marred only by the constant drone of traffic and the sometimes brisk winds. In the spring (Feb.-May), two-hour **wetland tours** are offered every other Sunday for $15, or $25 with lunch. Call the winery for more details and reservations. Tours of the winery itself are offered twice a day at 11am and 2pm and are free with the $5 tasting fee.

JACUZZI FAMILY VINEYARDS

Located across the road from Cline Cellars is another Cline family venture in the form of a giant Tuscan farmhouse, an homage to the family's Italian heritage. **Jacuzzi Family Vineyards** (24724 Arnold Dr., Sonoma, 707/931-7575, www.jacuzziwines.com, 10am-5:30pm daily, free tasting) was opened in mid-2007 and is modeled after the Jacuzzi family home in Italy—the same Jacuzzi family that invented the eponymous bubbling bathtubs. In that sense it could be considered as another Carneros producer of bubbly.

The Cline connection with Jacuzzi is not heavily publicized at the winery (and neither is the Jacuzzi connection to bathtubs), and unlike Cline, Jacuzzi focuses on classic Italian varietals such as nebbiolo, primitivo, and pinot grigio as well as the more common varietals in this part of the world like chardonnay, pinot noir, and merlot.

The flagship red wine is the winery's version of a super-Tuscan blend, albeit one incorporating the rather unusual combination of cabernet, malbec, barbera, and merlot. It is named after Valeriano Jacuzzi, the family patriarch who immigrated to the United States in 1907. The flagship white is named after Valeriano's wife, Giuseppina, and is a mellow example of a Carneros chardonnay. Surprisingly, tasting is free, but you can choose to spend a little and book an advanced reservation to have a private tasting and a tour ($20), or pair your wines with an assortment of cheese and chocolate wine shots ($40).

Jacuzzi is also the new home of Sonoma olive oil producer **The Olive Press** (www.theolivepress.com), which used to be based up in Glen Ellen. Its small tasting room is on the right as you enter the winery (for wine, turn left) and is the place to discover that olive oils can be as diverse in taste as wines. A small tasting bar usually features oils ranging from a light and grassy taste up to a rich, mellow one, with flavors generally determined by the olives used and where they're grown (sound similar to wine-grape lore?). The Olive Press is also a functioning production center, processing olives from growers across Northern California, and it sells a full range of oil-related gifts, from cookbooks and oil containers to soaps. Touring the facility is also an option for $40 and a reservation. Olive oil tasting is included, as well as a hearty selection of wines.

◀ CLINE CELLARS

Originally established across the bay in the East Bay, **Cline Cellars** (24737 Arnold Dr., Sonoma, 707/940-4061, www.clinecellars.com, 10am-6pm daily, free tasting) has come to thrive in southern Sonoma much like the lush, spring-fed garden oasis it calls home. The winery is now one of Sonoma's biggest makers of

Rhône-style wines and produces about 200,000 cases of wine a year from vineyards all over the Bay Area. Tasting-wise, the wines are a pleasant change from the Carneros staples of pinot and chardonnay, and most are pleasantly priced at $20 or less.

Despite being a relatively new member of the winery set in Carneros, Cline sits on some historic land. The tasting room is in a modest farmhouse with wraparound porch that dates from 1850. The area was also the site of a Miwok Indian village and later used by Father Altimira as a forward camp while investigating a site for what would become the Sonoma mission. Natural springs feed the three ponds and help sustain the giant willow trees, magnolias, and colorful flower beds surrounding small patches of lawn that are ideal for picnics. The tasting room contains a small deli, and the wines include several picnic-friendly options, including the Nancy Cuvee sparkling wine and a dry mourvèdre rosé.

The winery's colorful history comes alive in the three tours offered daily at 11am, 1pm, and 3pm. Celebrating the site's history as a temporary Spanish mission, the **California Missions Museum** (open 10am–4pm daily) is located in a barn right behind the tasting room and displays intricately detailed scale models of every single California mission, from the first in San Diego to the last just north of here in Sonoma.

GLORIA FERRER

At one end of Carneros is Artesa, the California outpost of one of the giants of cava production in Spain. At the other end is **Gloria Ferrer** (23555 Carneros Hwy., Sonoma, 707/933-1917, www.gloriaferrer.com, 10am–5pm daily, tasting $10), representing the other global Spanish bubbly producer, Freixenet, now the largest sparkling wine producer in the world. The fact that both these Spanish companies joined the largest French champagne houses in Carneros over the years is simply further testament to the ideal growing conditions here for the chardonnay and pinot noir grapes used to make classic sparkling wines.

The winery is styled much like a Spanish farmhouse, with stucco walls, tiled floors, and a large terrace that has sweeping views south over San Pablo Bay and far beyond. It can get crowded, but if you can snag a terrace table and it's not too foggy, there are few better places in Carneros to enjoy an early evening aperitif.

Gloria Ferrer now has the largest selection of champagnes in Carneros, priced from a modest $20 for the classic Brut or lively and aromatic Va de Vi up to $50 for the flagship Carneros Cuvée in a distinctly curvaceous bottle that matches its smooth elegance. In addition to the champagnes, the winery also makes an increasing quantity of still wines. There are four pinot noirs, as well as several chardonnays and small quantities of both syrah and merlot. Both still and sparkling regularly score above 90 with *Wine Enthusiast* and/or *Wine Spectator*.

Every day at 11am, 1pm, and 3pm, tours explore the long, cool cellars in the hillside behind the winery and are as good a lesson in how to make champagne as you'll find at any other sparkling wine producer. The cost is only $10 and comes with two sparkling wine tastes. Alternatively you can relax on the terrace with your choice of wines. The setup is more wine bar than tasting room—buy a glass of champagne, prices of which range $5-10 per glass, or taste the still wines in generous two-ounce pours for $2-3 each.

The visitors center shop is not only the place to buy wines but also to pick up all sorts of edibles, from picnic supplies and Spanish cooking ingredients to cookbooks and striking, pop art-inspired posters for some of the wines. You can also bring your own food, although you'll have to buy some wine if you want to eat it here and be happy sitting at a table.

ROBLEDO FAMILY WINERY

If you ever wondered about the fate of the laborers who hand-pick the grapes throughout the Wine Country, a visit to this winery will provide one answer. In the 1970s, Mexican immigrant Reynaldo Robledo was one of those laborers working in local vineyards, a job that was the beginning of his path to realizing the American Dream. He eventually formed a successful vineyard management company and finally created his dream winery, making his first commercial vintage in 1998.

The **Robledo Family Winery** (21901 Bonness Rd., Sonoma, 707/939-6903, www.robledofamilywinery.com, 10am-5pm Mon.-Sat., 11am-4pm Sun., tasting $5-10) is a low-key affair down a sleepy, semirural residential street off Highway 116 (Arnold Dr.) just north of the busy junction with Highway 121. Despite the lack of architectural flourishes of the big wineries nearby, the small tasting area with a giant oak communal table at its center is located in the barrel room, providing a wonderfully cool and intimate atmosphere in which to sample the wines. You're also likely to be served by one of the Robledo family, so be sure to ask about the story of Reynaldo.

The winery also boasts a large covered patio with long communal tables, perfect for picnicking and festive occasions. Thankfully, the tasting room stocks plenty of cheese and salami from the local Sonoma Vella Cheese Company. During your time here, you may also decide to take a tour of the vineyard. For $45 and a reservation, you'll learn about growing the grapes while tasting a selection of their reserve wines, which include chardonnay, merlot, and cabernet sauvignon, along with a barrel tasting.

BONNEAU WINES

Deli? Gas station? Tasting room? Actually, all three. **Bonneau Wines** (23001 Arnold Dr., Sonoma, 707/996-0420, www.bonneauwine.com, 11am-5pm Mon.-Fri., tasting $10) is operated by the third generation of the Bonneau family with a history that dates back to the early 1920s in the Sonoma-Carneros appellation. The Bonneaus arrived in America from Bordeaux, France, and began farming a 70-acre parcel of land just south of the town of Sonoma. After growing and providing chardonnay grapes to several well-known wineries in Sonoma and Napa, the family launched its own label in 2002. Tucked in the back of the Carneros Deli, this easily overlooked tasting room/wine bar at the juncture of Highways 121 and 116 offers "One of America's Best Chardonnays," according to *Wine & Spirits Magazine,* as well as an array of red varietals including the 2010 Sonoma Coast Pinot Noir, a gold medal winner at the San Francisco Chronicle Wine Competition. Taste wine, grab a pastrami sandwich, and fill the tank in one fell swoop!

SCHUG CARNEROS ESTATE

You might recognize the labels at the **Schug Carneros Estate** (602 Bonneau Rd., Sonoma, 800/966-9365, www.schugwinery.com, 10am-5pm daily, tasting $5-10). One of the Carneros region's elder statesmen, Walter Schug has made wine that's set the tone for California vintages for many years. The estate itself is worth a visit; the Tudor-esque barn sits in the middle of barns and fields of mustard (the brilliant yellow flowering plants) on the valley floor, with views of the surrounding mountains all around. Schug's hallmarks are chardonnays and pinot noirs, grapes that grow well in this cooler region, so be sure to try the latest releases of both.

ANABA

In a quaint, modest 100-year-old farmhouse near the intersection of Highways 121 and 116, **Anaba** (60 Bonneau Rd., Sonoma, 707/996-4188, www.anabawines.com, 10:30am-5:30pm daily, tasting $15) pours elegant wines that are handcrafted from premium Rhône and burgundian grape varietals grown on their Carneros Estate vineyard and on select vineyards throughout Sonoma County. Anaba's wines are artistic blends, inspired by the rugged earthiness of France's Rhône Valley and replicated in the rocky soils found in Sonoma. And as you might expect, the chardonnays and pinot noirs reflect the flavors and aromas that the gently sloping vineyards of the Burgundy, Sonoma Coast, and Carneros appellations are renowned. Producing just 4,500 cases per year, Anaba creates limited-edition, high-quality blends and single varietal wines. If you are looking for an intimate, unpretentious boutique winery, Anaba is a great place to kick back on the patio overlooking the vineyards and enjoy expertly crafted wine. The engaging and knowledgeable staff is an added bonus.

TIN BARN VINEYARDS

It might look like you are driving into a storage locker complex but don't be fooled by the industrial park setting. The tasting room at **Tin Barn Vineyards** (21692 8th St. E., #340, Sonoma, 707/938-5430, www.tinbarnvineyards.com, noon-5pm Fri.-Mon., tasting $10) is located in a spare, industrial-chic building near the Sonoma airport. There are no cutesy aprons or corkscrews with clichéd Wine Country sayings here. Instead, visitors see a modern tasting room with clean lines, corrugated ceilings, and large windows that overlook the adjacent wine production cellar. The staff is gregarious and knowledgeable. The name was derived from Tin Barn Road, a rocky appellation high atop the ridges of the Sonoma Coast, where the five friends and collaborators of the vineyard sourced their first grapes. The Tin Barn portfolio of wines includes a Russian River zinfandel, a Napa Valley merlot, and a Sonoma Valley zinfandel, as well as a syrah and sauvignon blanc.

MACROSTIE WINERY & VINEYARDS

On the south side of Sonoma, **MacRostie Winery** (21481 8th St. E., Sonoma, 707/996-4480, www.macrostiewinery.com, 11am-4pm Sat., call for appointment Mon.-Fri., tasting $10) makes 20,000 cases of highly regarded and elegantly understated chardonnay, pinot noir, and syrah from vineyards all over Carneros, including Steve MacRostie's own local Wildcat Mountain vineyard, a windswept hillside that he first planted in 1998. The tasting room, which doubles as a loading dock, is even less stylish than its Tin Barn neighbor and the vibe even more laid-back. The winery is only open to the public on Saturday, otherwise tasting is by appointment only (and only if someone in the office is free to pour wine). This is not a winery eager to woo wine tasters or to serve up a "Wine Country" experience, but it is worth a stop to taste some carefully crafted estate wines from a Carneros winemaking veteran.

LARSON FAMILY WINERY

To get to this historic patch of land, you must turn off Highway 121 and head toward the wetlands, down a small country road almost as far as dry land will take you. Only the whimsical, hand-painted signs along the way suggest there's civilization at the end of the road. The **Larson Family Winery** (23355 Millerick Rd., Sonoma, 707/938-3031, www.larsonfamilywinery.com, 10am-5pm daily, tasting $5) is situated next to Sonoma Creek at the edge of the San Pablo Bay, near what was once called Wingo, where steamships from San Francisco docked in the mid-1800s and disgorged their Sonoma-bound passengers. It's a pretty part of the world, but being surrounded by wetlands has its disadvantages. The area is prone to flooding during winter rains, and summer days can be a bit chilly this close to the water.

Today, the winery produces about 4,000 cases of wine from its 70 acres of Carneros vineyards, as well as a far larger amount under contract for the new owners of the Sonoma Creek brand. Despite the relatively small production of Larson wines, the portfolio is large and dominated by cool-climate Carneros wines including pinot noir, barrel-aged chardonnay, and a gewürztraminer. Standouts include a pinot noir rosé that got a nod at the state fair.

You won't find Larson wines on many reviewers' lists, but part of the fun of visiting here is the unique location and the down-home family-farm atmosphere that'll be a hit with kids and provide a refreshing contrast to the fancier wineries all around. The winery tasting room is in an old redwood barn with a small enclosure of goats and sheep right opposite and usually a couple of the winery dogs—Pete, Bubba, and Sonny—lounging nearby. You might also be lucky enough to see the pet llama.

There's also a regulation-sized bocce ball court and a grassy picnic and play area behind the tasting room to enjoy a bite to eat with a bottle of Larson's rosé or gewürztraminer. Jeep tours of the surrounding vineyards and wetlands are also sometimes available through an unaffiliated company—just look for the bright green Jeep in the parking lot.

Eastern Carneros
HOMEWOOD WINERY

Just a mile or so from the grandeur and glitz of Domaine Carneros, halfway down tiny Burndale Road, is the down-home atmosphere of **Homewood Winery** (23120 Burndale Rd., Sonoma, 707/996-6353, www.homewoodwinery.com, 10am-4pm daily, free tasting), which produces just 3,000 cases of reasonably priced wines a year.

The focus here is on small batches of a variety of mainly red wines like zinfandel, merlot, syrah, and Bordeaux-style red blends, Napa and Carneros chardonnays, and a couple of bottlings of pinot noir sourced from a neighboring Carneros vineyard. Most wines are very reasonably priced, with the best bang for the buck being the Flying Whizzbangers, a zinfandel-dominated red blend.

The staff will happily spend an hour or more with visitors in the tiny tasting room explaining the wines, conducting some vertical tastings, and teaching some tasting tricks, like how to identify the oak used in the barrels. That is, if no big groups arrive; otherwise the small indoor tasting area can quickly get claustrophobic, and it's best to spill out onto the back porch "lounge" if it's open. Be sure to check out the olive oils also sold at the winery.

NICHOLSON RANCH

Though just outside the Los Carneros appellation boundary by literally a few yards (it's technically in the Sonoma Valley appellation), the mission-style **Nicholson Ranch** winery (4200 Napa Rd., Sonoma, 707/938-8822, www.nicholsonranch.com, 10am-6pm daily, tasting $5-10) is perched on a small hill above the intersection of the Carneros Highway and Napa Road, putting it on the route of most visitors to Carneros or anyone heading to or from Napa beyond.

Nicholson Ranch is predominantly a pinot and chardonnay producer, and those two varietals account for much of the 10,000 cases of wine made each year. The chardonnays, and in particular the flagship Cuvée Natalie, garner some good reviews from critics, and bottle prices are generally reasonable. The winery also makes small quantities of syrah and merlot from local vineyards, both of which exhibit the classic aromas and restraint of cool-climate wines. For $5 you can taste three wines and for $10 you can bump it up to six. For just $5 more, you can take an appointment-only tour of the winery caves and winemaking facilities with a couple of extra tastes thrown in along the way.

The bright and spacious tasting room oozes sophistication, with limestone floors and a cherrywood central tasting bar topped with granite. Cheap gifts are nowhere to be seen, but a modest selection of picnic supplies are sold. There are tables on the veranda overlooking the surrounding hills and a grassy area next to the pond for those days when the weather's cooperating. When it's not, take time to peruse the Overlook Gallery, appropriately overlooking the tasting room. The airy space showcases local artists, sculptors, and photographers. The selection is well chosen and urbane, eschewing the typical wineglass still life. The tasting room is open later than most in the area, even in winter, so those on a hectic schedule should make this their last winery of the day.

◖ DOMAINE CARNEROS

The French heritage of one of California's premier champagne houses is obvious when you see the ornate château and its formal gardens on a low hill next to the main road. The **Domaine Carneros** estate (1240 Duhig Rd., Napa, 800/716-2788, www.domainecarneros.com, 10am-5:45pm daily, tasting $20-30) was built in the style of the 18th-century Chateau de la Marquetterie, home of one of the winery's principal founders, Champagne Taittinger. The sweeping staircase leading from the parking lot and the palatial interior leave no doubt about the winery's fancy French pedigree. It all feels a little over-the-top, particularly when contrasted with the rustic, windswept Carneros landscape on a foggy day. With some sun on a less crowded day, however, it can feel almost magical.

Then there is the magic of the flute.

Beginning at $20 you can taste a flight of three of their celebrated sparkling wines that include a regular brut, brut rosé, and the flagship Le Rêve blanc de blancs that is made from 100 percent chardonnay and considered one of California's top champagnes. The most interesting sparkler, however, is the LD (late-disgorged) brut, which has an extra creaminess and crispness that comes from leaving the lees in the bottle for longer before it is disgorged, essentially slowing down the bottle-aging process. Domaine Carneros also makes three different well-respected pinot noirs as well as unusual limited-release vintages that include the vermeil demi-sec, which is a lightly sweet sparkling wine. These are also available to taste.

To learn about how bubbly is made, there are three "The Art of Sparkling Wine" tours per day (11am, 1pm, and 3pm) that let visitors peer into the squeaky-clean, modern production and bottling areas after first sitting through a rather tiring PR-laden DVD presentation. At $30 per person, the tours offer the best value because they include a tasting of four wines along the way, and you get to keep the tasting glass. Reservations, while not required, are a good idea, especially during the busy summer months. If that sounds like too much effort, you can simply chill on the huge terrace overlooking the vineyards and let the bubbles do their work, perhaps with some caviar or a cheese plate ($18) to help the wines go down. Wines by the glass start at $7 and bottles hover around the $30 mark.

CUVAISON ESTATE

Right opposite the entrance to Domaine Carneros and its fancy French architectural excesses is the modern and minimalist home of **Cuvaison** (1221 Duhig Rd., Napa, 707/942-2455, www.cuvaison.com, 10am-4pm Sun.-Thurs., 10am-5pm Fri.-Sat., tasting $20), a winery that (rather ironically) takes its name from an old French term describing the part of the winemaking process that gives red wine its color. The contrast between the two neighboring wineries could not be starker: Where

Domaine Carneros surrounds visitors with ornate luxury that almost seems to enhance their luxurious sparkling wines, Cuvaison lets nature do the talking with an airy and contemporary concrete, wood, and glass indoor-outdoor tasting lounge from which you can almost reach out and touch the vines.

Also unlike its neighbor, Cuvaison is a bubble-free zone. Instead, you'll find Carneros-grown pinot, chardonnay, merlot, and syrah. The real treat, however, is the Napa Valley cabernet sauvignon, which is about as far from a fruit-bomb as a Napa cabernet can get. This is very much an Old World style of cabernet, with a balance, concentration, and structure typical of wines made from mountain-grown fruit.

Although Cuvaison advertises this tasting room as appointment-only, there's usually no problem rolling up unannounced. It's worth calling ahead if you can, however, because it can get crowded at certain times of the day. If you do decide to plan ahead, consider spending an extra $10 and booking a tour (9:30am Fri.-Mon.). It may seem a bit early for tasting wine, but wandering around the vineyards through the mist of the morning is a pretty magical way to start the day.

BOUCHAINE VINEYARDS

To get to this historic spot out on the scenic flatlands of Carneros, follow Duhig Road for about a mile (before Domaine Carneros), turn left on Las Amigas Road, and then right on Buchli Station Road. The current **Bouchaine** winery (1075 Buchli Station Rd., Napa, 707/252-9065, www.bouchaine.com, 10:30am-4:30pm daily Nov.-Apr., 10:30am-5:30pm May-Oct., tasting $15-35) was established in 1981, but there has been a winery on the site since 1934 and grapes have been grown here since 1899. Unfortunately, you won't see much evidence of that history here, just a cozy tasting room, refreshingly free of Wine Country paraphernalia, and a veranda that invites you to sit and enjoy some wine while overlooking the vineyards with San Pablo Bay in the distance.

The winery's official picnic area, however,

is reserved for its club members and those who preorder a "Table for Two" picnic lunch, which includes a wine tasting, a choice of five freshly prepared gourmet sandwiches complete with sides, and a bottle of wine. At $95 for two people, it's as good a way to have lunch as any in Carneros, particularly if the sun is out. The lunch option must be booked at least a day in advance, and is officially only offered May-October, but the winery often makes exceptions. Bouchaine is also a popular stop for bikers who relish the quiet, straight, and flat roads of the area.

Bouchaine offers a number of different tasting options that include their estate wines, pinot noir, chardonnay, and pinot gris. In their Bacchus Collection you can find more interesting wines like the light, flowery pinot meunier, a varietal that is normally used as a blending grape in champagne production. There's also a spicy syrah sourced from northern Sonoma vineyards and a good gewürztraminer from Mendocino's Anderson Valley.

ETUDE WINES

At the eastern end of Carneros and close to Napa is **Etude Wines** (1250 Cuttings Wharf Rd., Napa, 707/257-5300, www.etudewines. com, 10am-4:30pm daily $15-35), which, like many of the neighboring champagne houses has a decidedly French feel. The understated stone chateau-like winery is surrounded by trim grounds and lush vineyards and the tasting room has a Euro-chic air in its crisp lines and minimalist decor. High ceilings, blond wood, and modernist chandeliers complement the vertical (and artful) array of wines on display behind the bar. Style aside, the winery is known for its refined but pricey Carneros pinot noir, but also produces pinot blanc and pinot gris from local Carneros vineyards together with some Napa Valley merlot and cabernet. Tastings include five wines ($15) or five reserve wines ($25); during the week, opt for a seated tasting of reserve wines ($35). On the weekends, the appointment-only tasting includes food pairing on the lovely stone patio.

MICHAEL MONDAVI FAMILY ESTATE

Just down the road from the fake hill of Artesa, in a homey yet modern farmhouse, is a tasting room that can be either inspiring or intimidating, depending on your mood. **Michael Mondavi Family Estate** (1285 Dealy Ln., Napa, 707/256-2757, www.foliowinestudio.com, noon-5pm Mon.-Tues., 11am-5pm Fri.-Sun., tasting $10-20) is the home of no less than 35 different wines under seven different labels, all linked through Folio Fine Wine Partners and some sort of tie to Michael Mondavi.

The result is a dizzying array of wines on the tasting menu, many with names that offer no clue as to their style or origins. They are organized by varietal, which sounds helpful, except it means you might end up tasting a Carneros pinot alongside one from Oregon. Be sure to question the server thoroughly before deciding which of the wines to taste. That will help ensure you're less intimidated and more inspired by one of the more diverse tasting lineups in Carneros.

If you can afford it, go for the more expensive "artisan" tasting, which includes pinots from some of the best West Coast pinot-growing regions and a nice selection of old-vine zinfandels. If it's a quiet day and the weather's nice, then also be sure to make a beeline for the veranda at the back of the house through the door to the right of the main tasting bar. Piped music aside, it's a peaceful and cozy space overlooking a small secluded vineyard. Bring your own food and buy a bottle of rosé at the bar for a relaxing lunch.

ARTESA VINEYARDS & WINERY

A sure sign of how close this part of Carneros is to the Napa Valley, both geographically and culturally, is the marriage of wine, art, and design at **Artesa** (1345 Henry Rd., Napa, 707/224-1668, www.artesawinery.com, 10am-5pm daily, tasting $10-15), an outpost of the historic Spanish sparkling wine producer Codorníu. The grass-covered winery was designed by Barcelona architect Domingo Triay to blend in with the surrounding land, and to a certain extent he succeeded: Driving up tiny Henry Road through the vineyards, the only sign of the winery's presence is that one of the low hills happens to be peculiarly square-shaped.

Art is everywhere, from the sculptures and reflecting pools around the parking lot up to the gallery-like interior of the winery. The airy tasting room has a spacious indoor seating area and large (if breezy) patio overlooking the Carneros vineyards, and a small museum gives some history of champagne making and the Codorníu family.

There are several tasting options in the sleek tasting room with its adjoining patio overlooking the vineyards planted in chardonnay and pinot noir. You can try the lower tiers of wines or the limited releases, which include chardonnay, cabernet sauvignon, merlot, and syrah. Surprisingly, no sparkling wine is made here, but you can taste some cava from Spain, or do a horizontal tasting of pinots from both Carneros and the Russian River Valley that illustrates the subtle differences inherent to the wines from each region. Overall, however, the tasting options don't quite match the architectural and artistic scope of the winery, but tours are offered at 11am and 2pm daily ($20). Perusing the art is free.

WINERIES BY APPOINTMENT

Tucked away off the well-beaten path of the Carneros Highway are some notable appointment-only wineries that give more opportunities to discover some hot wines from the cool Carneros region.

The **McKenzie-Mueller** winery (2530 Las Amigas Rd., Napa, 707/252-0186, www.mckenziemueller.com, 10am-4:30 by appointment, tasting $10) is the family-run operation of Napa Valley wine veterans Bob and Karen Mueller. From their 50 acres of estate vineyards they produce only 2,500 cases of wine, encompassing many varietals, including merlot, pinot noir, malbec, and cabernet sauvignon. Standouts include an aromatic cabernet franc. The winery is on Las Amigas Road at the junction with Buchli Road, just up the road from Bouchaine.

Just down Las Amigas Road from McKenzie-Mueller is **Acacia Vineyard** (2750 Las Amigas Rd., Napa, 707/226-9991 or 877/226-1700, www.acaciavineyard.com, 10am-4pm Mon.-Sat. and noon-4pm Sun. by appointment, tasting $15), a much larger winery that has produced pinot and chardonnay wines since 1979 and now owns 150 acres of local vineyards. Recently, the 2009 chardonnay and pinot noir both received above 90 points by *Wine Spectator*. Acacia is on Las Amigas Road near the junction with Duhig Road.

The highly acclaimed wines made by **Truchard Vineyards** (3234 Old Sonoma Rd., Napa, 707/253-7153, www.truchardvineyards.com, Mon.-Sat. by appointment, tasting $20) come from its huge 270-acre Carneros vineyard where 10 varietals are grown, including cabernet, tempranillo, and zinfandel grapes that reflect the vineyard's location near the border with the warmer Napa Valley. Truchard sells most of its estate grapes to other wineries, using around 20 percent to make its 15,000 cases of premium limited-release wines, the best of which are the elegant syrah and pinot noir. A tour and tasting also provides the chance to see the winery's 100-year-old barn.

SIGHTS
◖ The di Rosa Preserve

When writer Rene di Rosa sought rural tranquility in 1960 and bought some old grazing land in Carneros, locals might have thought they were as likely to see cows walking on water as the eventual creation of the biggest collection of Northern California contemporary art and one of the largest regional art collections in the country. Thirty years later, they saw both.

The **di Rosa Preserve** (5200 Carneros Hwy./Hwy. 121, Napa, 707/226-5991, www.dirosaart.org, 10am-4pm Wed.-Sun. Nov.-Apr., 10am-6pm May-Oct., $5 donation) opened to the public in 1997 and now has more than 2,000 works on display throughout its 217 acres, including a colorful cow that has floated on the 35-acre lake since 1989, although it occasionally tips over. While Rene di Rosa passed away in 2010, the foundation continues his work collecting and displaying art from Northern California artists.

Visiting the preserve is to enter an eclectic, artistic wonderland, where giant sculptures march up into the hills, a car hangs from a tree, and every indoor space is crammed with photographs, paintings, and video installations of sometimes mind-bending strangeness. Even nature seems to do its part to maintain the sense of whimsy as the preserve's 85 peacocks (including two albinos) strut, screech, and occasionally crash-land around the galleries.

Don't expect labels to help make sense of the art because there are none, just a numbered catalog in each gallery. This is to ensure viewers approach each piece with no preconceptions. The only aspects that tie everything together are the Bay Area and di Rosa's love of maximal art over minimal. "The Bay Area is the pond in which I fish," he said. "The artists I like use the familiar as a hook to lead you into new realms. The best artists are like shamans who can take us to deeper truths."

The preserve is on the north side of the Carneros Highway (Hwy. 121), almost opposite the Domaine Carneros winery. Look for the two-dimensional sheep on the hillside. The $5 donation will get you into the Gatehouse Gallery, which displays rotating exhibits along with some pieces from the permanent collection, but to wander around the property or explore other indoor gallery space, including the 125-year-old winery and di Rosa's onetime home, you have to join a tour. Luckily, they are in abundance. Three to four are scheduled daily, depending on the time of year, and all last 1.5 or 2 hours and cost $12-15. During the dry summer months, the "Nature Hike" takes visitors up Milliken Peak, a 2.5-mile round-trip to the highest peak in Carneros. You might be able to sign up for one of the tours on the day, but chances are you'll need a reservation (call 707/226-5991 or visit www.dirosaart.org), especially on weekends.

Cornerstone Sonoma

It's hard to classify this sprawling collection of shops, studios, cafés, tasting rooms, and gardens, but **Cornerstone Sonoma** (23570 Arnold Dr., Sonoma, 707/933-3010, www.cornerstone-gardens.com, 10am-5pm daily, gardens 1pm-4pm daily) should certainly be on the list of any architecture or gardening enthusiast. The centerpiece of Cornerstone is a nine-acre plot of land that's a showcase for several dozen well-known landscape architects, each of whom designed and planted separate plots. The result is a fascinating blend of traditional and contemporary gardens that make art and sculpture out of plants. For $10 you can purchase a book giving information and background of each installation at the high-end hodge-podge store, **Zipper** (707/996-7956, www.zippergifts.com, 10am-5pm daily).

To get to the entrance to the gardens, you have to navigate through an ever-growing collection of fancy shops, restaurants, and most recently, tasting rooms. The growing retail presence is no doubt a necessary moneymaker, and the landscaped outdoor spaces along with some unique shops make it far more pleasant than your average Wine Country retail experience. The downside is that it sometimes feels more like a crowded shopping center than a celebration of the outdoors, particularly if several tour buses have just disgorged their hungry passengers in search of sustenance.

The **Sonoma Valley Visitors Bureau** has a useful outpost here (23570 Arnold Dr., Sonoma, 707/996-1090, www.sonomacounty.com, 10am-4pm daily) and is a first stop for many visitors to the region. Be sure to stop in and inquire about any discounted or free tasting passes to nearby wineries. The most fascinating of the shops and studios include **Artefact Design & Salvage** (707/933-0660, www.arte-factdesignsalvage.com, 11am-5pm Mon.-Fri., 10am-5pm Sat.-Sun.), which sells antiques and whimsical home and garden accessories made from salvaged materials (bar stools with a giant railroad springs in place of legs, for example), and **A New Leaf Gallery** (707/933-1300, www.sculpturesite.com, 10am-5pm daily), which is the showcase for some diverse sculptures from dozens of international artists. **Country by Eurasian Interiors** (707/933-8006, http://eurasianinteriors.com, 11am-6pm daily) is another. With its mix of Chinese and French antiques, incense, and handcrafted trinkets, it is a one-of-a-kind in Wine Country.

In the last few years, tasting rooms have also found homes here. The most recent additions are **Keating Wines** (707/939-6510, http://keatingwines.com, 10am-5pm daily, tasting $5-15) and **Meadowcroft** (707/934-4090, http://meadowcroftwines.com, 10am-5pm daily, tasting $5-10). Keating is a boutique winery whose wines have routinely won awards and scored above 90 points by *Wine Enthusiast.* Sourcing their fruit from the Napa and Sonoma Valleys, they make small batches of malbec, petite sirah, and zinfandel, but they are particularly known for their cabernet. Meadowcroft is a larger operation that produces two labels, Thomas Henry and Magito wines. Both make varietals from the Napa and Sonoma Valleys. Guests can enjoy their wine (some of which are not available anywhere else) inside the warm and airy tasting room or out on the terrace overlooking nearby vineyards.

EVENTS

Both big and small wineries open their doors during the **April in Carneros** event, usually held on the third weekend in April. Just visit one of the participating wineries for a ticket ($45), which gets you a glass and access to special tastings and events at all the other wineries, including many that are not usually open to the public. Later in the year there's a similar event called **Holiday in Carneros,** usually held on the weekend before Thanksgiving. For a list of wineries and more information about the events, visit www.carneroswineries.org. You can also purchase tickets in advance on the website for the discounted price of $39.

RECREATION
Infineon Raceway

Sleepy Carneros is the unlikely setting for one of the busiest racetracks in the country, the **Infineon Raceway** (29355 Arnold Dr., Sonoma, 800/870-7223, www.racesonoma.com), which usually has some sort of motorized vehicle racing round its two miles of track 340 days of the year. Born in 1968 as the Sears Point Raceway and rechristened in 2002 after San Jose-based Infineon Technologies bought the naming rights, the track is now part of the circuit for major national motor-sport events, including **NASCAR** in June (when the area is choked with traffic and best avoided in the late afternoon, when everyone leaves). It is also home to more than 70 motor-sport companies, from racing teams to parts suppliers. The raceway is on the way from San Francisco at the turnoff for Sonoma and Napa, hidden behind the hill at the intersection of Highways 37 and 121. It's not hard to find—just watch for the turbo-charged cow atop the giant raceway billboard at the junction. The entrance is a few hundred yards north on Highway 121.

Those who prefer a more hands-on approach to motor sports can try out the track through the **Russell Racing School** (800/733-0345, www.jimrussellusa.com), which is based at the raceway and offers driving, go-karting, and racing courses. Go-karting is the cheapest option at $500 for the day, but if you want to get behind the wheel of a racecar, expect to dole out upward of $1,500 for the pleasure.

Tubbs Island

When the tide comes in, large swaths of lower Carneros disappear underwater, so it's not surprising that the only hike in the area is through the wetlands at Tubbs Island, part of the San Pablo Bay National Wildlife Refuge. The path is on solid ground, so waders are not required, but it does get muddy in the winter. The eight-mile loop, open to hikers and bikers, is a dirt road that runs through farmland before reaching the edge of the bay and marshes.

It offers little in the way of memorable scenery or strenuous exercise, so the main reason to go is for the wildlife. Legions of migrating wetland birds call the tidal marshes home, particularly in the cold and wet winter months. Even in the slightly warmer summer months there are hawks, pelicans, and plenty of other interesting critters to see, including several endangered species, making the often bracing wind worth enduring.

The Tubbs Island gravel parking lot, where the trail begins, is on the south side of Highway 37, about 0.5 mile past the traffic lights at the junction with Highway 121 to Sonoma. Leaving the parking lot, you have to drive east almost all the way to Vallejo before you can turn around, so plan accordingly. For more information on the refuge, its wildlife, and the ongoing restoration projects, contact the Vallejo headquarters of the **San Pablo Bay National Wildlife Refuge** (707/769-4200, www.fws.gov/sfbayrefuges).

Flying

Elsewhere in the Wine Country, balloons might be the traditional way to see Wine Country from above, but Carneros has an altogether more adventurous way to take to the air. The **Vintage Aircraft Company** (23982 Arnold Dr., Sonoma, 707/938-2444, www.vintageaircraft.com, walk-in 10:30am-4pm Sat.-Sun., by appointment only Mon. and Thurs.-Fri.,) offers rides in its fascinating collection of old planes, which include biplanes and a World War II-era training aircraft.

Simply pick your adrenaline level for the biplane flights, and the FAA-certified pilots can oblige. For a modest rush, pick the 20-minute Scenic ride over the vineyards and mountains of the Sonoma Valley ($175, $270 for two people) or double the flying time (and price) for a trip out to the ocean, down to San Francisco, or over the Napa Valley. To really get the adrenaline pumping, try the Aerobatic ride with a few loops and rolls thrown in for fun for an additional $50. Acrobatics are free in the World War II SNJ-4 "Texan" plane, but flights in the navy fighter start at $399 for 20 minutes.

The Vintage Aircraft Company's home is the Sonoma County airport, a thriving base for vintage aircraft restoration and flights. You'll probably see an old plane or two parked close to the Carneros Highway as you drive by.

ACCOMMODATIONS

As the drive through the endless vineyards and fields of Carneros might suggest, there's not much in the way of lodging in this part of Wine Country. Carneros thinks of Sonoma as its main town, and that's where most of the "local" hotels can be found. There are, however, a couple of options at opposite ends of the price spectrum for those looking for either an out-of-the-way bargain or some out-of-this-world luxury.

$100-200

The refurbished **Vineyard Inn** (23000 Arnold Dr., Sonoma, 707/938-2350 or 800/359-4667, www.vineyardinnsonoma.com, $179-315) is one of the best values in southern Sonoma, although due to county regulations, it is closed November-May. The Spanish-style former motel has 22 modern and comfortable rooms just minutes from some of the biggest wineries in Carneros. The standard queen rooms are the cheapest, and the list of standard amenities includes private baths, satellite television, wireless Internet access, air-conditioning, breakfast, and use of the very small outdoor pool. The vineyard rooms in separate but adjoining bungalows have more space and additional features that include DVD players and fireplaces. Some rooms also have Jacuzzi tubs. There are also a handful of two-room suites and deluxe rooms with kitchenettes. One drawback is the inn's location at one of the busiest intersections in Carneros, which makes some of the cheaper rooms at the front of the building a bit noisy. Other than the constant traffic and a gas station opposite, there's not much else around, so you'll have to drive to dinner; Sonoma Plaza is only about 10 minutes away.

Over $200

The Carneros Inn (4048 Sonoma Hwy., Napa, 707/299-4900, www.thecarnerosinn.com, $450) is a new development of 86 individual cottages surrounded by vineyards at the eastern end of Carneros, providing a dose of contemporary luxury on a 27-acre site that used to be a trailer park. As you drive past the place on the

Sonoma-Napa Highway (Hwy. 121), the tall, stark walls resemble those of a prison, but on the other side of those walls is a luxury planned community with its own manicured streets, a town square, and some privately owned three-bedroom houses that share the spa, infinity pool, vineyard views, and other amenities with the resort cottages. Not surprisingly, there's a hefty price to pay in the Wine Country for a personal cottage that's bigger than some apartments and boasts cherrywood floors, a plasma TV, a fireplace, an alfresco shower, and a private garden. The cheapest places start at $395 per night. The price rockets past $600 for a vineyard view and up to four figures for the 10 walled compounds they call suites. The popularity of the place also means that rates change very little with the seasons, although you might find some special deals in winter. One of the on-site restaurants is the highly regarded and remarkably cheap (for the inn, at least) **Boon Fly Café** (707/299-4870, 7am-9pm daily, entrées $25), serving breakfasts that will make you feel instantly at home. The inn is

only about a 10-minute drive from downtown Napa or Sonoma, but the often cool and breezy Carneros weather can make the cottage fireplaces and down comforters essential features even in the middle of summer.

FOOD
California Cuisine

To be sure, Carneros is a funky place that is at the crossroads, literally, culturally and culinary. On one end of the spectrum is **The Carneros Inn** (4048 Sonoma Hwy., Napa, 707/299-4900), where once you are inside the walled compound, it can be hard to resist the pull of its luxury. If so, book a table at **The FARM** (4048 Sonoma Hwy., Napa, 707/299-4880, www.thecarnerosinn.com, daily 4pm-10pm, $35), the other restaurant at the Carneros Inn. Like the Boon Fly Café, it serves up the expected upscale California cuisine, complete with a chef's tasting menu and big white service plates topped with tiny artistic piles of food. The dining room feels more comfortable than many of its ilk, with cushy banquettes and padded

Boon Fly Café

chairs. Servers are friendly and good at their jobs, and can help you decipher anything on the menu that might be confusing. Do dress up just a little bit—despite its name, The FARM has a distinctly upscale vibe. But that's dinner. If you want to soak in the atmosphere but have a more casual experience, ask about the bar menu. You'll find a burger, flatbread, even grilled ham and cheese for considerably less.

Even more casual at The Carneros Inn is the ◖**Boon Fly Café** (4048 Sonoma Hwy., Napa, 707/299-4870, www.thecarnerosinn.com, 7am-9pm daily, entrées $25), whose bright red exterior brightens up the gray prison-like walls of the upscale inn on the Sonoma-Napa Highway. The food is rustic and full of fresh ingredients like those that might have been eaten by a local known as Boon Fly who used to farm the surrounding land. Breakfast and brunch are the fortes here and are priced low enough to make you want to fill up for the day, but it's also worth making a road stop in the evening to sample the simple but elegant main courses or the flatbread pizzas that excel in incorporating local ingredients. There is, of course, a healthy beer, wine, and cocktail menu, but the bar gives a careful nod to the rare non-drinker, with its "zero proof" beverages, such as the delicious pomegranate spritzer.

Casual Dining

Although it opened in 2002, the **Schellville Grill** (22900 Broadway, Sonoma, 707/996-5151, www.schellvillegrill.com, 8am-8:30pm Wed.-Mon., $12), at the intersection of Highways 12 and 121, has more of the old-school Carneros vibe. What you'll find are hearty plates of comfort food delivered by a crew of relaxed locals who seem unimpressed by all the Wine Country fuss. There is plenty of seating in the checkered tablecloth dining room, but if the weather is nice, take a table on the covered back patio. It's not a fancy space, but a very relaxed place to lunch, and there is even a bit of grassy backyard space for the kids to burn off any pent-up energy. This is primarily a sandwich joint with plenty of burgers, pulled pork, and fish sandwiches. There are lots of salads to

choose from, and for dinner there is steak and ribs on the menu. The real standout is the Hot Matty's Smoked Tri-Tip Sandy that bursts with strips of tender, flavorful meat.

For an even more down-home meal, head east past Boon Fly and look for the sign to the Napa River Resorts. Take Cuttings Wharf Road as far south as it will go, making sure you go left at the confusing fork in the road. There are no resorts at the river these days, but there is a popular juke-joint next to the boat ramp called **Moore's Landing** (6 Cuttings Wharf Rd., Napa, 707/253-7038, breakfast and lunch weekends, lunch Wed.-Fri., dinner Fri.-Sat., entrées $8-14). It serves American and Mexican comfort food to boaters, anglers, and the occasional stray winery visitor and has an idyllic deck right next to the river. The winter hours tend to be erratic, so call first. The food may not be anything to write home about, but the cheap beer and the scenery may scratch an itch for some down-home relaxing in upscale Wine Country.

Picnic Supplies

Carneros is often chilly and windy compared to the Napa and Sonoma Valleys just to the north and so might not be the most inviting part of Wine Country for a picnic, but there are plenty of places to stop for supplies if the weather's nice or you're en route to warmer climes.

Angelo's Wine Country Deli (23400 Arnold Dr., Sonoma, 707/938-3688, http://angelossmokehouse.com, 9am-5pm daily), almost opposite the entrance to the Gloria Ferrer winery, is renowned for its smoked meats but also sells a wide range of other deli food and has become a bit of a Carneros institution. Despite being small, the store is hard to miss—there's a large model of a cow on its roof.

Just up the road is the **Fruit Basket** (24101 Arnold Dr., Sonoma, 707/938-4332, 7am-7pm daily), which looks a little like a shack in the middle of its dusty parking lot but is actually a comprehensive open-air market and one of the best places to buy local in-season fruit and vegetables along with almost every other grocery staple, including bread, cheese, and a good selection of wine by the half bottle. There's a second Fruit Basket in Boyes Hot Springs (18474 Hwy 12., 707/996-7433, 7am-7pm daily).

And then, of course, there are the wineries. Most of the large wineries have a selection of deli meats, local cheeses, crackers, and even some prepared food. Both **Gloria Ferrer** (23555 Carneros Hwy., Sonoma, 707/933-1917, www.gloriaferrer.com, 10am-5pm daily) and **Robledo** wineries (21901 Bonness Rd., Sonoma, 707/939-6903, www.robledofamily-winery.com, 10am-5pm Mon.-Sat., 11am-4pm Sun.) have good selections, but the perhaps the best is found at **Viansa Winery** (25200 Arnold Dr., Sonoma, 707/935-4726, www.viansa.com, 10am-5pm daily), which sells a broad range of Italian-themed deli foods, soups, sandwiches, and even pizzas in its tasting room. There are some nice spots nearby to eat, but when the winery gets crowded in the summer months, you'd do better to flee to somewhere more peaceful.

If you fancy a picnic without the hassle of finding the food yourself, give **Bouchaine Vineyards** (1075 Buchli Station Rd., Napa, 707/252-9065, www.bouchaine.com, 10:30am-4pm daily) a call the day before and order one of its "Table for Two" picnic lunches. For $95, the winery includes a free wine tasting for two (worth $10), freshly prepared sandwiches and other treats, and a bottle of wine that can all be enjoyed at the scenic picnic area next to the winery.

INFORMATION AND SERVICES

Although you won't find much in the way of services here, you will find the **Sonoma Valley Visitors Center** (23570 Arnold Dr., Sonoma, 707/996-1090, www.sonomacounty.com, 10am-4pm daily) at Cornerstone Gardens. The visitors center is well stocked with maps, discounts on tastings, and general advice for where to go and what to do in the area.

GETTING THERE AND AROUND

Carneros sits at the tip of the San Pablo Bay and is the crossroads for many highways heading north-south and east-west. The region is also the gateway to the Sonoma Valley from San Francisco along Highway 121, and from Vallejo and the East Bay on Highway 12. Those two highways are the major roads through Carneros. While in the west, wineries hug Highway 121; in the east, many can be found off the main road (Hwy. 12) to the north or south. Here a bike is an alternative to the car, but otherwise expect to stay behind the wheel.

NORTHERN SONOMA

There's probably no other wine-producing region in California that has as much to offer visitors as northern Sonoma. Famed Victorian horticulturist Luther Burbank called this part of Sonoma the "chosen spot of all this earth as far as Nature is concerned," and he was pretty well traveled. For a man who tinkered with plants, this was paradise.

This is also a place where living off the land has always been, and still is, a way of life. That land provides some of California's best wine and food and countless recreational possibilities. You can mix wine with almost anything outdoors here: kayaking, mountain hikes, apple picking, camping, fishing, lounging on a sandy beach, flying, or even a safari.

While "Hop Country" and "Prune Country" don't have quite the same ring as "Wine Country," those crops and others once dominated the land but have long since vanished (at one point in the last century, a silkworm farm was planned, and a frog farm briefly found fame with its edible amphibians). There's even a major road named after the slowly disappearing Gravenstein apple. It would be easier to name crops that had *not* at some point been grown on these hills and valleys, helped along by the vast number of microclimates. There are probably more here than in any other part of the Wine Country—which is saying something in this climate-challenged part of the world. One day vines too might disappear, only to be replaced by the next big agricultural cash generator.

That's not to say that all is peace and rural tranquility—far from it. The freeway that was carved through the region in the 1960s has

© ELIZABETH LINHART VENEMAN

HIGHLIGHTS

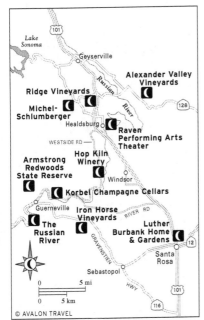

© AVALON TRAVEL

LOOK FOR ◖ TO FIND RECOMMENDED SIGHTS, ACTIVITIES, DINING, AND LODGING.

◖ **Hop Kiln Winery:** The towering hop kilns are so well preserved that this small winery could almost produce beer in addition to its unusual range of well-priced wines (page 81).

◖ **Korbel Champagne Cellars:** In a forest clearing in Victorian times, two Czech brothers started making wine. Their historic stone winery still makes sparkling wine fit for presidents and plebeians alike (page 83).

◖ **Iron Horse Vineyards:** An unassuming barn off the beaten track is home to some of the Russian River Valley's best sparkling wines and a view to die for (page 84).

◖ **Luther Burbank Home & Gardens:** Learn about the Victorian horticulturist who created hundreds of new plants in his greenhouses and see many of those plants in the historic gardens (page 91).

◖ **Armstrong Redwoods State Reserve:** Take a break from the car and the heat on a short hike through the cool, damp redwood forest in this historic park (page 96).

◖ **The Russian River:** Rent a canoe for a day and drift along the Russian River, stopping at the many secluded beaches (page 97).

◖ **Ridge Vineyards:** This winery, built with rice-straw bales, takes the principle of organic wines to a whole new level (page 116).

◖ **Michel-Schlumberger:** Producing some of the best cabernet in a valley dominated by zinfandel, this winery is housed in a beautiful mission-revival building tucked away down a scenic canyon (page 117).

◖ **Raven Performing Arts Theater:** Visit this historic theater for performance art or a movie and support the artists that help keep Healdsburg real (page 126).

◖ **Alexander Valley Vineyards:** Incorporating part of the homestead of the valley's first settler, Cyrus Alexander, the grounds of this winery are peppered with historic buildings (page 144).

brought with it the kind of suburban sprawl and rush-hour traffic that sucked the soul out of the largest city, Santa Rosa. But while Santa Rosa continues to bulge outward, it doesn't take much to get back to the land and step back in time. Less than a half hour away, deep in the woods, are towns like Guerneville and Occidental that still retain some feeling of the frontier towns they once were, even as they become overrun in the summer by an unlikely mix of urbanites, hippies, bikers, and ranchers who all seem to coexist happily for a few months.

Even the Victorian town of Healdsburg has

managed to keep in touch with its historic past, despite trying ever so hard to sell its soul to those marketing an imaginary Wine Country lifestyle.

The whole area is slowly being dragged up-market, however, as the burgeoning Bay Area population seeks out bigger backyards. At the southernmost edge of this part of the Wine Country, Sebastopol is starting to resemble a hip San Francisco neighborhood. Property prices everywhere are soaring, slowing down the mechanisms of change that have continually transformed the land since European immigrants first arrived here in the 1800s and carved out a life for themselves in the soil and forests.

Winemakers still produce wines to rival the best in the world, but as the cost of doing so rises, the conglomerates are beginning to take over, much as they've already done in the Napa and Sonoma Valleys. You increasingly have to be big to survive in the wine world here, and many new winemakers are looking farther north in Mendocino and Lake Counties for a chance to get in on the action.

Nevertheless, there's still plenty of life left in the northern Sonoma scene, with an amazing diversity of wine, scenery, and activities. There might be trouble in paradise, but it's still paradise to visit.

PLANNING YOUR TIME

Parts of northern Sonoma are easy to get around, others are not. The **Russian River Valley** is definitely in the "not" category. This sprawling appellation encompasses forests and mountains, hills and dales, and has the navigational inconvenience of a large river cutting almost straight through the middle of it. A map is essential, as is a bit of planning to ensure you spend more time in wineries than backtracking on the roads. The Russian River Wine Road (707/433-4335 or 800/723-6336, www.wineroad.com) publishes one of the best maps, which can usually be found free at wineries.

The **Dry Creek Valley** and **Alexander Valley** are relatively straightforward to navigate by comparison, with most of the wineries strung along a few long, relatively straight

roads. These valleys are almost like miniature Sonoma or Napa Valleys as far as climate, shape, and scenery, and it's easy to get a good feel for the area in a day or even a half day.

The three main appellations are like night and day when it comes to wine, which makes planning a wine route either exciting or daunting. Sample some velvety Alexander Valley cabernets, for example, before crossing into the Dry Creek Valley and tasting the subtly different cabernets there. Or try the warm-climate chardonnays in the Alexander Valley, then head down Westside Road to try some leaner, cool-climate versions in the Russian River Valley.

Alternatively, try to find your favorite Dry Creek zinfandel from the hundreds on offer in the valley, or hunt out the next big pinot noir in the Russian River Valley.

If all the possibilities just seem too overwhelming, there's always the option of staying in **Healdsburg,** which has enough tasting rooms to satisfy the most fussy wine drinker, as well as plenty of shops and restaurants to occupy those less curious about the region's wines. Healdsburg is also the most central town in the region, and the large number of good hotels and restaurants make it an almost essential staging post for any trip to this part of the world.

As in other parts of the Wine Country, wineries generally open late and close early, so don't expect to get started until late morning, and plan to be finished touring by about 5pm, closer to 4pm during the winter. Unlike the rest of Sonoma and Napa, free tasting is still fairly commonplace but is getting increasingly less so. But even when there is a fee for tasting regular or reserve wines, it will be far more palatable than in some other parts of Wine Country.

And of course, non-wine-related activities also abound. Check out the burgeoning Santa Rosa Arts District, or the multitude of hiking options in wilderness areas such as Armstrong Redwoods State Reserve.

GETTING THERE
By Car

The railroad came and left this part of Sonoma

before most of us were even born, leaving the car and sporadic bus services as the only real options for getting around.

U.S. 101, which runs down the center of this region, might be a bit of an eyesore as it snakes up otherwise picturesque valleys, leaving strip malls in its wake, but it's a pretty convenient way to get places fast. The drive time from San Francisco up the freeway to almost every major Russian River Valley town is usually not much more than an hour, to Healdsburg and beyond about an hour and a half.

From the freeway, **Highway 116** West runs up through Sebastopol to Guerneville. In the Santa Rosa area, River Road runs west to Forestville, though it tends to get choked during rush hour. The Healdsburg Avenue exit leads straight into downtown Healdsburg, and the Westside Road exit is the entry to the Dry Creek Valley and Russian River regions. The next four exits serve Dry Creek and Alexander Valleys before the freeway reaches Cloverdale and then heads into the hills toward Hopland and Mendocino.

By Bus

Although most people come to this part of the Wine Country by car, there are other transport options. Both Santa Rosa and Sebastopol are well served by **Golden Gate Transit** (415/455-2000, www.goldengatetransit.org), which runs scheduled bus service to and from San Francisco hourly for much of the day. From Santa Rosa, **Sonoma County Transit** (707/576-7433 or 800/345-7433, www.sctransit.com) runs regular services to Healdsburg, Geyserville, and Guerneville. From Sebastopol there's service to Guerneville through Graton and Forestville. Things are so spread out in the Russian River Valley, however, that once you arrive there by bus you'll still need some mode of transport to see anything.

GETTING AROUND
By Car

The Russian River Valley is roughly square in shape, with an arm stretching from its northeastern corner up to Healdsburg. The major towns are Guerneville, in the northwest corner of the square, Sebastopol on the southern edge, Occidental on the western edge, and Santa Rosa on the eastern side. In the middle is a patchwork of farmland and vineyards, together with the hamlets of Graton and Forestville. Highway 116, also called the **Gravenstein Highway,** is the main road running north-south through them.

Wineries are spread mainly along Eastside and Westside Roads, which both run on either side of the river from Healdsburg down toward Guerneville, and throughout the patchwork in the middle of the area. Many of the region's food and lodging options lie in Healdsburg and around the edge of this Russian River square. Unlike in the Dry Creek and Alexander Valleys farther north, roads here tend to meander as they follow the river and hills, often making driving times longer than anticipated.

By comparison, the Dry Creek Valley could be navigated with your eyes shut. Just two roads run the length of the valley, and the wineries are roughly spread out along them, making it the easiest part of northern Sonoma to visit in a day, even without a map. Along the other side of the freeway is the longer and wider Alexander Valley. Even here, the wineries are concentrated along Geyserville Avenue on the western side of the valley and along Highway 128 on the eastern side.

By Bike

Of course, driving is not the only way to get around. Wine Country would not be complete without cycling. The compact, flat **Dry Creek Valley** and relatively flat **Westside Road** from Healdsburg down into the Russian River Valley are two of the most bikeable routes. The Alexander Valley is also relatively flat, but distances between wineries are greater. In all areas, temperatures get high in the summer, so plenty of water is essential.

The best place to rent bikes is in Healdsburg, where there are several options. The friendly folks at **Spoke Folk Cyclery** (201 Center St., Healdsburg, 707/433-7171, www.spokefolk.com, 10am-6pm Mon.-Fri., 10am-5pm

THE GRAVENSTEIN HIGHWAY

Although almost every imaginable fruit and vegetable seems to be grown in Sonoma, the most celebrated crop in the Russian River Valley (apart from grapes) is perhaps the apple, and in particular the small yellow and red Gravenstein with its strong aroma and taste.

Highway 116, which runs through Sebastopol and Graton, is also called the Gravenstein Highway for the large number of orchards it used to pass. The orchards are now disappearing, along with the Gravenstein apple itself, as growers favor bigger and more easily transported varieties of apple like Fuji and golden delicious.

At one point apple orchards covered 14,000 acres of Sonoma County, but by 2011 there were less than 3,000 acres left, and Gravensteins accounted for only one-third of that total. Slow Food Russian River, the local chapter of the Slow Food movement, is now campaigning to raise the profile of this humble little apple among consumers, retailers, and restaurants to slow any further decline.

Nothing specifically links the Gravenstein apple to this area—it is actually believed to have originated in Germany. It just happens to grow particularly well here and has been doing so for almost 200 years.

The Gravenstein is the earliest-ripening apple in the region, so look for it starting in late July. Other apple varieties tend to ripen August-December. Farms offering apples and other seasonal produce are generally clustered around Sebastopol and Graton. Many are open only during the summer and fall.

In the Forestville/Graton area they include **Kozlowski Farms** (5566 Gravenstein Hwy. N., Forestville, 707/887-1587, www.kozlowski-farms.com, 9am-5pm Mon.-Fri., 10am-5pm Sat.-Sun. year-round), **Gabriel Farm** (3175 Sullivan Rd., just off Graton Rd., Sebastopol, 707/829-0617, wwww.gabrielfarm.com, 10am-3pm Sat.-Sun. Aug.-Oct.), and **Walker Apples** (10966 Upp Rd., off Graton Rd., Sebastopol, 707/623-4310, 9am-5pm daily Aug.-mid-Nov.), which sells a staggering 27 varieties of apples. Just south of Sebastopol on Pleasant Hill Road is **Twin Hill Ranch** (1689 Pleasant Hill Rd., Sebastopol, 707/823-2815, www.twinhill-ranch.com., 9am-4pm Mon.-Sat. year-round), and halfway between Sebastopol and Occidental is **Ratzlaff Ranch** (13128 Occidental Rd., Sebastopol, 707/823-0538, 8am-5pm Sun.-Fri. year-round), which grows Gravensteins along with other apples and pears.

Between Sebastopol and Graton on the Gravenstein Highway, you will also likely find a bountiful supply of apples at the big roadside produce store called **Andy's Market** (1691 Gravenstein Hwy. N., Sebastopol, 707/823-8661, www.andysproduce.com, 8:30am-8pm daily). But perhaps the sweetest place to find them is at **Mom's Apple Pie** (4550 Gravenstein Hwy., Sebastopol, 707/823-8330, www.momsapplepieusa.com, 10am-6pm daily), where the homemade pies are made with a flaky double crust and the celebrated Gravensteins August-November and Granny Smiths the rest of the year.

More information about all the fruits and vegetables grown here and the farms that sell them is available from **Sonoma Country Farm Trails** (707/837-8896, www.farmtrails.org). You might also see the free *Farm Trails* map and guide at wineries and farms in the region.

Sat.-Sun.) will rent you a bike ($50/day) and send you on your way with maps for biking routes that range from leisurely 12-mile loops in Dry Creek Valley to 40-mile adventures down to Guerneville. At the other end of town next to the Old Roma Station winery complex, **Wine Country Bikes** (61 Front St., Healdsburg, 707/473-0610, www.winecountrybikes.com, 9am-5pm daily) rents bikes and also has a couple of options for organized tours, including a day tour of local organic farms and wineries during the spring and summer ($139) and a longer day tour for more avid bikers, which takes in scenery and wineries in both the Dry Creek and Russian River Valleys on its 45-mile loop ($149).

Russian River Valley

The Russian River Valley is one of Sonoma's largest and most diverse geographic regions. It covers about 150 square miles of forest, orchards, vineyards, and pastureland from trendy Sebastopol in the south to chic Healdsburg in the north, and from the suburban freeway sprawl in the east to rural Occidental in the west. Running right through it is the mighty Russian River, shaping the climate, scenery, and recreational opportunities in the region.

The Russian River Valley attracted immigrants in the late 1800s to exploit its vast forests, and many of the towns that exist today were established as logging or railroad outposts. Once the redwood forests had been largely cleared, sheep ranches, cattle pasture, orchards, and even hop farms took over the land. The Gravenstein apple, now an endangered piece of local agricultural history, was embraced as the region's very own, though its roots remain somewhat ambiguous.

It wasn't until the 1980s, when the cool growing climate was recognized as ideal for the increasingly fashionable pinot noir and chardonnay grapes, that the area's wine industry took off, and the Russian River Valley has long since been recognized as one of the best cool grape-growing regions in California.

This is not an easy part of Wine Country to explore compared to the relatively self-contained valleys elsewhere in Sonoma, however. Roads wind through forests, over hills, and along the snaking river, making wineries sometimes hard to find. Large parts of the region are rural, dotted with small communities like **Forestville** and **Graton,** which hide their already small populations very well in the surrounding hills and woods.

The center of the action is **Guerneville** and neighboring **Monte Rio,** both slightly faded Victorian resort towns that are transformed each summer into a surreal scene of leather-clad bikers and plaid-clad outdoorsmen, hipsters, and hippies. Guerneville is something of a gay mecca and party town, and the rustic resorts and bars often pulsate with the beat of dance music and drunken hordes on summer evenings.

The eastern and western edges of the appellation could not be more of a contrast. The suburban sprawl of **Santa Rosa** is just outside the eastern boundary of the appellation and is almost a poster child for how not to grow a city. It is by far the biggest city in the region—a place where culture meets characterless malls—but a far cry from the peaceful and remote Bohemian Highway running along the appellation's western edge, where the picture-postcard town of **Occidental** exists in the midst of dense forests.

The Wines

Almost a third of all the grapes grown in Sonoma County come from the Russian River Valley, but there's the potential for it to be a far higher proportion. Only 12,000 acres, or about 10 percent, of the 125,000 acres in the valley are actually planted with vineyards. The rest is still pasture, forest, and the occasional town.

The river and the valley it carved through the coastal mountain ranges over millennia provide the region with the unique climate that is perfect for growing grapes that like cool conditions. There's enough strong sunlight each day to ensure the grapes ripen, but the air remains cool, often downright chilly at night, and keeps a lid on the fruit's sugar levels.

Pinot noir and chardonnay are the dominant varietals in this part of the Wine Country, but zinfandel is almost as important, and the resulting wines have a subtlety that is often lacking in the brawny zins from the warmer valleys to the north. Growers are also having increasing success with syrah and some other Rhône varietals, while gewürztraminer is also starting to make more of an appearance. The ubiquitous cabernet sauvignon and merlot are largely absent, however, except on the warmest eastern hills of the region.

The cool layer of damp marine air from the Pacific Ocean just a few miles west is the region's natural air-conditioner and was a big factor in the granting of the **Russian River Valley**'s AVA status in 1983. Marine fog rolls down the river valley during the summer, snaking into gullies and canyons and keeping the temperature here lower than any other inland portion of Sonoma County. As the ripening process slows, the fruit can gain in complexity and retain enough acidity to keep the wines interesting. Grapes are usually harvested several weeks later here than in some hotter Sonoma regions.

The river is also responsible for the area's unique soils, depositing deep, well-drained sandy and gravelly sediments over millions of years. The combination of relatively cool microclimates, no summer rain, and a patchwork of soils is a grape grower's dream and a reason there are so many styles of pinot made here.

Within the southwest corner of the Russian River appellation, closest to the ocean, is the even cooler **Green Valley** AVA. This is just about as cool as a climate can be and still ripen grapes, and it is the source of some of Sonoma's best pinot noir.

WINERIES

Many of the Russian River wineries are south of Healdsburg down the meandering Westside Road, which has been dubbed the "Rodeo Drive of Pinot Noir" due to the number of high-end pinot producers strung along it. Once Westside Road reaches River Road, a map is an essential tool to find the hidden gems around Forestville, Graton, and beyond.

FOPPIANO VINEYARDS

The first major winery south of Healdsburg on the Old Redwood Highway is also one of the few historic wineries that continued to operate right through Prohibition. **Foppiano Vineyards** (12707 Old Redwood Hwy., Healdsburg, 707/433-7272, www.foppiano.com, 11am-5pm daily, tasting $5) remains a family-owned affair, best known

for its powerful, inky petite sirah, which has been very highly rated in recent years. Other wines include the estate pinot noir, chardonnay, and a dry rosé made from petite sirah and pinot noir.

All are well worth tasting, and not only because tasting is only $5. Unusually, most are aged in American oak barrels that impart a stronger tannic punch than the French oak more commonly used by Russian River wineries. The tannins will mellow over time, but those who are impatient should try the softer reserve petite sirah, which is the only Foppiano wine aged in French oak.

Although there are no official tours, visitors are free to wander off into the vineyards on a self-guided tour, leaflets for which can be found in the tasting room.

RODNEY STRONG VINEYARDS

Founded in 1959 as Sonoma County's 13th bonded winery, **Rodney Strong Vineyards** (11455 Old Redwood Hwy., Healdsburg, 707/431-1533, www.rodneystrong.com, 10am-5pm daily, tasting free-$15) comprise 12 estate vineyards in the Russian River Valley, Alexander Valley, Chalk Hill, and the Sonoma Coast. The name belongs to Rod Strong, a distinguished Broadway dancer and pioneering Sonoma County vintner, who was the first to plant pinot noir in the Russian River Valley. The dapper, silver-haired Strong was a well-respected champion of the California wine industry and a passionate promoter of Sonoma wines in particular. In 1989, Rodney Strong Vineyards was purchased by Tom Klein, a fourth-generation California farmer and Stanford graduate. Today, the winemaking team maintains old man Strong's level of excellence with a myriad of accolades and awards to support their portfolio of cabernet sauvignon, pinot noir, chardonnay, and meritage wines. Advocates of sustainable practices, their solar energy system is one of the largest of any winery worldwide, and they were the first carbon-neutral winery in Sonoma County. Winery tours are held daily at 11am and 3pm.

NORTHERN SONOMA

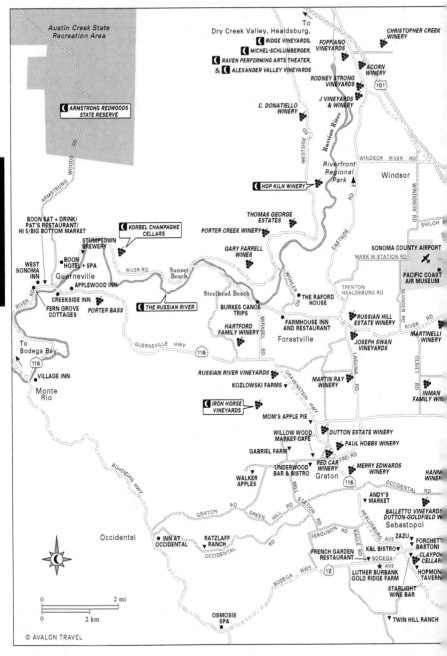

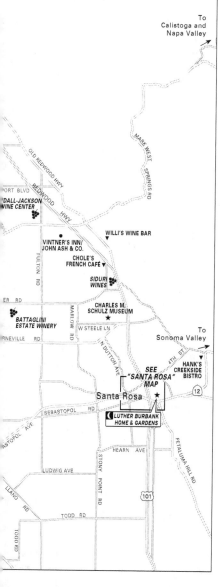

RUSSIAN RIVER VALLEY

To
Calistoga and
Napa Valley

OLD REDWOOD HWY

PORT BLVD

REDWOOD HWY

'DALL-JACKSON
WINE CENTER

MARK WEST SPRINGS RD

WILLI'S WINE BAR

VINTNER'S INN/
JOHN ASH & CO.

CHOLE'S
FRENCH CAFÉ

FULTON RD

SIDURI
WINES

ER RD

MARLOW RD

CHARLES M.
SCHULZ MUSEUM

BATTAGLINI
ESTATE WINERY

W STEELE LN

RNEVILLE RD

N DUTTON AVE

To
Sonoma Valley

4TH ST

SEE
"SANTA ROSA"
MAP

HANK'S
CREEKSIDE
BISTRO

Santa Rosa

12

SEBASTOPOL RD

LUTHER BURBANK
HOME & GARDENS

ASTOPOL AVE

HEARN AVE

PETALUMA HILL RD

LUDWIG AVE

STONY POINT RD

LLANO RD

101

TODD RD

TODD RD

J VINEYARDS & WINERY

Just south of Foppiano, the giant parking lot shared with the neighboring Rodney Strong Winery can be a magnet for busloads of tourists, but there's a relative oasis and some delicious food to be found inside the sleek and modern **J Vineyards & Winery** (11447 Old Redwood Hwy., Healdsburg, 707/431-3646, www.jwine.com, 11am-5pm daily, food and wine tastings $20-65).

At the main tasting bar, $20 buys generous pours of five wines from the lengthy menu of red, white, sparkling, and dessert wines. If the spacious tasting room is overrun, a common occurrence on weekends, the more exclusive Bubble Room takes the tasting experience (and the price) up a notch. Monday-Wednesday, a seated tasting of six reserve wines is offered on the hour ($30), and for an additional $20, it can be paired with cheese and charcuterie. Later in the week, the price goes up to $75, but guests will enjoy three courses, plus a cheese and dessert course paired with the winery's reserve wines. The food is filling and inventive (smoked sunchoke, squid, and pork belly with a lime vinaigrette paired with a pinot noir), making it a worthwhile stop for both oenophiles and foodies alike. There are four seatings each day Thursday-Sunday, and reservations are mandatory. If it's already booked up, there's a similarly structured but slightly less indulgent tasting menu ($40/couple) available on the outdoor terrace Friday-Sunday during the summer.

J specializes in sparkling wines and pinot noir from the Russian River Valley, but it also produces respectable chardonnay and pinot gris. Its portfolio of bubbly includes a late-disgorged brut and the flagship Vintage Brut, which is the signature wine here. The sparkling winemaking process is the focus of the 30-minute appointment-only tours that finish with a wine tasting.

HOP KILN WINERY

Between Westside Road and the Russian River is one of Sonoma's best-preserved old hop kilns, a towering wooden building where hops were once dried before being used to make beer. The hop vines of Sonoma have long since been re-placed by grapevines, but the **Hop Kiln Winery** (6050 Westside Rd., Healdsburg, 707/433-6491, www.hopkilnwinery.com, 10am-5pm daily, tasting $7) has kept much of the cavernous interior of the 1905-era building intact, including the old stone drying ovens.

Belying its giant home, the winery itself is a fairly small operation, producing reasonably priced pinot grigio, chardonnay, pinot noir, pinot noir rosé, and a sparkling, you guessed it, pinot noir rosé. Two proprietary blends round out their portfolio: Big Red, which is as big as its name suggests—a rambunctious blend of zinfandel, cabernet, and syrah; and Thousand Flowers, a more delicate white blend of chardonnay, gewürztraminer, and riesling. The once-common Napa gamay red grape is also represented under its more accurate name of valdiguié. Very few wineries still make it, and it's an acquired taste.

There are plenty of picnic tables around the building, including some next to a rather murky pond. The winery stocks a host of vinegars, oils, and mustards, but not much in the way of more filling picnic fare, so you'll have to bring your own.

THOMAS GEORGE ESTATES

One of the valley's newer large wineries is **Thomas George Estates** (8075 Westside Rd., Healdsburg, 707/431-8031, www.thomasgeorgeestates.com, 11am-5pm daily, tasting $15), opened in 2009 in the former Davis Bynum winery, which was once a 1920s hop kiln. The winery still produces a large number of varietals including several different pinots, chardonnays both oak and stainless steel fermented, sauvignon blanc, pinot blanc, zinfandels from Dry Creek, and a Sonoma Valley viognier.

Part of the change in ownership resulted in a new 8,000-square-foot cave that boasts a reserve tasting room, a library, and beautifully redone main tasting room just inside the entrance. If you want a bit of sunshine, the winery has also made its outside picnic areas a priority. Tables with bright red umbrellas dot the

stately open glen, perfect for opening a bottle of pinot blanc.

PORTER CREEK WINERY

Serious cork dorks recommend the tiny tasting room at **Porter Creek Winery** (8735 Westside Rd., Healdsburg, 707/433-6321, www.portercreekvineyards.com, 10:30am-4:30pm daily, tasting $10), which casual tasters might otherwise miss at the bend on a twisting road. Turn onto the dirt driveway, passing a farm-style house (that's the owner's family home), and park in front of a small converted shed—*that's* the actual tasting room. This is Sonoma wine tasting, old school. Porter Creek has been making its precious few cases of rich red wine each year for the last 30 years or so. You can find it at the occasional local restaurant, but if you like what you taste you'd better buy it right here at the winery. Porter Creek's wines are almost all red, made from grapes grown organically within sight of the tasting room. You might even see the owner-winemaker walking through his vineyards with his family on a sunny afternoon in the off-season.

GARY FARRELL WINES

If you find yourself touring the Russian River area on a wet winter day, consider calling ahead to make an appointment at **Gary Farrell Wines** (10701 Westside Rd., Healdsburg, 707/473-2909, www.garyfarrellwines.com, 10am-4:30pm daily, tasting $15-25). November-March, the winery hosts fireside tastings ($25) of its reserve wines next to a large picture window overlooking the vineyards. On days when the mist hangs in the redwoods and the river rushes swollen with rain, there is no better place to be. And the wine is good, too.

Pinot noir and chardonnay dominate the tasting menu, but limited-release sauvignon blanc, zinfandel, and syrah are usually poured as well. In the summer when the weather gets hot, the seated tastings move outside to the terrace where you can soak in the sun and the views, as well as the wine. For an additional $10, you can tack on a tour to either tasting,

Korbel's historic winery on the Russian River

lumber business. Wine production gradually took over from their other businesses as the quality of their sparkling wines and brandies improved and word spread.

Now the winery makes close to 1.7 million cases of the fizzy stuff a year in a dizzying array of styles. It has also added some respectable table wines to its portfolio, as well as brandy and port, all of which can only be bought at the winery.

The Korbel family connection is long gone, but Korbel wines remain the tipple of both presidents and plebeians alike. The champagne has been poured at five presidential inaugurations, and is claimed to be the most popular premium champagne in the United States.

From the bone-dry top-of-the-line Le Premier to the sweeter Sec, Korbel's 10 or so champagnes are eminently affordable, as are the cabernet, pinot noir, chardonnay, and zinfandel table wines, and even the barrel-aged port. After the tasting room bubbles have gone to your head, the prices look even better. It's hard to leave without at least a couple of bottles.

How the bubbles get into the wine and how the Korbel brothers got into the wine business are both covered in an entertaining tour offered daily. A tour of the sweet old rose garden is offered twice a day Tuesday-Sunday mid-April-mid-October, and after all that touring you can lounge on the deck of the small delicatessen, shaded by redwood trees with a gourmet sandwich and even a beer.

HARTFORD FAMILY WINERY

A little off the beaten track about a mile up Martinelli Road and surrounded by lush gardens and redwood forest is the big white barnlike winery and mansion of this pinot noir and chardonnay specialist. **Hartford Family Winery** (8075 Martinelli Rd., Forestville, 707/887-8011 or 800/588-0234, www.hartfordwines. com, 10am-4:30pm daily, tasting $15) makes about 20,000 cases of some serious point-scoring regional and single-vineyard wines from the Sonoma Coast, Russian River Valley, Carneros, and (unusually) Marin County to the south.

The portfolio of wines is very compact,

offered daily at 10:30am and 1pm. Of course, there is always the Traditional Tasting, which only costs $10 for five generous pours of single-vineyard wines, while overlooking the spectacular views. These happen rain or shine, winter and summer, and are well worth the effort.

KORBEL CHAMPAGNE CELLARS

This is one of the most impressive of the 19th-century wineries in Sonoma—a collection of solid, imposing stone and brick buildings at the edge of redwood forests. If you're a fan of sparkling wines, it's a place worth visiting—it might not have the acclaim of top producers like Iron Horse, but **Korbel** (13250 River Rd., Guerneville, 707/824-7000, www.korbel. com, 10am-4:30pm daily, free tasting) offers perhaps the best value for money among sparkling wine producers and has a fascinating history.

Three Korbel brothers, immigrants from the Bohemia region of what is now the Czech Republic, founded the winery in 1882 after making their money in the local redwood however, comprising only pinot noir, chardonnay, and zinfandel, all from cool-climate vineyards and all well worth tasting. For the price of a tasting you get a flight of six wines—three are multi-vineyard, and three are single vineyard. On nice days, an outside seated tasting is available for the same price, but if you want a tour plus a more formal seated tasting, you'll have to call ahead and shell out an additional $20.

RUSSIAN RIVER VINEYARDS

Ironically, **Russian River Vineyards** (5700 Gravenstein Hwy., Forestville, 707/887-3344, www.russianrivervineyards.com, 11:30am-4:30pm daily, free) really isn't on the Russian River; it sits in the coastal hills of nearby Forestville that nurture the Sonoma Coast vineyards and wineries. The property doesn't look like a typical high-end winery—the elderly wooden buildings seem almost to be falling apart. (Don't worry, the tasting room has been shored up.) Sadly, the funky old Victorian house behind the tasting room isn't open for tours—it's part of the private production facility.

The staff is friendly and creates a classy small-winery tasting experience. Russian River Vineyard's small list of only red wines reflects their locale—tasters enjoy full-bodied, fruity pinot noirs and interesting varietals from the southern reaches of Europe. The charbono tastes especially good. For lunch, ask for a table in one of the two small dining rooms, divided by the brushed-metal tasting bar. Brunch or light afternoon fare is available every day, as is dinner that includes a three-course prix fixe option.

■ IRON HORSE VINEYARDS

One of the southernmost wineries in the Green Valley appellation, **Iron Horse Vineyards** (9786 Ross Station Rd., Sebastopol, 707/887-1507, www.ironhorsevineyards.com, 10am-4:30pm daily, tasting $10-15), is also well off the beaten track down Ross Station Road (off the Gravenstein Hwy.), a one-lane road that winds through orchards, over a creek, and

(perhaps) past some wild turkeys before climbing up the palm-lined driveway to the winery.

The rustic simplicity of the barnlike building and its indoor-outdoor tasting bar belies the pedigree of the sparkling wines made here—they have been served to presidents and won numerous accolades from wine critics over the past 30 years. Tours ($20) are offered by appointment weekdays only at 10am, and on Friday they are led by the winemaker, David Muskgard. But with such panoramic views over the valley from right behind the tasting area, you might be content just to sit back and relax in the bucolic setting.

Today, the winery is still run by the Sterling family that built it in the 1970s and makes about 20,000 cases of sparkling wines a year, most priced at $30 and up. They include the ever-popular Wedding Cuvée and a series of late-disgorged wines, including the flagship Brut LD, which are bottle-aged for four or more years in contact with the lees to give them a rich aroma and flavor. All the grapes for the sparkling wines are sourced from the winery's vineyards in the surrounding Green Valley AVA, the coolest part of an already cool Russian River Valley appellation.

It's an ideal place to grow chardonnay and pinot noir, both of which Iron Horse also bottles as outstanding still wines that are worth tasting. Try the unoaked chardonnay—one of the best examples of this new breed of food-friendly chardonnays.

DUTTON ESTATE WINERY

The modest tasting room (8757 Green Valley Rd., Sebastopol, 707/829-9463, www.sebastopolvineyards.com, 10am-5pm daily, tasting $10-15) of the Dutton family, just off the Gravenstein Highway, barely hints at the renown of their Dutton Ranch in the Green Valley AVA for producing highly rated, limited-production wines.

Sauvignon blanc, chardonnay, pinot noir, and syrah are the only wines made here, but there are lots of different versions of them made from specific vineyards and sometimes specific blocks within a vineyard. Discovering some of the nuances of the tiny Green Valley sub-appellation with the more expensive vineyard-specific wines entails a higher tasting fee, but there is also a wine and cheese pairing offered for $20.

MERRY EDWARDS WINERY

Merry Edwards was the first woman to earn a degree in enology (winemaking) from the prestigious UC Davis program in 1993. After working as a winemaker for numerous Sonoma vintners and developing her own pinot noir grape clone with the help of the facilities and staff at UC Davis, Merry finally gave in and opened her own winery. The **Merry Edwards Winery** (2959 Gravenstein Hwy., Sebastopol, 707/823-7466, www.merryedwards.com, 9:30am-4:30pm daily, free tasting) offers tastings in its two glass-walled tasting rooms. Anxious to avoid the overcrowded, under-attended Napa tourist tasting model, each member of Merry Edwards's tasting staff will work with only one party of tasters at a time. Instead of forcing your way through a crowd to garner 12 inches of bar space, you'll be led to a table with comfortable chairs that's already set with four glasses ready to hold the four different pinot noirs you'll sip. (That's four examples of the same varietal, plus a bonus sauvignon blanc served at the end of the tasting.) It's easy to spend an hour at Merry Edwards, soaking up the luxury of a completely different tasting experience. Perhaps most amazingly of all, tasting at Merry Edwards is free. However, you probably won't make it out the door without purchasing at least one bottle of Merry's stellar wine.

RED CAR WINERY

Vintage Hollywood comes to the Gravenstein Highway at **Red Car Winery** (8400 Graton Rd., Sebastopol, 707/829-8500, www.redcarwine.com, 10am-5pm daily, tasting $15). Red Car was founded in 2000 by a Los Angeles-based team—film producer Carroll Kemp and screenwriter Mark Estrin. With a single ton of grapes grown in Santa Barbara County, the pair produced their first 50 cases of syrah. Fast-forward a few years: Kemp and Estrin

discovered the magic of the Sonoma Coast and purchased Red Car Estate Vineyard on a mountaintop in Fort Ross. By 2009 all wines were made with Sonoma fruit. They have received recognition for their well-balanced artisan blends and burgundian varietals pinot noir and chardonnay. Though the wines showcase Sonoma's bounty, Hollywood continues to be a muse. The winery's name is an homage to the red electric trolley cars that crisscrossed Los Angeles during the last century, and a tragic romance novella set in 1940s LA is played out on wine labels of their Amour Fou pinot noir. The hip tasting room has a rustic-chic appeal, with comfortable couches, antiques-store memorabilia, and vinyl spinning on a turntable.

CLAYPOOL CELLARS

For a wine experience you won't soon forget, check out the **Claypool Cellars** Fancy Booze Caboose (6761 Sebastopol Ave., #500, Sebastopol, 707/861-9358, http://claypoolcellars.com, 1pm-5:30pm Sat.-Sun., weekdays by appointment, tasting $10). This is the tasting room of Les Claypool, best known as the eccentric bassist and frontman of the rock band Primus. Turns out he also makes wine! Located in Gravenstein Station in the quirky heart of Sebastopol, the repurposed train car is the official tasting zone for Pachyderm wines, Claypool's personal brand. Inside the Southern Pacific caboose you might rub elbows (literally, it's tiny) with artists and local bohemians. Sip Purple Pachyderm pinot noir and Pink Platypus rosé, nibble M&Ms, and immerse yourself in the artwork that lines the walls, some by Claypool himself. What started as a money-saving endeavor evolved into a viable undertaking for Claypool, who describes himself as "not much of a wine guy" until moving to the Russian River Valley. Fans of Primus needn't worry though, the band continues to record and tour.

BALLETTO VINEYARDS AND DUTTON-GOLDFIELD WINERY

An industrial-looking modern building is an unlikely setting for two wineries with deep roots in the grape-growing business in the Russian River Valley. Both only recently started making wines from their renowned vineyards, and together they offer a remarkable range of Russian River Valley wines in terms of both price and style in their new tasting room.

The **Balletto** family (5700 Occidental Rd., Santa Rosa, 707/568-2455, www.ballettovineyards.com, 10am-5pm daily, tasting $5) started out as fruit growers in the 1970s, then became grape growers, and finally began making small quantities of wine from their four Russian River Valley vineyards in 2001. The new winery was completed in 2006 and now produces a modest 5,000 cases of Balletto wines. Pinot noir and pinot gris account for much of the output, with zinfandel and chardonnay making up the balance. All are decent enough and made all the more palatable by their reasonable prices—the pinot noir is the most expensive at $25. The best of the four are undoubtedly the two reds.

The vineyards are also home to the **Dutton-Goldfield Winery** (tasting room at 3100 Gravenstein Hwy. N., 707/827-3600, 10am-4:30pm daily, tasting $10), which makes limited-production wines positioned at the other end of the price spectrum. Founded in 1998 by Dan Goldfield, a well-known winemaker, and Steve Dutton, a member of the family that farms the renowned vineyards that make up the Dutton Ranch, the winery produces about 5,000 cases of high-end wines that garner some glowing reviews.

Pinot noir accounts for most of the production, both a blended Russian River Valley version and several exquisite single-vineyard bottlings that are made in such limited quantities and win such stellar reviews that they usually sell out fast. Chardonnay, zinfandel, and syrah make up the balance of the production. The syrah and zinfandel, in particular, are elegant and earthy cool-climate examples of the varietals and well worth trying.

HANNA WINERY

The specialty at **Hanna Winery** (5353 Occidental Rd., Santa Rosa, 707/575-3371, www.hannawinery.com, 10am-4pm daily, tasting $10-25) is a crisp, steel-fermented sauvignon blanc. Not only is it a hit with critics, but it is exactly what you want to drink soaking in the Russian River sun either on the winery's wraparound front porch or beneath the great live oak out front.

Inside, the tasting room makes the most out of the views and sunlight with large picture windows. Tastings include wines from its full portfolio from the 250 acres of vineyards it owns around its two winery locations (the other is in Healdsburg) and high up in the Mayacamas Mountains at its Bismark Ranch vineyards above Sonoma Valley—claimed to be the highest-elevation vineyard in Sonoma. The Bismark red wines, including cabernet sauvignon, cabernet franc, and zinfandel, are powerful and often highly rated by critics. At the other end of the scale is the fruity rosé made from petite sirah and zinfandel, an ideal accompaniment to a picnic.

A flight of five red and white wines is available for $10, while another $10 will get you into some of the reserve wines. Private seated tastings are available by appointment and cost $15-25. You can also add a cheese pairing to any tasting option (an extra $15), or a custom boxed lunch prepared by the Jimtown Store ($25 extra), but you must call in advance for that.

KENDALL-JACKSON WINE CENTER

The **Kendall-Jackson Wine Center** (5007 Fulton Rd., Fulton, 707/571-7500, www.kj.com, 10am-5pm daily, tours 11am, 1pm, and 3pm, tasting fee $5-15) surprises even serious oenophiles with the quiet elegance of its tasting room and the extensive sustainable gardens and demonstration vineyards surrounding the buildings. Inside, choose between the moderately priced regular wine tasting and the $30 per person Food & Wine Pairing (order at the tasting bar, then wait to be seated at one of the small bistro tables nearby). KJ's Food & Wine Pairing might be the very best example of this new Wine Country tasting trend. A staff of full-time chefs prepares a fresh selection of small bites that pair with the day's selection of reserve and estate wines. The wines are delicate and tasty, but it's the food that stands out—brought out hot and perfect by one of the chefs, who will tell you all about the preparation of each luscious mouthful. (Expect one or two goodies that aren't on the menu.) Locals sometimes stop by the high-ceilinged tasting room and make a lunch out of the Food & Wine Pairing here. Just be aware that in high season you might need to make a reservation in advance—KJ doesn't boast too many tables. Take a tour of the gardens in the spring and the summer, and try a taste of fresh wine grapes during the fall harvest season.

RUSSIAN HILL ESTATE WINERY

A narrow drive wends its way up a hill covered in meticulously manicured vines. At the top, a stately, colonnaded building is home to **Russian Hill Estate Winery** (4525 Slusser Rd., Windsor, 707/575-9453, www.russianhillestate.com, 10am-4pm daily, tasting $50). This family-owned and operated winery is dedicated to the production of world-class pinot noir and syrah, but the crisp, fruit-forward chardonnay is also worth a taste. In contrast to the heavy oak found in other Sonoma regions, Russian River chards have higher acid levels, resulting in dry, refreshing wines. At the helm of winemaking at Russian Hill Estate is Patrick Melley, a self-taught winemaker who makes elegant wines that have the unmistakable imprint of the valley where the fruit was grown. The tasting room patio offers spectacular views of rolling hills, historic hop kilns, California oaks, and the cool coastal fog that contributes to this region's climate and rich soil. That combination creates the perfect conditions for growing pinot noir and other "cool climate" grape varieties, resulting in lively, much sought-after wines.

JOSEPH SWAN VINEYARDS

If you're looking to taste some famous Russian River pinot noir, be sure to stop by **Joseph Swan Vineyards** (2916 Laguna Rd., Forestville, 707/573-3747, www.swanwinery. com, 11am-4:30pm Sat.-Sun., by appointment weekdays, tasting $10). Joseph Swan got into the winemaking game when he bought a run-down farm in Forestville in the late 1960s with a plan to grow grapes and make wine during his retirement. He went about it with such a perfectionist passion and with so many good winemaking connections, however, that he became one of a small group of pinot pioneers in the Russian River Valley—a group that helped put the region firmly on the world pinot noir stage. Today his son-in-law continues Swan's legacy, producing beautifully crafted single-vineyard pinots as well as an excellent-value Russian River Valley blend called Cuvée de Trois, which usually sells out fast. Also worth trying are the equally elegant single-vineyard zinfandels. For those who like white, Swan also produces single-vineyard gewürztaminer, pinot gris, and a roussanne-marsanne. The small, rustic winery tasting room is off the beaten path, down tiny Trenton Road at the northern end of Laguna Road.

MARTINELLI WINERY

One of the most noteworthy zinfandels made in the Russian River Valley comes from the Jackass Vineyard of **Martinelli Winery** (3360 River Rd., Windsor, 707/525-0570 or 800/346-1627, www.martinelliwinery.com, 10am-5pm daily, tasting $5), planted in the 1800s and still going. That notable vineyard's name has absolutely no historical significance, instead referring to the sort of farmer who would consider farming such a steep and rugged slope.

The Martinellis have been a fixture here since the early 1900s as grape and apple growers. In fact, apples can be found alongside the wines and other gourmet food in the rather chaotic winery gift shop inside the big red barn, a former hop barn. (This Martinelli apple-and-wine clan is, however, unrelated to the Martinelli clan that supplies cheap apple cider to your local supermarket.)

Not much of the popular, if expensive, Jackass zin is made each year, however, so chances are it will have sold out. There are plenty of other wines to try in the huge

NORTHERN SONOMA

portfolio. So many different wines are made here that it's hard to believe total production is only about 10,000 cases. The portfolio of pinot noir stretches to more than a half-dozen wines, most sourced from the Russian River Valley or Green Valley and most being big, earthy, and full-bodied affairs. Others worth tasting include the sauvignon blanc and an intensely aromatic muscat, both unusual wines for this area.

MARTIN RAY WINERY

Although housed in the oldest continually operating winery in Sonoma and named after one of California's pioneering modern winemakers, the **Martin Ray Winery** (2191 Laguna Rd., Santa Rosa, 707/823-2404, www.martinray-winery.com, 11am-5pm daily, tasting free or $5-10) is actually a relatively modern operation with few links to the site's historic past or the man after whom it is named. Nonetheless, it makes some good wines from mountain fruit and has some fascinating historic features and heritage that make it worth visiting.

The winery itself dates back to 1881, and a few of the massive redwood fermenting tanks from the early 1900s are still on display outside the modest tasting room at the end of the long driveway. Since then it has undergone countless transformations, including as a maker of sacramental wines during Prohibition.

Today the winery makes several hundred thousand cases of wine, a size that's evident from the huge warehouses and water tower on the site. The wines cover just about every major varietal and growing region in Northern California, with an emphasis on mountain fruit. From a historical and quality perspective, the most interesting are the expensive reserve cabernet sauvignons from vineyards in the Santa Cruz Mountains, Martin Ray's old stomping ground, and Diamond Mountain in the Napa Valley. Both are intensely flavored mountain wines, each with the distinctive character of its region. They're worth paying the modest reserve tasting fee to try. The best pinot noir in the lineup, from the Russian River Valley, is also a reserve wine. The cheaper

nonreserve Martin Ray wines include a nice Russian River chardonnay and Mendocino pinot gris along with a series of less unique wines from Napa Valley vineyards.

Cheaper wines sold under the Angeline label account for the vast majority of total production here and are a good value but not in the same league as the reserves.

INMAN FAMILY WINES

The focus of the **Inman Family Wines** (3900 Piner Rd., Santa Rosa, 707/293-9576, www.inmanfamilywines.com, 11am-4pm Thurs.-Mon., tasting $10) is wine that is nurtured and cultivated in small lots in Sonoma's prestigious Russian River Valley. Healthy soil, natural winemaking, and sustainable business practices are hallmarks here. Owner/general manager/winemaker Kathleen Inman's passion for the pinot noir grape is evident in the bright, balanced wines she produces. Inman prides herself on her hands-on approach to the business—she has a hand in everything from growing grapes and driving the forklift to sales and accounting. You might even see this multitasking entrepreneur pouring her beloved pinots in the tasting room. Kathleen's dedication to sustainability and preserving the environment goes beyond farming to eco-friendly labels, recyclable packaging, and using suppliers that share the Inman family's vision and philosophy. In keeping with that, for a modest fee visitors who drive electric automobiles can charge up at Sonoma County's first privately owned public charging station while sipping Russian River Valley pinot noir or the snappy Sonoma chardonnay.

BATTAGLINI ESTATE WINERY

Many large Russian River wineries make a wine out of every varietal under the hot Sonoma sun, but **Battaglini Estate Winery** (2948 Piner Rd., Santa Rosa, 707/578-4091, www.battagliniwines.com, 10am-5pm daily, tasting $10) has chosen instead to specialize. Inside the cute wood-paneled tasting room with the homey cluttered bar, you'll find only zinfandels, chardonnays, and petite sirahs. However, the expression of each of these grapes approaches perfection. You'll also see a few unusual manifestations, such as a late-harvest dessert chardonnay. For the most fun you can have during the crowded harvest season, join Battaglini in the fall for a "Stomp" event, during which you'll literally take off your shoes and start stomping in a bucket of grapes. If you're in the area in the fall, check out the Annual Barrel Tasting Event, where you can sample wines still in the barrel and meet the winemaker.

WINERIES BY APPOINTMENT

Tucked away inside an anonymous unit in the middle of an industrial estate on the northern edge of Santa Rosa, **Siduri Wines** (980 Airway Ct., Ste. C, Santa Rosa, 707/578-3882, www.siduri.com, 10am-3pm daily by appointment) has quietly carved out a huge reputation for its single-vineyard pinot noirs sourced from just about every great pinot-growing region on the West Coast. Owners Adam and Dianna Lee have followed a dream of making their favorite wine fervently, since they first left their native Texas in their twenties. After years gaining experience working for small wineries, they leased their first acre of vineyards, made their first 100 cases of wine in 1994, and, through a chance meeting with critic Robert Parker, won what would be the first of countless stellar ratings.

The portfolio runs to more than 15 single-vineyard pinots sourced from the Willamette Valley in Oregon all the way down to the Santa Rita Hills near Santa Barbara. Anywhere from a few hundred to 1,000 cases are made of each wine, but all are richly extracted and regarded as among the cream of West Coast pinots. The big news is when Siduri *doesn't* receive a 90-plus point rating for one of its wines, which generally cost $30-50 per bottle. Visiting the winery is a refreshing change from Wine Country chintz—in such an industrial setting you can't help but focus solely on what's under your nose, which might well be one of the keys to Siduri's success. That and perhaps the fact that the winery is named after the Babylonian goddess of wine.

The setting does make finding Siduri challenging, however. From Piner Road just west of U.S. Highway 101, go north on Airway Drive, into what looks like (and is) a light industrial area. The first road on the right is Airway Court, and Siduri is in the warehouse right at the end of the street, through the gates, on the right.

From Healdsburg via Argentina to Graton might seem like a tortuous route for a winemaker, but the founder of **Paul Hobbs Winery** (3355 Gravenstein Hwy. N., Sebastopol, 707/824-9879, www.paulhobbswinery.com, 10am and 1:30pm Mon.-Tues. and Thurs.-Fri. by appointment, tour and tasting $30) picked up some valuable winemaking experience along the way from Simi Winery near Healdsburg and Vina Cobos winery in Mendoza, Argentina, before establishing his wine label in 1991. Now Hobbs makes highly rated, vineyard-designate chardonnay, syrah, and pinot noir from Russian River vineyards, and a cabernet sauvignon using Napa fruit. Prices of the wines, like their ratings, are high. Tasting here is more like Napa Valley than Sonoma and the Russian River. The price for a tour and tasting of five wines is a hefty $30, and for the same price you can have a flight of Hobbs Argentinian wines. For $75, your flight can be paired with food on Tuesday and Thursday at 1pm.

Acorn Winery (12040 Old Redwood Hwy., down a gravel driveway just south of Limerick Ln., Healdsburg, 707/433-6440, www.acornwinery.com, 10am-4pm daily, tasting $10), with its modest tasting bar in the corner of Bill and Betsy Nachbauer's garage, couldn't be further from the winemaking behemoths of Rodney Strong and Foppiano nearby. The Nachbauers are former corporate lawyers who bought their 26 acres of vineyards here in 1990 and started making their own wine six years later using equipment at other wineries but barrel aging (and tasting) in their garage. Production now is about 3,000 cases a year and a thoroughly Italian affair. Wines include zinfandel, sangiovese, dolcetto, and field blends including Medley, a blend of 15 varietals that redefines the term "complex." Being popular, however, most of the wines sell out fast each year.

NORTHERN SONOMA

tasting at Porter Bass

If it's a sunny day and you are passing through Guerneville, make an appointment to taste at **Porter Bass** (11750 Mays Canyon Rd., Guerneville, 707/869-1475, www.porterbass.com, free tasting). Tucked up into the mountains, surrounded only by vineyards and redwood forest, this one-man operation makes less than 1,000 cases of estate chardonnay, zinfandel, and pinot noir a year. Luke Bass is the owner, farmer, winemaker, and tour guide, and has lived on the property since his parents (who still live there) bought it and planted it in grapes in the early 1980s. His stints away, however, include getting a degree in economics at UC Santa Cruz and time spent in South America where he learned to make wine.

Today the land is certified biodynamic, and when you visit, Bass is happy to explain the process of biodynamic farming, show off the small cave and bottling room, and talk about his family's history on the land. The tasting room is a plank of hardwood beneath a walnut tree surrounded by camping chairs, where Bass pours healthy tastes of anything he has available. If you're lucky, you might even get a vertical tasting of his lemony chardonnay. Appointments are easy to come by and can be made a day in advance, and even hours before on Saturday. Bottle prices range $40-55, while Bass's cheaper non-estate wines under the Poco a Poco label can be enjoyed at nearby restaurants such as Big Bottom Market (16228 Main St., Guerneville, 707/604-7295, www.bigbottommarket.com, 8am-5pm Sun.-Mon. and Wed.-Thurs., 8am-6pm Fri.-Sat., $10) in Guerneville.

SIGHTS

The Russian River Valley is full of beautiful natural sights, from rivers to fir-covered mountains, but most of the cultural sights in the region are clustered around Santa Rosa. The biggest city in Wine Country, and the largest in the North Bay, Santa Rosa is more preoccupied with big-city issues than with wine tasting. One of the plusses to Santa Rosa's size is that there are plenty of museums and things to do with or without kids. The downside is that it is also not very compact, meaning that it has been susceptible to sprawl and can be difficult to navigate: Destinations can feel, and often are, far flung. The closest thing to a central tourist area is **Railroad Square,** around which some of Santa Rosa's precious few pre-1906-earthquake buildings have been restored and now house restaurants and shops. The square is also a part of the larger **Arts District** where galleries and public art installations showcase regional contemporary art. The area hosts art-themed events, including open studios throughout the year. For more information, visit www.sofas-antarosa.com

Railroad Square

The Railroad Square district encompasses 3rd, 4th, and 5th Streets in downtown Santa Rosa, just west of U.S. 101. The center of the Railroad Square district is the **Northwestern Pacific Railroad Depot,** a small stone station house built in 1904 to replace an earlier wooden structure that burned down. Like many of the basalt stone buildings in the surrounding blocks, the depot is as solid as it looks and withstood the 1906 earthquake that leveled much of downtown Santa Rosa. Its claim to fame was acting as a backdrop in the Alfred Hitchcock film *Shadow of a Doubt,* and it is now home to the **Santa Rosa Convention & Visitors Bureau** (9 4th St., Santa Rosa, 707/577-8674 or 800/404-7673, 8:30am-5pm Mon.-Fri., 10am-3pm Sat.-Sun.).

Pick up a walking map from the visitors bureau to see some of the other historic buildings made from the locally quarried basalt stone. The buildings now house dozens of antiques stores, jewelry stores, and other boutiques; 4th Street is particularly rich in historical storefronts.

Old Towne Jewelers (125 4th St., Santa Rosa, 707/577-8813, 10am-5:30pm Mon.-Sat.) specializes in glamorous vintage jewelry and watches, from Victorian and Edwardian to mid-century and 21st-century periods. **Whistlestop Antiques** (130 4th St., Santa Rosa, 707/542-9474, 10am-5:30pm Mon.-Sat., 11am-5pm Sun.) is a collective of dozens

of antiques dealers worth visiting not least because of its antique home—a 1911 brick-and-steel building that won the city's first merit award for historical preservation and is typical of many of the surrounding edifices.

For timeless pieces that you can wear, stroll over to **Hot Couture Vintage Fashion** (101 3rd St., Santa Rosa, 707/528-7247, www.hot-couturevintage.com, 10am-6pm Mon.-Sat., 11am-5pm Sun.), where clothes mostly from the 1940s to the 1970s fill the racks, and hats for both men and women line the shelves along the walls. This store takes great pride in selling fashionable vintage clothing in great condition, so as not to be confused with just any old used clothing store.

Wine tasting has arrived to the square thanks to **Cellars of Sonoma** (133 4th St., Santa Rosa, 707/578-1826, www.cellarsofsonoma.com, noon-8:30pm Sun.-Mon., 11am-8:30pm Tues.-Wed., 11am-10:30 Thurs.-Sat., tasting $10-20). You'll find numerous pinot noirs and zinfandels, along with some coastal chardonnays from small mom and pop wineries. Among the wines from the nine vintners represented, the standout is La Sirena from winemaker Heidi Peterson Barrett. Along with having a long Wine Country pedigree (including ties to the Judgment of Paris), Barrett is best known for making cult cabernets such as Screaming Eagle, a six-liter 1992 vintage that sold at the Napa Valley Wine Auction in 2000 for $500,000. So, if any of Barrett's cabernets are available to try, do so.

◖ Luther Burbank Home & Gardens

Apples and pears, grapes and hops, plums and peaches—as Sonoma County's rich agricultural history suggests, pretty much anything will grow here. Pioneering horticulturist Luther Burbank recognized this when he made Sonoma County his home in 1875. Burbank's cross-breeding experiments at his Santa Rosa and Sebastopol greenhouses are credited with creating more than 800 new strains of flowers, fruits, trees, and other plants over his 50-year science career, including the big white

Shasta daisy, a spineless cactus, the blight-resistant Burbank potato, and the plumcot, a cross between an apricot and a plum. He was well connected in scientific circles of the time, counting Thomas Edison and Henry Ford, among others, as friends. Ford sent him the first tractor off the company's production line as a gift in 1918.

Santa Rosa was proud to have Burbank, and he in turn was happy to be part of the city's self-promotion. A Santa Rosa promotional brochure in the 1920s described him as "California's best citizen," and borrowed one of his many famous Sonoma quotes: "I would rather own a piece of land the size of a good healthy house lot in Sonoma County than an entire farm anywhere else on earth."

Burbank's own healthy house lot, where he lived until 1906, is preserved along with a small greenhouse and the gardens as part of the 1.6-acre National and State Historic Landmark in Santa Rosa (204 Santa Rosa Ave., just across the street from city hall, 707/524-5445, www.lutherburbank.org). The gardens contain many of Burbank's horticultural creations and are open 8am-sunset every day. The **museum** and **greenhouse** (10am-4pm Tues.-Sun. Apr.-Oct., $4) include some of his tools and explain the significance of his work. **Guided tours** (adults $7, children under 12 free) are available during opening hours April-October. Check the website for a list of what's in bloom during your visit, as something will be showing off its finest flowers every month of the year!

Also open about a half mile west of downtown Sebastopol is the 15-acre **Gold Ridge Experiment Farm** (7781 Bodega Ave., Sebastopol, 707/829-6711, daily year-round, cottage 9am-noon Wed., free), where Burbank did many of his horticultural experiments and where there is now a historical collection of some of his creations. The replica cottage (the original was destroyed in 1906) and gardens have a rather unflattering modern setting in the middle of a retirement community. Take a self-guided hike or join a docent-led tour (by appointment year-round).

Museums

Santa Rosa has only a modest number of cultural attractions, but being the biggest city in Sonoma County does mean it's the rightful home of the **Sonoma County Museum** (425 7th St., Santa Rosa, 707/579-1500, www.sonomacountymuseum.org, 11am-5pm Tues.-Sun., $7, children under 12 free). Located in the city's historic former main post office building, the museum includes permanent exhibits of historic artifacts and photos that help tell the story of the county alongside temporary local art and photography exhibits. There's also an unlikely collection of art from world-famous artists Christo and Jeanne-Claude that was donated to the museum in 2001 by their longtime assistant Tom Golden, who's from nearby Freestone. This unexpected acquisition dovetailed nicely into the permanent collection inherited from the Sonoma Museum of Contemporary Art, which closed its doors in 2005. Now, the Sonoma County Museum has become a more balanced art and history museum that even boasts a sculpture garden that was completed in 2011.

A slightly offbeat cultural attraction is the **Charles M. Schulz Museum** (2301 Hardies Ln., Santa Rosa, 707/579-4452, www.schulzmuseum.org, 11am-5pm Mon.-Fri., 10am-5pm Sat.-Sun. summer, 11am-5pm Mon. and Wed.-Fri., 10am-5pm Sat.-Sun. fall-spring, adults $10, kids $5, 3 and under free), for the man who drew the beloved *Peanuts* comic strip for almost 50 years and called Sonoma home from 1958 until his death in 2000. Inside the 27,000-square-foot building, which somehow manages to look like it comes from a four-inch comic strip, you'll find an incredible wealth of multimedia art, original drawings, and changing exhibitions based on the works of Charles Schulz. No matter how many times you visit, you're likely to see something new. The museum owns most of the original *Peanuts* strips, a large collection of Schulz's personal possessions, and an astonishing array of tribute artwork (everyone from other comic-strip artists to urban installation designers the world over). Outside the building, the grounds include attractive gardens, the Snoopy Labyrinth, and even the infamous Kite-Eating Tree.

Schulz's influence is felt outside the museum property as well. Across the street you can skate at Snoopy's Home Ice. (Schulz was an avid hockey player for most of his life.) And throughout downtown Santa Rosa, especially in historic Railroad Square, you'll see colorful sculptures depicting favorite members of the *Peanuts* gang brightening the streets, making people smile.

Nearby, the **Pacific Coast Air Museum** (2230 Becker Blvd., Santa Rosa, 707/575-7900, www.pacificcoastairmuseum.org, 10am-4pm Tues., Thurs., and Sat.-Sun., adults $9, children 6-17 $5, under 5 free) is worth a stop even if you're not an aviation buff. Through interpretive and photographic exhibits, you can learn about the history of aviation in America. Spend some time studying the cutaways and bits and pieces to enhance your understanding of the mechanics of powered flight. And finally, fantasize about flying the fine examples of F-series fighters and the many other military and civilian aircraft on display. Many of the planes here are examples of modern war machines—such as those you'd see on the deck of an aircraft carrier in the Persian Gulf today. Or if you prefer to see civilian craft, check out the funky little Pitts aerobatic plane, the sort of thing you'll see doing impossible-looking tricks during the museum's annual **Wings over Wine Country** air show, held each August.

ENTERTAINMENT

Santa Rosa's entertainment scene is somewhat dispersed, but the city does have a well-established local theater group. **The Imaginists Theatre Collective** (461 Sebastopol Ave., Santa Rosa, 707/528-7554, www.theimaginists.org, $15-25) puts on an eclectic series of original and imaginative plays year-round at a small theater that was once home to an auto-repair shop. The evening performances are usually concentrated in a two-week stretch each month. Check the website for a performance schedule.

One of the most popular live music venues in the city is the **Last Day Saloon** in the Railroad Square area (120 5th St., Santa Rosa, 707/545-5876, www.lastdaysaloon.com, bar and restaurant Tues.-Sat. until late and other times when a show is scheduled). It's a fairly big and somewhat grungy venue with a decent bar and basic restaurant at the front, but most people come here for the DJs or the live music—generally rock and blues with some fairly big-name bands sometimes appearing. It also boasts the biggest dance floor of any venue in the area, which is not saying much. Check the website for upcoming shows and other events.

Guerneville and Sebastopol are two other local towns to visit for some late-night fun. Guerneville and its environs have probably the most diverse entertainment scene in the Russian River Valley, befitting the eclectic population that swells in the summer with an influx of both gay and straight revelers. Sebastopol's action is a little more mainstream. Much of Guerneville's nightlife caters to the gay scene with a curious mix of rustic bars enhanced with Day-Glo furnishings, all open late (and a few open unusually early, too) and all along a three-block stretch of Main Street downtown. **The Rainbow Cattle Company** (16220 Main St., Guerneville, 707/869-0206, www.queersteer.com, 6am-2am daily) is one of the oldest, with a big outdoor patio and legendary quarts of Long Island iced tea to get patrons in the mood. The poolside bar at the **Russian River Resort** (16390 4th St., Guerneville, 707/869-0691, www.russianriverresort.com, from 3pm Mon.-Fri. and noon Sat.-Sun.), also known as the Triple-R, is a popular drinking location for the gay masses and has some form of entertainment on weekend nights during the summer and Friday nights during the winter.

A few miles east of Guerneville and almost an institution in the area is the **Rio Nido Roadhouse** (14540 Canyon 2 Rd., off River Rd., Rio Nido, 707/869-0821, www.rionidoroadhouse.com), which combines a rustic bar, restaurant, and poolside entertainment. Here you

NORTHERN SONOMA FESTIVALS AND EVENTS

Whatever the time of year, there's always some sort of festival or wine-related event going on in this part of the world.

JANUARY

Wineries have to think of something to bring in customers in the depths of winter, hence the **Winter Wineland** event (707/433-4335, www.wineroad.com), held around the middle of the month. More than 100 of the region's wineries take part. For the ticket price of $35-45, visitors get the VIP treatment and samples of limited-release wines. There's even a special designated-driver ticket price of $5.

MARCH

The region's annual **Barrel Tasting** (707/433-4335, www.wineroad.com), held on the first two weekends of the month, is a great excuse to visit as many wineries as possible in a day and sample wines straight from the barrel, whether you're interested in buying wine futures or not. Tickets are $30 in advance, $40 at the door, and $5 for any designated drivers.

APRIL

The **Passport to Dry Creek Valley** ($70-120), held on the last weekend of the month, gets visitors into almost every winery in the valley, even those usually open by appointment only. Every one of them has some sort of theme for the weekend and puts on quite a party, with plenty of food and, of course, wine. The mock passports are stamped at every winery; passports are limited so book early. Contact the Winegrowers of Dry Creek Valley (707/433-3031, www.wdcv.com) for more information.

MAY

At the end of the month, on Memorial Day weekend, Healdsburg's antiques sellers set up shop on the plaza for the one-day, free **Healdsburg Antique Fair** (707/433-6935, www.healdsburg.com).

JUNE

Before wine there was the Wild West, which is celebrated every year at the **Russian River Rodeo** (707/865-9854, www.russianriverrodeo.org, tickets $10-12), held the third weekend of the month at the Duncans Mills Rodeo, a 15-minute drive west of Guerneville. Over in Healdsburg, the beginning of June marks the

can lounge on a lawn next to bikers and aging hippies, surrounded by redwoods, soaking up the alcohol and the last rays of sun while tucking in to some freshly barbecued ribs and listening to a local blues band. It can be quite a trip, even for Guerneville. Bands play most weekend evenings throughout the year, and the pool is open Memorial Day-Labor Day.

About 15 minutes west on Highway 116, Monte Rio is a sort of miniature Guerneville on acid, a self-proclaimed "Vacation Wonderland" with more going on than its scrappy cluster of downtown buildings suggests.

Hard to miss is the brightly painted, neon-signed hump of the **Rio Theater** (20396 Bohemian Hwy., at Hwy. 116, Monte Rio, 707/865-0913, www.riotheater.com, Fri.-Sun.), an old World War II-era Quonset hut, one of 170,000 churned out for emergency housing and warehousing in the 1940s. The theater now shows a program of current films that would put any big-city independent theater to shame. The Sunday matinees ($5) start at 3pm, and the evening shows, which run on Friday and Saturday nights ($7), begin at 7pm. Check the website or call the theater for the regularly changing schedules.

If you think a movie theater satiates the cultural requirements of tiny Monte Rio, think again. Monte Rio is also home to an active beginning of the annual **Healdsburg Jazz Festival** (707/433-4633, www.healdsburgjazz-festival.com), a weeklong series of concerts at venues around the city.

AUGUST

They named a highway after this apple, so why not have a festival in its honor as well? The **Gravenstein Apple Fair** (800/207-9464, www.gravensteinapplefair.com, tickets $12) in Sebastopol is held around the middle of the month at the town's Ragle Ranch Park. The event includes music, crafts, and plenty of apple-flavored fun. More raucous fun can be had farther down the road at the **Russian River Beer Revival and BBQ Cook Off** (707/869-0705, www.stumptown.com, $80) at the Stumptown Brewery. The annual event features live music, beer tasting from 30 different breweries, and lots and lots of barbecue.

SEPTEMBER

The big blowout wine event of the year is the **Sonoma Wine Country Weekend** (800/939-7666, www.sonomawinecountryweekend.com), a three-day wine, food, and arts extravaganza

held during the beginning of the month at the region's wineries. The main event is the **Taste of Sonoma County,** which is usually held at a winery near Healdsburg.

Celebrate the end of summer on the beach in Guerneville at the **Russian River Jazz and Blues Festival** (707/869-1595, www.omegaevents.com, $50-80), usually held the third weekend of the month. Top jazz musicians, fine wine, late summer sun, and the option of simply floating on the river all combine to make a unique experience. Tickets for the weekend event are available starting in April from the festival organizers.

NOVEMBER

With all the creative names for food and wine events apparently exhausted for the year, this month's reason to eat and drink to excess is called simply **A Food & Wine Affair.** Many of the region's wineries match their wines with all sorts of food on the first weekend of the month. All you have to do is get from one winery to another. Tickets ($50-70, $30 designated drivers) and information are available from the Russian River Wine Road (707/433-4335, www.wineroad.com).

nonprofit theater group, the **Pegasus Theater Company** (4444 Wood Rd., Monte Rio, 707/583-2343, www.pegasustheater.com, $15) established in 1998 by some veteran regional actors. It puts on plays and readings during the year, most from well-known playwrights (except the holiday variety show). Each runs for about six weeks at the snug Rio Nido Lodge in Monte Rio.

Live local bands, DJ dance nights, and the occasional open-mike night are the main forms of entertainment at the **Hopmonk Tavern** (230 Petaluma Ave., 707/829-7300, www.hopmonk.com, 11:30am-close daily) in Sebastopol. There's something going on

nearly every night, particularly in summer, when the dance action can also sometimes spill out onto the patio. Check the website for upcoming events. Covers for live bands range $5-30, and most come on around 8pm. There's also a late-night menu for anyone looking for some food to wash down the microbrews made here.

RECREATION

Two big wilderness areas, miles of river, tracts of forest, and a limited population make almost any sort of outdoor pursuit possible in the Russian River Valley, whether on land, on water, or in the air.

Armstrong Redwoods State Reserve

This 805-acre reserve is just a few miles up Armstrong Woods Road from the center of Guerneville and is, as its name suggests, home to some neck-twistingly tall redwoods. The shady and damp forest provides welcome relief from the summer heat and is now the largest remaining old-growth redwood forest in Sonoma County. Some of its trees survived the region's vast 19th-century logging operations and were ironically saved by a lumberman—Colonel James Armstrong—who bought the land in the 1870s to preserve the last tracts of the very same forest he profited from.

Visitors with little time or energy can make a short trek on groomed paths from one of the three parking lots to some fine redwood specimens, including the 308-foot-tall **Colonel Armstrong Tree,** which is believed to be about 1,400 years old and the oldest in the park. If craning your neck is too strenuous, relax at one of the picnic tables scattered among the trees.

One hike is a relatively quick loop (2.2 miles) that illustrates the wide range of vegetation and microclimates. The **East Ridge Trail** climbs steeply from just behind the visitors center up to a warm ridge that ducks in and out of the sun before descending back into the redwoods (head downhill at the first signposted trail junction, or the hike will become a half-day ordeal). Once back in the redwoods it's an easy walk down the road or the **Pioneer Trail** back to the visitors center. Another moderate loop is the 2.3-mile **Pool Ridge Trail,** which climbs 500 feet up a series of switchbacks before looping back down into the forest.

The more adventurous can choose from any number of longer hikes up out of the redwoods to the oak and madrone forests on the ridges higher up and continue on into the Austin Creek State Recreation Area, which is north of the reserve.

The reserve is open sunrise-sunset, and there's a $8 day-use fee for cars. Alternatively, park at the **visitors center** (17000 Armstrong Woods Rd., Guerneville, 707/869-2958, www. parks.ca.gov, 11am-3pm daily) and walk in on the road or a trail to avoid the fee. Dogs and bikes are not allowed on any of the trails.

Austin Creek State Recreation Area

Adventurous outdoorsy types might want to drive straight through Armstrong Redwoods to **Austin Creek State Recreation Area** (17000 Armstrong Woods Rd., Guerneville, 707/869-2015, www.parks.ca.gov, day use $8), a 5,700-acre wilderness with 20 miles of hiking trails, chaparral and oak woodlands, rolling hills, and meandering creeks.

The steep, switchbacking Armstrong Woods road (no trailers or vehicles over 20 feet) ends at the Bullfrog Pond Campground but stops at several trailheads on the way up, including the **Gilliam Creek Trail,** which dives down to Schoolhouse Creek and toward a handful of primitive creek-side campgrounds. The closest of these is almost four miles, so allow plenty of time.

Horseback riding is allowed on all of the Austin Creek trails, but unless you own your own horse the only option for getting on one is with the **Armstrong Woods Pack Station** concession (707/887-2939, www.redwoodhorses.com), which operates by reservation only from the Armstrong Redwoods reserve. Two-hour rides ($90) up to full-day trips ($160-200) are available year-round (weather permitting). There's usually a four-person minimum for the rides in the summer, though if there are not enough riders booked, there's also the option of a two-person ride for double the normal price.

Riverfront Regional Park

About three miles south of J Vineyards on Eastside Road, **Riverfront Regional Park** (7821 Eastside Rd., Healdsburg, 707/565-2041, www.sonoma-county.org/parks, sunrise-sunset, $8) is the perfect retreat to stretch your legs or sit in the shade of a redwood grove next to the parking lot and enjoy a picnic. The former gravel-mining operation here left behind a series of small lakes that look very inviting on a

the Russian River

hot summer day but are strictly off-limits to swimmers. Several miles of trails around the 300-acre park give plenty of chances to see the wildlife on and around the lakes, however, and fishing for bass in the lakes is allowed with a current license. There are picnic areas, with restroom facilities and barbecue pits, along with a volleyball court and a horseshoe pit. Just beyond that is the Russian River, where you can swim if you're brave enough. There's no official river access and no real beach, but it's easy enough to get down to the water if you're desperate to cool off.

The Russian River

With the Russian River gently snaking through the vineyards and forests toward the sea, it's not surprising that canoeing and kayaking are popular summer activities here. The river flow is relatively smooth this far downstream, even in the winter when the water is higher and faster, so don't expect any adrenaline-pumping rapids. Do expect to have to slather on the sunscreen on a hot summer day, however, and not to care

if you tip over and take an unexpected dip in the river.

One of the least strenuous ways to experience the river's meandering pace is to rent a canoe at **Burkes Canoe Trips** (8600 River Rd., Forestville, 707/887-1222, www.burkescanoetrips.com, May-Sept., $60/day). Paddle or simply float 10 miles downriver, stopping at the many secluded beaches along the way, to Guerneville, where courtesy shuttles run back to base every half hour all day long.

Near the small enclave of Monte Rio, **Johnsons Beach & Resort** (16241 1st St., Guerneville, 707/869-2022, www.johnsonsbeach.com, 10am-6pm daily, May-Oct.) rents canoes, kayaks, and pedal boats for $30 a day or $10 per hour. Inner tubes are also available ($5/day), but can only be used at the beach. To make this more appealing, Johnson's Beach also has a safe, kid-friendly section of the riverbank that is roped off for small children; parents and beachcombers can rent beach chairs and umbrellas for use on the small beach. The boathouse sells beer and snacks, rounding out what you might need for a beach day on the Russian River.

Kayaks and canoes can also be rented for a day or more from **Kings Sport & Tackle** (16258 Main St., Guerneville, 707/869-2156, www. kingsrussianriver.com, 8am-5pm daily). Single kayaks cost $35 per day, doubles are $55, aluminum canoes cost $55. From Guerneville's Johnson's Beach, it's four miles to Monte Rio downstream or eight miles to Forestville upstream. Make it a round-trip or pay $15 for the store to send a shuttle for pickup or drop-off. The store also sells a variety of beach and river gear, including inflatable boats and inner tubes. Floating down the river is popular here, and you'll see many locals relaxing in inner tubes, often with a six pack or even a bag of white wine tethered to the back and chilling in the river (although drinking on the river is not recommended).

Fishing for the river's bass, bluegill, catfish, and steelhead salmon is also popular from a rented canoe or one of the many beaches, though a California fishing license is required. One-day, two-day, and longer licenses can be bought at Kings Sport & Tackle in Guerneville, which also rents fishing equipment and offers daylong guided fishing and fly-fishing trips ($75-200) in the area. Also ask about the myriad rules and regulations. Barbed hooks cannot be used, for example, only artificial lures (no bait) are allowed during the summer, and chinook salmon must be released immediately if hooked.

Ballooning

While not as plentiful as in the Napa Valley area, there are still plenty of opportunities to take to the air in this part of the Wine Country, and, arguably, the aerial views of vineyards, mountains, rivers, forests, and the distant ocean are more impressive than in less scenically diverse Napa.

Taking to the air in Wine Country, of course, usually means ballooning, which entails getting up before the crack of dawn (balloons typically take off not long after sunrise), spending several hundred dollars, waiting around as the balloon is set up, and having little idea of which way it will drift once it does get airborne. Almost everyone thinks the reward, however, is worth it, as the initial adrenaline surge from lifting off yields to a sense of relaxation from being in a still and silent world thousands of feet above the stress of daily life.

Flights usually last about an hour, but expect the whole experience, including a postflight brunch, to take up about half a day. Also expect to have to make reservations up to a month in advance during the summer and be held to a strict cancellation policy. Full directions to the meeting place along with any flight-related updates are provided once you make a reservation.

Wine Country Balloons (707/538-7359 or 800/759-5638, www.balloontours.com, $225/person) usually flies from the Sonoma County airport near Santa Rosa and meets passengers at Kal's Kaffe Mocha where the postflight brunch is served. **Up and Away** (707/836-0171 or 800/711-2998, www.up-away.com, $235/person) also meets passengers at the Sonoma County airport, though balloons may take off elsewhere, depending on the weather. Both companies' balloons fly year-round and usually carry 6-8 people, though private flights can also be arranged for a lot more money.

Golf

Stroll among the redwoods without donning hiking boots at the **Northwood Golf Club** (19400 Hwy. 116, Monte Rio, 707/865-1116), just west of Guerneville. The historic par-36, nine-hole course was conceived by members of the exclusive gentlemen's retreat Bohemian Grove, just across the road, designed by famous course architect Alistair McKenzie (who also designed the Augusta National course), and completed in 1928. Weekend greens fees start at $26 for nine holes, $39 for 18.

Russian River Spas

The spa destination in the Russian River Valley is as alternative as its remote location on the Bohemian Highway just south of Occidental suggests. The mud baths at **Osmosis** (209 Bohemian Hwy., Occidental, 707/823-8231,

RUSSIAN RIVER BEACHES

It can get hot in the summer—too hot for even a chilled chardonnay to take the edge off. Luckily, the cool waters of the Russian River are always only a short drive away (though perhaps best experienced without being inebriated). As summer temperatures soar and the water level falls, the river is relatively calm and benign compared to the swift torrent it can become in the winter and spring. It's still fairly cold though, with plenty of hidden obstacles underwater. The dozens of small beaches exposed as the water level falls in the summer are technically public land, but getting to them usually involves crossing private or restricted areas. That puts many out of reach unless you're floating down the river in a canoe—the best way to experience some summer river fun. It is still possible to get to some key beaches from the road, however.

- **Geyserville Bridge:** In the Alexander Valley (Hwy. 128 west of Geyserville) there is space for a few cars to park off the side of the road at both ends. The easiest way down to the river is a short trail at the southwest end of the bridge that leads down to a gravelly beach area and stretches for quite a ways downstream.

- **Memorial Beach:** A better place for swimming in the area is at this beach at the southern end of Healdsburg, just across the Memorial Bridge. This family-friendly beach has a swimming lagoon and canoe rentals. There's parking ($7), which can fill up quickly in the summer. Finding free parking anywhere near the beach is usually tough. The best alternative is to park on 1st Street in Healdsburg and walk back over the bridge.

- **Wohler Bridge:** The historic bridge on Wohler Road (just off the southern end of the Westside Rd.) has a small parking lot, a boat ramp on the west side of the bridge, and some limited parking along the road. Walk back to the other side of the bridge, hop over the steel gate, and follow the gravel trail for

about 0.5 mile, past the Water Agency yard. Bear right at a small fork until you reach the meadow and generally sandy beach just beyond. This is a popular beach with nude sunbathers and has gained a reputation as a gay cruising area.

- **Steelhead Beach:** To reach this beach, drive southeast on Wohler Road, past the Raford House B&B, and turn right on River Road. About one mile farther, on the right, is the entrance ($7 day-use fee). The large parking lot and boat ramp at the main beach hint at the spot's popularity for fishing and canoeing. A couple of trails heading east from the parking area lead to a more secluded stretch of beach that is better for swimming.

- **Hacienda Beach:** Farther along River Road, just west of the junction with Westside Road, is this hidden beach off tiny residential Sunset Avenue. Parking on Sunset is illegal unless you live there, but there's usually plenty of space on the wide shoulder along River Road. At the first bend on Sunset Avenue there's a dusty trail off to the right leading down to a wide, gravelly beach and a good swimming hole. From there you can walk farther downstream to additional, more secluded beaches. However, plenty of parking can be found at **Sunset Beach,** about a quarter mile down the road. There are chemical toilets and picnic areas here, as well as a day-use fee of $7.

- **Johnson's Beach:** This family beach in the middle of Guerneville, just a few hundred yards off Main Street, is where a makeshift dam is set up each summer to create a lagoon for swimming or paddling around in a rented canoe. It's crowded in summer, but the big parking lot is free, the food plentiful, and the atmosphere fun. This is the spot to rent canoes, kayaks, inflatables, and beach umbrellas, as well as the site of the town's Fourth of July bash and the annual Jazz on the River festival.

www.osmosis.com, 9am-8pm daily) are of the dry variety, in which hundreds of enzymes are mixed with rice bran and ground-up cedar leaves to ferment the impurities out of the skin. The warm, relaxing treatment is best enjoyed before consuming the local fermented grape juice, however; otherwise an early hangover might be the only result. The enzyme baths cost from $80 each for couples ($90 for a single person) and include a pretreatment tea service in the peaceful Zen garden. Massages and facials are available to complete the rejuvenation process, and full packages incorporating two or three treatments start at $199.

Exchange cedar for seaweed at Sebastopol's **Mermaids** (115 S. Main St., Sebastopol, 707/823-3535, www.mermaidsspa.com, 10am-5pm Sun.-Mon., 10am-8pm Wed.-Sat.). In the thick of downtown, this spa is not the luxury compound that you find at other spas in Wine Country. The atmosphere is decidedly more New Age healing than over-the-top personal pampering. Still, you will be greeted by a heated lavender neck pillow to help you relax while you peruse the long (and certainly luxurious) treatment menu. Choose between Pacific kelp or Mediterranean seaweed for a bath infused with essential oils and mineral salts, or go earthy with a mud bath of Italian volcanic ash and pine needle extract. Either way, spending 30 minutes or an hour soaking in the tubs will only set you back $55 or $80, respectively, and include a foot massage. If you want more than just a foot rub, there are multiple massage options from shiatsu to foot reflexology to hot stone therapy. You can opt for 30 minutes, an hour, hour and a half, or two hours and prices run $60-165. Putting it all together, the spa's combination packages are the best bargain, starting at $125 and topping out at $410.

ACCOMMODATIONS

The main city in these parts is Santa Rosa, and it has perhaps more rooms than any other town, although mostly in chain hotels. But the bohemian resort town of Guerneville and the surrounding area offer the widest range of accommodations, from so-called river resorts that have seen better days to some classier and reasonably priced inns and B&Bs. As usual, camping is by far the cheapest option, and there's plenty of the great outdoors to choose from, including the wilds of the backcountry and the relative comforts of the grounds of some of those resorts along the river.

If all else fails, there are usually rooms to be found in the string of motels along the freeway and to the south in Sebastopol. Just be sure to drink a glass of wine to remember that this is indeed Wine Country and not some random freeway exit to Anywhere, USA.

Under $150

The **Creekside Inn** (16180 Neely Rd., Guerneville, 707/869-3623, www.creeksideinn. com, $98-165) is indeed right beside the creek otherwise known as the Russian River. It is just a few minutes' stroll to Guerneville's Main Street but also even closer to noisy Highway 116. Nevertheless, the rooms with the shared bath in the main house are the cheapest, while the suites, which boast a small sitting area, balcony, and private bathroom, go for only $175. The several acres of grounds include a pool and eight cottages, from studios to two-bedrooms, all of which are equally affordable, never rising above $250. While this may seem spendy, the rooms at the high end are actually solar-powered suites that come with fully equipped kitchens and can sleep four.

Rather like a funky Guerneville version of an 1830s resort, **Fern Grove Cottages** (16650 Hwy. 116, Guerneville, 707/869-8105, www. ferngrove.com, $90-165) offers equal measures of tranquility and activity among the redwoods at the far western end of town. The collection of well-spaced cottages includes studio, one-bedroom, and two-bedroom accommodations with some twists including wet bars, hot tubs, and fireplaces. They are relative bargains, though the somewhat sparse decor is a reminder that they were built in the 1920s as a cheap family resort. On-site amenities include a pool, a bar, and a giant picnic area that's a hive of activity in the summer.

$150-250

The **West Sonoma Inn** (14100 Brookside Ln., Guerneville, 707/869-2470, www.west-sonomainn.com, $149-179) is a refreshing change from the rustic nature of many cheap lodging options in the area. The 36-room self-styled resort and spa is surprisingly cheap considering its relatively central location in Guerneville and the modern decor and amenities that include down comforters, fireplaces in most rooms, luxury bathrooms, and nice views. It would almost fit in to the chic Healdsburg scene. The cheapest are the two Vineyard rooms and two Creekside rooms, while the best value is the Deluxe Vineyard or Courtyard rooms, which are more spacious and have either panoramic views or a cozy fireplace. More expensive suites are available as are full cottages.

In a pretty part of the valley en route to Armstrong Redwoods State Reserve, the **Boon Hotel + Spa** (14711 Armstrong Woods Rd., Guerneville, 707/869-2721, www.boonhotels.com, $180) is the antithesis of Guerneville's woodsy funkiness. In almost a rebuff to the area it resides in, Boon Hotel + Spa is spare in the extreme with white walls devoid of painting or artwork, square armless couches, and beds vast enough to get lost in the fair-trade organic cotton sheets. The palette is slate, chrome, and white offset by slashes of red and orange. Many of the 14 rooms have freestanding cast-iron fireplaces, private patios, and refrigerators. Good to its name, there is a pool and hot tubs (both saline for a little twist) and plenty of facial and massage options to take out the kinks. In the morning, you can wake up to a press pot of locally roasted coffee and in the evening, chill out with a cocktail by the pool. Downtown Guerneville is about a half mile away, which is easily walkable but best navigated using one of the hotel's cruiser bikes that can be rented for a modest daily or half-day fee.

A few miles west of Guerneville in Monte Rio is the **Village Inn** (20822 River Blvd., off Bohemian Hwy., Monte Rio, 707/865-2304, www.villageinn-ca.com, $115-200), a tastefully restored Victorian home set in the redwoods on the south bank of the river not far from the infamous Bohemian Grove, an exclusive country club for America's elite and powerful. All 11 rooms have private bathrooms and a view of something, whether trees or the river. The bargains here are the three queen studios in the main inn, which have comfy club chairs and views of the river from their private balconies. The cheapest rooms are in the separate lodge, while the most expensive deluxe king studio has a big private deck overlooking the river. Amenities include TVs and VCRs, wireless Internet access, and mini-fridges so you can chill a bottle of Russian River chardonnay to enjoy on the balcony.

Standing sentinel at a sharp bend in Wohler Road just half a mile south of Wohler Bridge is the historic ◖ **Raford House** (10630 Wohler Rd., Healdsburg, 707/887-9573 or 800/887-9503, www.rafordinn.com, $170-235), once part of a huge hop-growing estate in its Victorian heyday but now a charming inn with verandas overlooking acres of vineyards. All six rooms have private bathrooms and are decorated in a tasteful and fairly restrained Victorian style. The biggest (and priciest) rooms have their own fireplaces, while the largest of all, the Bridal Room, has a private covered porch overlooking the valley. Rooms at the front of the house have the best views. Standard amenities include a CD player/radio, wireless Internet access, an evening wine reception, and a hot organic breakfast served every morning in the dining room.

One of the larger independent hotels in Santa Rosa is the **Hotel La Rose** (308 Wilson St., Santa Rosa, 707/579-3200 or 800/527-6738, www.hotellarose.com, $129-189), an imposing basalt stone building that's part of the historic Railroad Square development downtown, within walking distance of many of the city's sights and restaurants. The 29 guest rooms in the main building and Carriage House across the street (built in 1985) cater to the tourist and business crowd alike and so are well equipped and businesslike with minimal frills on the Victorian-style decor. Top-floor rooms in both buildings are the most interesting, with either vaulted or sloping ceilings.

NORTHERN SONOMA

NORTHERN SONOMA

Over $250

A bit like staying on a French country wine estate, the **Vintners Inn** (4350 Barnes Rd., Santa Rosa, 800/421-2584, www.vintnersinn. com, $360) sprawls amid 50 acres of manicured gardens and vineyards just a few miles north of Santa Rosa. It's ideally located for exploring the Russian River Valley, and quick access to the freeway (River Road exit) gives easy access to Healdsburg and beyond (though also some freeway noise). All 44 rooms and suites are cozy and luxurious, some with fireplaces and all with either balconies or patios. Breakfast is always included in the room rates, but on weekends you could also indulge with a sumptuous brunch at the inn's renowned **John Ash & Co.** restaurant, one of the eateries credited with starting the California "Wine Country cuisine" style of cooking that so many other restaurants now mimic.

A little off the beaten track is the neat former railroad town of Occidental, and just off the main road on the edge of the forest is a delightfully rambling Victorian homestead that is now the ◖ **Inn at Occidental** (3657 Church St., Occidental, 707/874-1047, www.innatoccidental.com, $239-379), a quirky yet luxurious bed-and-breakfast. None of the 16 whimsical rooms and suites are alike, although all have fireplaces and are stuffed with odd pieces of folk art, as are many of the inn's common areas.

A little piece of the Mediterranean landed in the redwoods just south of Guerneville in the form of the **Applewood Inn** (13555 Hwy. 116, Guerneville, 707/869-9093 or 800/555-8509, www.applewoodinn.com, $195-375). Three salmon-pink villas are nestled around a manicured central courtyard, the oldest of which is the 1922 Belden House with the cheapest (and smallest) rooms, starting at just under $200. The more modern Piccola Casa and Gate House, both built since 1996, contain the bigger and more expensive rooms, costing over $300. At those prices, the tranquil surroundings, swimming pool, in-room luxuries, and available spa therapies are to be expected. The big building at one end of the courtyard houses the hotel's Michelin-starred restaurant, offering classy Mediterranean-influenced California food and an extensive local-wine list.

Just a stone's throw from the Russian River, tucked away in the woods just off busy River Road, is the **Farmhouse Inn and Restaurant** (7871 River Rd., Forestville, 707/887-3300 or 800/464-6642, www.farmhouseinn.com, $345-545). Nestled among the trees, and near the Main House (which dates back to 1872), are brightly painted cottages that house the 10 cheapest rooms and the larger suite and luxury king rooms; these have their own fireplaces and saunas or steam showers. A barn was added on the site in 2007, containing seven more luxurious guest rooms that are even more expensive but include every amenity you could imagine, from radiant heating and fireplaces to steam showers and jetted tubs. In keeping with maximum luxury, the inn also boasts a highly celebrated restaurant and a spa. Treatments start at $125 for a one-hour massage to $410 for the three-hour Beeyond Bliss honey-based package.

Camping

There are plenty of resort campgrounds along the Russian River, but many cater to summer crowds and RVs and usually charge a premium price for the extensive services and facilities they offer. In all cases, reservations are essential during the busy summer months.

One of the more reasonable is **Burkes Canoe Trips** (8600 River Rd., Forestville, 707/887-1222, www.burkescanoetrips.com, $10/person/day), hidden in the redwoods right next to the river (and the road) just north of Forestville. The full-service campground, open May-October, has 60 sites for tents or RVs for $10. This is also a popular place to rent canoes. The year-round **Hilton Park Family Campground** (10750 River Rd., Forestville, 707/887-9206, www.hiltonparkcampground.com) is one of the smaller of the riverside resort campgrounds, with 49 open or secluded sites for tents ($35/night, $40 for the premium riverside sites) and small RVs ($45), all in a lush, woodsy setting. There are also eight "camping cottages" that just about sleep three people and have space for a tent outside, but cost a relatively steep $69 per night.

The more scenic campgrounds are generally off the beaten track—well off the beaten track in the case of the primitive but scenic creek-side campgrounds high up in the Austin Creek State Recreation Area. The road up into the park through Armstrong Redwoods State Reserve ends at the **Bullfrog Pond Campground,** with 23 sites ($25), toilets, and drinking water. No vehicles over 20 feet long are allowed into the park, so the camping experience here is relatively free of humming RVs. Unfortunately, the park does not take reservations and camping is first come, first serve. To register for a campsite, stop by the **Armstrong Redwoods** park office (17000 Armstrong Woods Rd., Guerneville, 707/869-2958, 11am-3pm daily) on the way up into the Austin Creek area. You can also inquire about, or get permits for, the three backcountry sites ($25) that are roughly four miles from the parking lot. If you arrive after hours, you can register (for the Bullfrog Pond sites, at least) at the self-pay kiosk at the campground.

FOOD

The food scene in the Russian River Valley is one of the most varied in northern Sonoma, as would be expected from a place that is effectively the produce basket of Northern California. It certainly has its share of pricey, stylish establishments, particularly in the many inns hidden away in the woods. But since it's a down-to-earth, outdoorsy sort of place, there are also plenty of cheap and homey establishments where the lack of an uptight reservation system can make the experience instantly relaxing.

Guerneville

Guerneville has always been known for having solid diner, burger, and beer fare. Although the food is good, often hitting the spot, the small riverside town has not been what you would call a dining destination. Things are changing. Recently, San Francisco money has begun to move into town, adding a bit of polish and urban sensibility to the rustic restaurant scene here.

Representing the Guerneville old guard is the landmark **River Inn Grill** (16141 Main St., Guerneville, 707/869-0481, 8am-2pm daily, $10). Its cozy booths, acres of Formica, hunks of ham, and piles of pancakes seem right out of a 1950s movie. Another Guerneville establishment is **Main Street Station** (16280 Main St., Guerneville, 707/869-0501, www.mainststation.com, noon-9:30pm Mon.-Thurs., noon-10:30pm Fri.-Sun. May-Oct., noon-8pm Mon.-Thurs., noon-9pm Fri.-Sun. Nov.-Apr., $16), which offers a big menu filled with homey, casual grub. The mainstay is handmade pizza; you can grab a quick slice for lunch, or bring friends and order a whole pie for dinner. In the evenings, locals and visitors come down to munch sandwiches and pizza, drink beer, and listen to live entertainment on the small stage. Though folk, jazz, blues, and even comedy happen every single night, this tiny venue gets crowded when a popular act comes to town. Consider making reservations in advance to ensure you'll get a seat. **Pat's Restaurant** (16236 Main St., 707/869-9905, www.pats-restaurant.com, 6am-3pm daily, $10) is the kind of diner that travelers hope to find. It's homey, casual, and the place the locals come to sit at the counter and have breakfast all day long.

At night it is another restaurant entirely, and that's not speaking figuratively. The diner is home to **Hi 5** (5pm-10pm Sun. and Wed.-Thurs., 5pm-11pm Fri.-Sat., $15-25), a Korean pop-up. Here, comfort food (short ribs, hamburgers, fried chicken) are served up Korean style with crazy twists such as deep-fried pickles, kimchi aioli, Saki ice cream, and hash browns with a seafood medley. It doesn't stop with the desserts, either. The specialty? A peanut butter sandwich, dipped in pancake batter, and fried with Pop Rocks candy. Not joking. And it's delicious. If you want a stiff one to go with your KFC (Korean Fried Crack, or Korean-style fried chicken served with a Captain Crunch waffle), you can order a large cocktail from the bar next door. Hi-5 is easily the hippest restaurant in Wine Country.

Another newcomer, but decidedly less avant-garde, is **Big Bottom Market** (16228 Main St., Guerneville, 707/604-7295, www.bigbottommarket.com, 8am-5pm Sun.-Mon. and Wed.-Thurs., 8am-6pm Fri.-Sat., $10), a café that serves its coffee via French press and has a small but select local wine list. The food to go with your beverage of choice includes excellent cold and hot pressed sandwiches, savory bread pudding, and a wide assortment of biscuits, so dense and satisfying they can almost stand in for a meal on their own. There are plenty of artisan jams, jellies, chocolates, and other treats for sale (perfect to bring home as gifts), but the atmosphere, with touches of brushed metal on the beautiful wood-topped tables, will make you want to linger.

Next door, the **Whitetail Winebar** (16230 Main St., Guerneville, 707/604-7449, www.whitetailwinebar.com, 4pm-9pm Thurs.-Fri., 2pm-9pm Sat., 2pm-7pm Sun., $10) finally brings home the fact that Guerneville is in the heart of Wine Country—although it does it with a decidedly Guerneville funkiness. Open beams and a great antique brass chandelier complement the metal bar, touches of reclaimed wood, and the odd heap of bleached antlers here and there. The wine list is aimed toward the small boutique wineries of the valley. If you're hungry, small bites, flatbreads, and ceviche are available.

Guerneville now may be on the culinary map of Wine Country, but it was **Boon Eat + Drink** (16248 Main St., Guerneville, 707/869-0780, http://eatatboon.com, lunch 11am-3pm Thurs.-Tues., dinner 5pm-9pm Sun.-Thurs., 5pm-10pm Fri.-Sat., dinner entrées $14-25) that first got it there. Light and airy with splashes of metal and bright colors, this bistro is related to the nearby (and equally hip) **Boon Hotel + Spa** (14711 Armstrong Woods Rd., Guerneville, 707/869-2721, www.boonhotels.com, $180), where some of the vegetables are grown. Since opening in 2007, Boon has lured diners to queue the sidewalks in anticipation of local, organic, and sustainable cuisine served with simple elegance. Lunch usually consists of a simple menu of panini, small plates, and the grass-fed Boon burger ($11). For dinner, hearty mains combine lamb shank with mint pesto or flat iron steak with truffle fries. You really can't go wrong here—unless you can't get in!

One of the few saviors of beer drinkers in this part of Wine Country is the **Stumptown Brewery and Smokehouse** (15045 River Rd., Guerneville, 707/869-0705, www.stumptown. com, 11am-midnight Sun.-Thurs., 11am-2am Fri.-Sat., $10), just east of Guerneville in Rio Nido, which serves juicy ribs, brisket, and sandwiches for less than $15. Its heady microbrews, like Red Rocket and Racer 5, will get you drunk as fast as their names suggest and are best enjoyed while chilling on the giant deck out back.

Just south of Guerneville, things get classier and more romantic at the **◖ Applewood Inn** (13555 Hwy. 116, Guerneville, 707/869-9093, www.applewoodinn.com, dinner 5:30pm-8:30pm Wed.-Sun., entrées $27-38). Seasonal dishes like braised rabbit with olives and Humboldt Fog cheese are inspired by local produce and classic French cooking. As would be expected, the wine list is a who's who of local growers and regularly wins *Wine Spectator*'s Award of Excellence, while the restaurant itself earned a Michelin star in 2011 and 2012.

Monte Rio and Duncans Mills

About a 15-mile drive west of Guerneville in the two-block hamlet of Duncans Mills is the **Cape Fear Café** (25191 Hwy. 116, Duncans Mills, 707/865-9246, 10am-3pm Mon.-Thurs., 9am-8:30pm Fri.-Sun., dinner entrées $16-24), where Sonoma seafood meets Southern soul food. Many dishes in this cozy restaurant have a Cajun twist, and the grits make it worth an early morning drive for breakfast or a weekend brunch.

A scenic place to grab a bite halfway between Guerneville and Duncans Mills is the **Village Inn Restaurant** (20822 River Blvd., off Bohemian Hwy., Monte Rio, 707/865-2304, http://villageinn-ca.com, dinner 5pm-close Wed.-Sun., entrées $14-25) in Monte Rio.

The beautifully restored building and its dining patio peek out from the redwoods onto the banks of the river. Most of the bistro-style main courses are hearty, rustic Italian-inspired dishes that can be washed down with wine from the award-winning list.

Forestville

You would not expect world-class food to find a home out in the woods east of Guerneville, but that's fast becoming the reputation of the restaurant at the luxurious **Farmhouse Inn and Restaurant** (7871 River Rd., Forestville, 707/887-3300 or 800/464-6642, www.farmhouseinn.com, dinner 5:30pm-close Thurs.-Mon., entrées $28-42). Chef Steve Litke, a proponent of the Slow Food movement, lets the veritable treasure trove of local produce do the talking here, with dishes like oven-roasted bluenose sea bass, or squab and wild mushroom terrine. Following the trend of many high-end Wine Country restaurants, Litke has exchanged the traditional menu for a prix fixe menu. The menu changes nightly and diners get to choose two or three courses, each with one dessert course. With prices at $69 and $84, respectively, plus additional for wine pairing, this "slow food" will quickly empty your wallet. The exception is the three-course prix fixe menu that is often offered on Monday nights for a more modest $49.

Graton

Halfway between Forestville and Sebastopol is the tiny rural town of Graton, home to some big names in Russian River Valley dining. The best known is the **Underwood Bar & Bistro** (9113 Graton Rd., just west of Hwy. 116, Graton, 707/823-7023, www.underwoodgraton.com, 11am-10pm Tues.-Sun., dinner entrées $19-27), where lots of dark wood, plush red booths, and a nickel-plated bar add some unique luxury beyond the rustic exterior. The Mediterranean-inspired bistro menu features tapas plates (you can't beat the oysters) and hearty main dishes like Catalan fish stew and duck confit with pancetta and an orange reduction. There's a late-night tapas menu served after 10pm on weekend nights.

Across the road (and sharing the same owners) is a rustic local gathering spot that doubles as a country store, the **Willow Wood Market Café** (9020 Graton Rd., Graton, 707/823-0233, www.willowwoodgraton.com, 8am-9pm Mon.-Sat., 9am-3pm Sun., $15). The well-priced breakfast, lunch, and light dinner menu is always popular with locals, and the polenta ($11-15) is legendary in these parts. It is becoming a victim of its own success, however, with lines that snake out the door on the busiest lunchtimes, although the back patio provides a bit more space. On a Sunday morning, this is where those in the know come for a brunch of Willow Wood Monte Cristo washed down with a mimosa.

Sebastopol

For years, Sebastopol was not known for its food, its many eateries catering to commuting locals. However, things have changed. The Barlow, the town's version of Napa's Oxbow Market, opened downtown in 2013 and aims to be the focal point of the Russian River foodie crowd.

One of the restaurants anchoring The Barlow is the area's hippest farm-to-table (and nose-to-snout, for that matter) restaurants, **ZaZu** (6770 McKinley St., Sebastopol, 707/523-4814, lunch 11am-2:30pm Wed.-Fri., dinner 5-9pm Sun.-Mon. and Wed.-Thurs., 5-10pm Fri.-Sat., brunch 9am-2pm Sat.-Sun., dinner entrées $16-25). In its original Santa Rosa location, Zazu earned a reputation for inventive Italian/Northern California cuisine and for its house-cured bacon and salumi made from an heirloom variety Black Pig, which the owners and chefs not only raise but founded. The pork-heavy menu changes daily and is infused with twists such as eggplant combined with cocoa nibs or cauliflower with turmeric. Like the ingredients that fill its plates, the wine list is locally sourced and there is always a $5 glass of red and white available to help keep the check down.

Wine is the main attraction at the

◖**Starlight Wine Bar** (6761 Sebastopol Ave./ Hwy. 12, Sebastopol, 707/823-1943, www.starlightwinebar.com, 5:30pm-9pm Tues.-Sat., entrées $12-28), inside a 1950s Southern Pacific railroad car now permanently stationed at the Gravenstein Station mall. The many small plates of tapas or cheese might be enough to satisfy as you explore the fascinating and reasonably priced wine list from the comfort of a booth. More filling fare comes in the form of pizzas and Southern-influence comfort food like gumbo or chicken pot pie. If you think this gloriously restored railroad relic resembles a movie set, you will not be surprised to learn that the co-owners of the restaurant are former Hollywood visual effects artists.

If something more filling is needed, the popular **K&L Bistro** (119 S. Main St., Sebastopol, 707/823-6614, http://klbistro.com, lunch 11:30am-2:30pm Mon.-Sat., dinner 5:30pm-9pm Mon.-Sat., 4pm-8pm Sun., dinner entrées $14-28) serves classic French-style bistro food, including french fries that are probably the best in the region. Equally suited to the relaxed, if slightly cramped, setting is K&L's famous mac and cheese, which can be ordered either as a main dish or a side.

Walking into downtown's ◖ **Forchetta/ Bastoni** (6948 Sebastopol Ave., Sebastopol, 707/829-9500, http://forchettabastoni.com, $12-30) presents a difficult decision. On one side is the South Asian street food (banh mi sandwiches, noodle bowls, and curry plates). On the other side, the fare is rustic Italian to the tune of wood-fired pizzas, pastas, and salads, all with the usual California cuisine twist. The twin restaurants are both smartly decorated: Bastoni (the Asian side) has skinny communal tables, colorfully worn stools, and cans of chopsticks; over in Forchetta (the Italian side), the decor is a bit more urbane with warm wood walls, exposed vents, and simple but artsy glass chandeliers. A full bar takes up most of Bastoni and is happily filled by locals grabbing a quick bite, drink, or chat. If you are torn between the two, Bastoni is frequently less busy, but both sides often find space at the chef's tables that face the open kitchens where, if you're lucky, you can exchange quips with the chefs while they prepare your meal. The name translates to "forks/sticks" in Italian, and both restaurants keep different hours: Forchetta is open 5pm-9pm Thursday-Monday, and Bastoni is open 11:30am-9pm Sunday-Thursday and 11:30am-10pm Friday-Saturday.

On the western edge of town, the **French Garden Restaurant** (8050 Bodega Ave., Sebastopol, 707/824-2030, http://frenchgardenrestaurant.com, lunch 11:30am-2:30pm, dinner 5pm-9:30pm Wed.-Sun., entrées $25) offers some French sophistication in an unlikely setting. The appeal here is the simple, beautifully crafted Mediterranean-inspired food by Arturo Guzman, the former executive sous chef at Napa's Meadowood. Guzman's cuisine takes full advantage of the wide range of produce grown on a neighboring 16-acre farm run by the restaurant owners, while remaining as precision oriented as his pedigree suggests. The ambience in the main dining room is as awkward as the faux-Renaissance building, which formerly housed a family-style Italian restaurant, might suggest. Outdoors on the large patio is the best place to ask for a table, or you can order some of the filling appetizers from the full menu in the cozy bar warmed by a large fireplace. Sunday brunch here is accompanied by a farm stand selling much of the same produce used in the restaurant. The menu is filled with the greatest hits of pubs, such as meatloaf, fish-and-chips, grilled chicken, and burgers, but the main draws are entertainment and beer, both in-house and domestic brews. The entertainment ranges from open-mike nights to DJs and live music. There's also a late-night menu. If you go for the New York steak from the menu, there's a modest wine list with plenty of middle-of-the-road wines at reasonable prices to help wash it down.

Occidental

At first glance, picture-postcard Occidental would seem to be the sort of town teeming with celebrated chefs ready to turn its sleepy Victorian charm into the next big food destination. Instead, the rural counterculture is alive and well here and so, evidently, is the Italian culture. There are almost as many Italian restaurants here as organic-labeled eateries and services (organic housecleaning, anyone?.).

Find mountains of cheap Italian comfort food and surroundings in need of some updating at **Negri's** (3700 Bohemian Hwy., Occidental, 707/823-5301, www.negrisrestaurant.com, 11am-9:30pm daily, entrées $9-15). Specialties include the "world-famous" homemade ravioli, made from an old family recipe, alongside plenty of other pasta, chicken, and fried seafood dishes.

Similar family-style food with pizza thrown into the mix can be found in the homey dining room of the historic **Union Hotel** (3731 Main St., Occidental, 707/874-3555, www.unionhotel.com, 11am-9pm daily, dinner entrées $12-20). There is also a café, open at 6am, that makes a mean espresso and serves tasty homemade muffins and pastries, and a saloon where the stiffer drinks start flowing at 11am. Curiously enough, the Union Hotel also offers free overnight RV parking with dinner.

A breath of garlic-free fresh air is provided by the tiny French-inspired **Bistro des Copains** (3782 Bohemian Hwy., Occidental, 707/874-2436, www.bistrodescopains.com, 5pm-9pm Wed.-Sun., entrées $16-25). Classic bistro dishes include escargot served in puff pastry with bordelaise sauce or braised cloverdale rabbit in mustard sauce with butter noodles. The wine list is dominated by Russian River Valley and Sonoma Coast wines, including more than a dozen pinot noirs, and if you bring your own bottle of Sonoma wine on Thursday, the normal $20 corkage fee ($10 if from Sonoma) is waived.

Santa Rosa

With vast expanses of Napa and Sonoma Counties to explore, there are few reasons to head into Santa Rosa. One reason, however, is the city's restaurant scene, in particular French restaurants, which might eventually persuade people to linger for longer downtown.

Some of the best restaurants are around the historic Railroad Square development near downtown. The location was obviously an inspiration when naming **La Gare** (208 Wilson St., Santa Rosa, 707/528-4355, www.lagarerestaurant.com, 5pm-9pm Tues.-Sun., $25), which serves simple but sophisticated French-Swiss food, including some lavish steaks, in an old-school setting of starched white tablecloths (the French influence) and mountain ambience (the Swiss). It was established in 1979, and such longevity is rare for a Sonoma restaurant, which means it must be doing something right.

One of the most popular restaurants on the Santa Rosa scene is **Bistro 29** (620 5th St., Santa Rosa, 707/546-2929, www.bistro29.com, 5pm-9pm Tues.-Thurs., 5pm-9:30pm Fri.-Sat., entrées $19-26). The food is inspired by Breton regional cuisine from northwestern France (29 is the number of the Département, or district, called Finistère in Brittany) and includes an assortment of savory buckwheat crepes and old French standbys like cassoulet and *steak frites*. The modern decor hints at French country style, and the wine list also gives a nod to French regional wines, with choices from Bandol, the Rhône, the Loire, and Languedoc complementing the extensive Northern California options. Ask about the three-course prix fixe dinner menu ($29) that is offered midweek.

A favorite if slightly out-of-the-way breakfast and lunch spot for locals is **Chloe's French Café** (3883 Airway Dr., Ste. 145, Santa Rosa, 707/528-3095, www.chloesco.com, 8am-5pm Mon.-Fri., sandwiches $7-9), tucked into an anonymous unit at the back of a medical building on the northern edge of the city. It has a plain-looking commercial café interior, but the gourmet cold and grilled sandwiches made from fresh local ingredients are what draw legions of fans. Chloe is not the owner but the name the Pisan family gave to their trusty old Citroën truck that they shipped over from France.

Also just north of Santa Rosa, **Willi's Wine Bar** (4404 Old Redwood Hwy., just south of River Rd., Santa Rosa, 707/526-3096, 11:30am-9:30pm Tues.-Thurs., 11:30am-10pm Fri.-Sat., 5pm-9:30pm Sun.-Mon., $7-15) is

NORTHERN SONOMA

BEER BEFORE WINE

It's hard to imagine a time before vineyards in Sonoma, but another type of vine was once the mainstay of the agricultural economy in the Russian River Valley. From Sebastopol to Healdsburg and up into Mendocino, hop vines rather than grapevines once lined the roads and covered the hillsides. All that is left to remind us now are the tall hop kilns that rear up over the landscape from Guerneville to Hopland, some long since converted into wineries.

The conditions were perfect here for hop growing. Rich alluvial soils and the cooling influence of the fog favored the hop vines just like they favor chardonnay and pinot noir grapevines today. Hops were first planted in the region around 1880, and by 1930 almost 3 million pounds were harvested each year. That's enough to make more than 100 million gallons of beer, by some estimates.

The small green fruit, resembling a miniature pine cone, was harvested, dried (or "toasted") in the giant kilns, and used in the making of beer. A resin-like substance from the hops called lupolin is what gives beer its distinctive bitter taste.

Market forces, disease, and (ironically) a mechanical invention by a local hop grower all spelled doom for the local hop industry. After World War II, demand and prices for hops plummeted as the public started to prefer less bitter beer (call it the Budweiser effect). Adding to growers' misery, downy mildew started to thrive in the damp, foggy air and infected the soil in the 1950s, killing vast tracts of hops.

The final nail in the hop growers' coffin was the invention of an automated hop harvesting machine in the 1940s by Santa Rosa grower Florian Dauenhauer. It quickly made the small, hand-harvested growing lots that were common in Sonoma far less economical. Growers sought out bigger plots of land elsewhere in California and the Pacific Northwest that could be machine-harvested, and by the 1960s the Sonoma hop industry was dead.

All that is left of the beer-related industry in northern Sonoma these days is a handful of brewpubs, many of them now buying hops from the Pacific Northwest or further afield. In Healdsburg, the **Bear Republic Brewing Company** (345 Healdsburg Ave., Healdsburg, 707/433-2337, www.bearrepublic.com) is right behind the Hotel Healdsburg and has a quiet, sunny outdoor patio, the perfect place to tap into its Racer 5 IPA. In Guerneville, the **Stumptown Brewery** (15045 River Rd., Guerneville, 707/869-0705, www.stumptown. com) offers such potent-sounding microbrews as Red Rocket and Death and Taxes.

Over in Santa Rosa, the **Third Street Ale Works** (610 3rd St., Santa Rosa, 707/523-3060, www.thirdstreetaleworks.com) challenges drinkers to take the plunge with Brass Parachute Barleywine and Puddle Jumper Pale Ale. A few blocks away is the **Russian River Brewing Company** (725 4th St., Santa Rosa, 707/545-2337, www.russianriverbrewing. com), which was actually founded by a winery (Korbel) in 1997 but now goes it alone, brewing dozens of ales and lagers with names that probably sound funnier when drunk, like Hop 2 It, Pliny the Elder, and Blind Pig IPA. Down in Sebastopol the beer legacy is kept alive by the **Hopmonk Tavern** (230 Petaluma Ave., Sebastopol, 707/829-7300, www.hopmonk.com) with its modest portfolio of four brews, along with a hearty selection of other West Coast microbrews.

Santa Rosa's favorite small-plate restaurant. Here, sipping wine or cocktails is as much a part of the fun as nibbling on one of the many dishes on the menu. Willi's shares the same owners as **Willi's Seafood and Raw Bar** in Healdsburg (403 Healdsburg Ave., Healdsburg, 707/433-9191, 11:30am-9pm Sun.-Thurs.,

11:30am-10pm Fri.-Sat., small plates $8-13) and has a relaxed ambience that creates a perfect backdrop for the globally inspired small dishes, few of which are over $10.

Still in the vineyards, but closer to the Russian River, **John Ash & Co.** (4350 Barnes Rd., Santa Rosa, 707/527-7687, www.

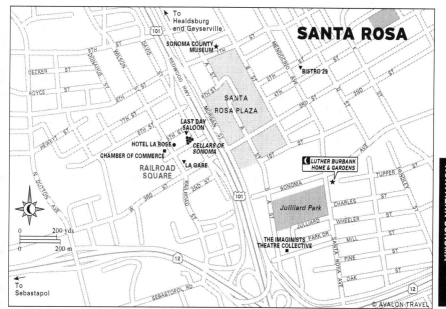

vintnersinn.com, lunch 11:30am-2:30pm Wed.-Fri., dinner 5pm-9pm Sun.-Thurs., 5pm-9:30pm Fri.-Sat., $33) stands out as one of the best high-end California cuisine restaurants in the Russian River region. This large dining room is part of the **Vintners Inn** (4350 Barnes Rd., Santa Rosa, 800/421-2584, www.vintnersinn.com, $360), and the only unappetizing thing about it is its location across the street from a power plant. The elegant dining room is done up in Mediterranean style, and the food runs to pure California cuisine, with lots of local and sustainable produce prepared to show off its natural flavors. The menu is fairly short, making it easy to choose from each of the three courses (often highlighting seafood, beef, lamb, and seasonal specialties). And of course, the wine list at John Ash & Co. is something special, with some amazing local vintages that are tough to find anywhere outside of the Russian River Valley.

Picnic Supplies

There is no shortage of supermarkets, including organic ones, in most of the region's towns, but a few smaller stores are worth searching out for more unusual options. The **Korbel Delicatessen** (13250 River Rd., Guerneville, 707/824-7316, 10am-4:30pm daily), right next door to the winery's tasting room, makes fat sandwiches and gourmet salads to go. Eat on the small deck outside or head off into the wilds.

The **Kozlowski Farms** store (5566 Hwy. 116, Forestville, 707/887-1587, www.kozlowskifarms.com, 9am-5pm Mon.-Fri., 10am-5pm Sat.-Sun.), hidden down a driveway a few yards north of Ross Station Road, has a deli and offers a different kind of tasting—the countless jams, jellies, sauces, and chutneys it makes. A little farther toward Sebastopol is the barnlike **Andy's Market** (1691 Hwy. 116, Sebastopol, 707/823-8661, www.andysproduce.com, 8am-8pm daily), which is part organic produce market and part grocery store. In addition to the piles of fresh produce, the market sells breads, cheeses, olives, and sandwiches. In late summer it's the place to find countless varieties of local apples, and throughout the summer you'll often find a barbeque fired up outside.

And in downtown Guerneville, almost thumbing its nose at neighboring 24-hour Safeway, is the little organic grocery store **Food for Humans** (1st St. at Mill St., Guerneville, 707/869-3612, 9am-8pm daily), an eminently better place to buy produce. Down the street, **Big Bottom** Market (16228 Main St., Guerneville, 707/604-7295, www.bigbottommarket.com, 8am-5pm Sun.-Mon. and Wed.-Thurs., 8am-6pm Fri.-Sat.) has delicious take-out sandwiches, plus plenty of chips, dips, and drinks for any picnic basket.

In Santa Rosa, head to **Chloe's French Café** (3883 Airway Dr., Ste. 145, Santa Rosa, 707/528-3095, www.chloesco.com, 8am-5pm Mon.-Fri., sandwiches $7-9) just north of downtown for gourmet sandwiches to go. In the heart of the downtown area, **Arrigoni's Deli** (701 4th St., Santa Rosa, 707/545-1297, 7am-4pm Mon.-Fri., 7am-3pm Sat., sandwiches $7-10) has a good selection of sandwiches and other deli items needed for a gourmet picnic.

There is also no shortage of tranquil places to have a picnic, from the beaches of the Russian River to the shade of the redwoods at the Armstrong Redwoods State Reserve just north of Guerneville. Or head to one of the many picnic-friendly wineries and pick up a bottle of wine to go with lunch. Some of the better picnicking wineries include Davis Bynum, Hop Kiln, and Foppiano.

Farmers Markets

With so many small towns in this agricultural region, there's a farmers market almost every day of the week, usually Memorial Day-Labor Day. On Friday (4pm-dusk June-Oct.) it's **Occidental**'s turn, downtown in front of the Howard Station Café. **Sebastopol**'s farmers market is held on Sunday mornings (10am-1:30pm year-round) at the Sonoma Plaza on Weeks Way, and **Duncans Mills** has its own on Saturday (11am-4pm May-Oct.) behind the Blue Heron Restaurant on Steelhead Boulevard. Just down the road, **Guerneville**'s farmers market runs every Thursday evening

(3pm-7pm May-Oct.) at the Safeway parking lot on 1st Street.

Santa Rosa has two farmers markets worth checking out. The **Santa Rosa Downtown Market** includes chef demonstrations and other entertainment alongside farm stands. It is held on 4th Street from Mendocino Avenue to E Street on Wednesday evenings (5pm-8:30pm May-Aug.). The more traditional **Santa Rosa Farmers Market,** without the fun and games, can be found year-round on Wednesday (8:30am-noon) and Saturday (8:30am-1pm) in the parking lot of the Wells Fargo Center for the Arts (50 Mark West Springs Rd.), just northeast of the downtown area.

INFORMATION AND SERVICES

The most important tool for visiting the Russian River Valley is the excellent free map published by the **Russian River Wine Road** (707/433-4335 or 800/723-6336, www.wineroad.com), an organization representing wineries and other businesses throughout northern Sonoma that is based in Healdsburg. The map is pretty easy to find at all major wineries and covers all the major roads in the Russian River Valley and up into the Dry Creek and Alexander Valleys.

More detailed and specific information about the Russian River Valley can be found in the free guide published by the **Russian River Valley Winegrowers Association** (707/521-2534, www.rrvw.org), also widely available. Neither organization has offices open to the public.

Maps and other information about the region are available at the drop-in office of the **Russian River Chamber of Commerce** in the center of Guerneville (16209 1st St., at the old bridge, Guerneville, 707/869-9000 or 877/644-9001, www.russianriver.com, 10am-5pm daily). There's also an outpost at the Korbel winery (13250 River Rd., Guerneville, 707/869-4096, 10am-4pm daily summer, 10am-3pm Tues.-Sun. fall-spring) in the old station house that is now the ticket office.

In downtown Santa Rosa, the **Santa Rosa**

Convention & Visitors Bureau (9 4th St., Santa Rosa, 707/577-8674 or 800/404-7673, www.tastesantarosa.com, 9am-5pm Mon.-Sat., 10am-5pm Sun.) offers countless maps and brochures about accommodations, food and wine, and activities in the city and surrounding regions.

The serious local daily newspaper is the *Santa Rosa Press Democrat* (www.pressdemocrat.com); check the Living and Entertainment sections for tourist information.

As a major city, Santa Rosa has plenty of available medical services. If you need help, try to get to **Santa Rosa Memorial Hospital** (1165 Montgomery Ave., Santa Rosa, 707/546-3210, www.stjosephhealth.org), which includes an emergency room.

For banking needs, there is a **Bank of America** at 10 Santa Rosa Avenue and a **Wells Fargo** at 200 B Street, both in the heart of downtown Santa Rosa. If you are in Guerneville, the locations are 16390 Main Street and 16405 River Road, respectively. Mailing a letter is as easy as dropping by the **post office** at 730 2nd Street in Santa Rosa or 14060 Mill Street in Guerneville.

GETTING THERE AND AROUND

The Russian River Valley sits to the west of U.S. Highway 101. The southern end is Santa Rosa, which is 50 miles north of the Golden Gate Bridge and San Francisco, while the northern border is roughly River Road, 4 miles north. Be aware that traffic on 101 can get sticky, particularly during the morning commute and 3pm-7pm It is also slow on sunny summer afternoons when all the folks seeking to cool themselves along the Russian River return to their Bay Area homes. Still, unlike the two-lane roads elsewhere in Wine Country, especially Highway 29 in the Napa Valley, the side roads taking you to various tasting rooms and recreation spots are seldom overcrowded.

Taking exit 489 toward downtown Santa Rosa will get you to the historic districts, and downtown is located on the east side of the freeway. Wineries sit on the west side of town and can be accessed by taking Highway 12 west and the River Road and Guerneville exits off U.S. Highway 101. Other east-west roads include Sebastopol, Occidental, and Guerneville Highways, which conveniently enough terminate at their namesake towns. Highway 116, also called the Gravenstein Highway, runs diagonal from Cotati, south of Santa Rosa, 22 twisty miles through Sebastapol, Graton, and Forestville to emerge onto River Road in Guerneville. You can also get to Guerneville by taking the River Road/Guerneville exit and following River Road west for 15 miles to downtown Guerneville. Worth noting is that there are virtually no gas stations west of Sebastopol and Guerneville, so fill up in Forestville or Sebastopol if you plan to venture out to the coast.

To avoid traffic headaches, **Golden Gate Transit** (routes 70/71/80/72/74, 415/455-2000, http://goldengatetransit.org/schedules, $10.25) runs buses between San Francisco and Santa Rosa.

NORTHERN SONOMA

Dry Creek Valley

This compact valley is perhaps one of the easiest parts of northern Sonoma to visit in a day, and certainly one of the easiest to get around by car or bike.

At its southern end is the Victorian town of **Healdsburg**, with plenty of Wine Country frills but still relatively crowd-free even on summer weekends. It also has a staggering number of downtown tasting rooms, so many in fact that you can't help but wonder whether they'll all survive. You could tour northern Sonoma's wineries, never venturing more than a few blocks from the plaza, but that would mean missing out on the rustic charms of places like the Dry Creek Valley.

Although Healdsburg is the only place to shop, stay, or eat, getting out of the town is essential if you plan to experience the area. At its hot northern end, the Dry Creek Valley is dominated by the huge Lake Sonoma Recreation Area, which offers some of the best outdoor recreation opportunities in Sonoma County. Between Healdsburg and the lake, there are vineyards, barns, and small wineries full of character, many run by eccentric characters.

Although the wine industry got an early start here when French and later Italian immigrants planted grapes in the late 1800s, Prohibition killed everything off, and for much of the 20th century the valley was full of plum and pear orchards. It was not until the early 1970s that grape growing started to pick up again, and the 7,000 acres of prune orchards that once filled the valley with their bounty shriveling in the hot sun are now long gone.

During that agricultural transition, little else apparently changed in the valley, and the only development seems to have been winery related. Just two main roads run up the valley, on either side of Dry Creek itself: West Dry Creek Road and the original Dry Creek Road, which eventually becomes Skaggs Springs Road and heads off over the coastal hills to the ocean. Apart from a couple of roads traversing the valley and cutting through the eastern hills to the freeway and Alexander Valley beyond, that's about it.

Development did significantly change one thing: the valley's eponymous creek. Dry Creek used to dry up to nothing more than a few puddles by the end of the summer, like the many smaller creeks running down the valley sides still do today. Since the dam that created Lake Sonoma was completed in the 1980s, however, Dry Creek has become wet year-round.

The Wines

Dry Creek is perhaps best known for its zinfandels, which can sometimes take on an overbearing, jammy style in the hotter parts of the valley. But zinfandel vines do not dominate the valley as much as the wine's prevalence might suggest, and account for only about a quarter of the almost 10,000 acres of vineyards in the **Dry Creek** AVA. That's a big total acreage for such a small and narrow valley, especially when you consider the sprawling Russian River Valley AVA to the south only contains a few thousand acres more.

About 4,000 acres in the Dry Creek Valley are planted with cabernet sauvignon and merlot, particularly on the cooler western hillsides around places like the renowned Bradford Mountain. The hotter valley floor with its richer, alluvial soils grows excellent sauvignon blanc and, increasingly, semillon. Other varietals hint at the valley's French and Italian heritage, with syrah and petite sirah coexisting with small amounts of sangiovese and carignane.

The ideal mix of growing conditions for so many grape varietals results from the two ranges of low mountains that flank the valley—the 1,500-foot coastal hills on the valley's western side and the lower hills on the eastern side that separate it from the Alexander Valley. These hillsides have thousands of acres of benchland and canyons where growers can usually find just the right degree of heat needed

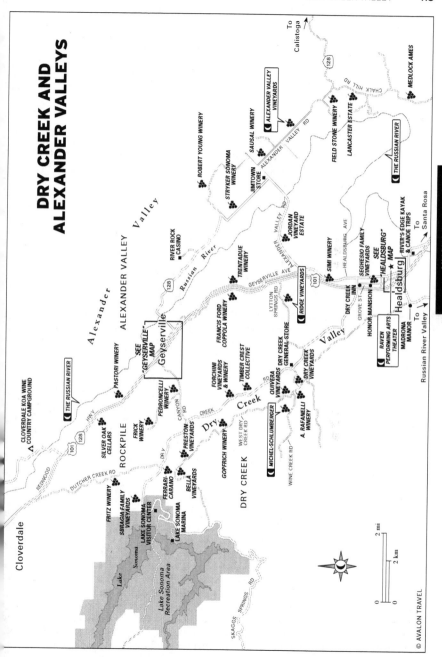

DRY CREEK AND ALEXANDER VALLEYS

To Calistoga

128

MEDLOCK AMES

CHALK HILL RD

ALEXANDER VALLEY VINEYARDS

FIELD STONE WINERY

LANCASTER ESTATE

THE RUSSIAN RIVER

SAUSAL WINERY

ROBERT YOUNG WINERY

STRYKER SONOMA WINERY

JIMTOWN STORE

ALEXANDER VALLEY RD

To Santa Rosa

Santa Rosa

RIVER'S-EDGE KAYAK & CANOE TRIPS

JORDAN VINEYARD ESTATE

SIMI WINERY

HEALDSBURG AVE

SEGHESIO FAMILY VINEYARDS

SEE "HEALDSBURG" MAP

Alexander Valley

RIVER ROCK CASINO

Russian River

TRENTADUE WINERY

GEYSERVILLE AVE

RIDGE VINEYARDS

LYTTON SPRINGS RD

DRY CREEK INN

Healdsburg

GROVE ST

HONOR MANSION

MADRONA MANOR

RAVEN PERFORMING ARTS THEATER

To Russian River Valley

ALEXANDER VALLEY RD

128

Geyserville

SEE "GEYSERVILLE" MAP

PASTORI WINERY

FRANCIS FORD COPPOLA WINERY

TIMBER CREST COLLECTIVE

FORCHINI VINEYARDS & WINERY

QUIVIRA VINEYARDS

DRY CREEK GENERAL STORE

Valley

DRY CREEK VINEYARDS

A. RAFANELLI WINERY

MICHEL-SCHLUMBERGER

WEST DRY CREEK RD

WINE CREEK RD

PEDRONCELLI WINERY

CANYON RD

FRICK WINERY

PRESTON VINEYARDS

GOPFRICH WINERY

Dry Creek

DRY CREEK

Creek

THE RUSSIAN RIVER

CLOVERDALE KOA WINE COUNTRY CAMPGROUND

SILVER OAK CELLARS

ROCKPILE

REDWOOD HWY

101

128

DUTCHER CREEK RD

FRITZ WINERY

SBRAGIA FAMILY VINEYARDS

FERRARI-CARANO

BELLA VINEYARDS

LAKE SONOMA VISITOR CENTER

LAKE SONOMA MARINA

Cloverdale

Lake Sonoma

Lake Sonoma Recreation Area

SKAGGS SPRINGS RD

0   2 mi

0   2 km

© AVALON TRAVEL

for ideal ripening of most grape varietals. The hills also shield the valley from direct influence of the cold coastal air, yet just enough cool air and fog is funneled up from the Russian River Valley to prevent things from getting too hot and sticky, particularly at night.

At the far northern end of the valley, on the hot rocky ridges overlooking Lake Sonoma, is the aptly named **Rockpile** AVA, established in 2002. Don't expect to be visiting wineries here, though, because there are none. In fact, there are few paved roads. The 200 acres of vineyards are planted predominantly with zinfandel and cabernet, producing intensely flavored wines for the few wineries lucky enough to own land here.

WINERIES

This part of the world offers perhaps the most eclectic mix of wineries, from rustic homespun operations of families that have been making wine for generations to the splashier newcomers reflecting the increasing popularity of the Dry Creek Valley as a major wine destination. Most wineries (even some newcomers) are fairly small, and many still offer some sort of free tasting, although more are now charging a modest fee for a basic tasting, usually $5. Nearly all the wineries also have some sort of outdoor space for picnics.

FRITZ UNDERGROUND WINERY

At the top of the valley, **Fritz Underground Winery** (24691 Dutcher Creek Rd., Cloverdale, 707/894-3389 or 800/418-9463, www.fritzwinery.com, 10:30am-4:30pm daily, tasting $10-15) bills itself as an "underground winery"; and that doesn't stand for some radical politics to match its earthship aesthetic. In fact, the winery owes its name and styling in part to the energy crisis of the late 1970s when it was built by Jay and Barbara Fritz. The patio and domed tasting room are above two levels of winery workings deep underground, so no pumps, coolers, or air-conditioning are needed, saving power and adding to its modern-day green credentials. If seeing the extent of this subterranean marvel sounds intriguing, make sure you visit Fritz on a weekend and book a tour, which takes you "top to bottom" and often includes a barrel tasting (Sat.-Sun. only, $20)

While the inner workings of the winery occur deep underground, the tasting room has lovely views of the vineyards, with a stone patio for picnicking and tasting just outside. The estate and other Dry Creek Valley vineyards provide grapes for zinfandel, sauvignon blanc, and cabernet, including a rich cabernet from the tiny Rockpile appellation just north of here. The Russian River wines include chardonnay and pinot noir, both of which have become as highly regarded as some of the Dry Creek wines. Don't miss the two tasty Vino Valpredolabeled proprietary blends—one a cabernet and zinfandel blend and the other sauvignon blanc and chardonnay.

SBRAGIA FAMILY VINEYARDS

Sbragia Family Vineyards (9990 Dry Creek Rd., Geyserville, 707/473-2992, www.sbragia.com, 11am-5pm daily, tasting $10-20) makes the most of its southern exposure, offering sweeping views of the Alexander Valley below. Thankfully, the wines are as beautiful as the scenery.

While very much a family operation, the winery has a serious pedigree. Ed Sbragia spent 32 years at Beringer Vineyards in the Napa Valley, where he earned a reputation for producing some of Napa's greatest cabernets. His skill at creating highly extracted yet elegant wines, together with his connections to some of the best growers in Sonoma and Napa, make Sbragia, which produces roughly 12,000 cases per year, one of the best wineries in the valley. All the wines made here are single-vineyard versions from both the family's own vineyards and other growers.

Two tasting options are offered. For $10, you can taste four of the winery's Dry Creek wines that include a merlot and a highly rated chardonnay from the 20-acre Home Ranch vineyard in the southeast part of the valley. The Gino's Vineyard zinfandel is a quintessentially spicy and jammy Dry Creek zin from the vineyard named after Ed's grandfather, and the cabernet sauvignon comes from the bench-land Andolsen Vineyard owned by the family's doctor. A Napa Valley flight ($20) is also on the menu, and this includes an intense cabernet from the Monte Rosso vineyard atop the Mayacamas Mountains above Sonoma Valley, and a powerfully flavored chardonnay from Gamble Ranch in the Napa Valley. There are also wines from Howell Mountain and Mount Veeder.

The winery recently remodeled its tasting room, which opens out onto a large concrete deck overlooking the valley. There are plenty of shaded tables to either taste or picnic at. While the winery sells some light picnic fare in its tasting room, it does welcome outside food.

FERRARI-CARANO VINEYARDS AND WINERY

Ferrari-Carano (8761 Dry Creek Rd., Healdsburg, 707/433-6700 or 800/831-0381, www.ferraricarano.com, 10am-5pm daily, tasting $5-15) might sound like it was established by one of the old Italian wine-making families of northern Sonoma, but this is actually the flagship winery of a hospitality empire built up by the Carano family in the last 40 years. Sister businesses include the Eldorado Hotel and Casino in Reno and the **Vintners Inn** (4350 Barnes Rd., Santa Rosa, 800/421-2584, www.vintnersinn.com, $360) in Santa Rosa.

Despite its lack of historic pedigree, the pink Italianate mansion known as Villa Fiore (which translates to House of Flowers, a fitting name when the spring bulbs are in full bloom) and the acres of manicured gardens evoke a grandiose past, albeit one that's a little out of sync with the rustic charm of most Dry Creek wineries. Equally grandiose is the huge vaulted cellar that can house up to 1,500 barrels of aging wine down the grand stairs from the main tasting room. As you wander in the lush gardens, be careful not to trample any of the flower beds, or you might meet the same fate as a wild boar that once did and is now memorialized by a statue outside the tasting room.

The 160,000 cases of wine made each year are sourced from the 1,200 acres of vineyards that Carano owns throughout Sonoma, including its rapidly growing Alexander Valley mountain estate. They include a whole raft of highly rated single-vineyard chardonnays and a wide range of reds, from single varietals to blends including the Bordeaux-style Tresor blend. There are also two decadent dessert wines, including the Eldorado Noir, made from black muscat.

Those are among the best wines that can be tasted downstairs (for a price) in the Enoteca Lounge, a sumptuous den that has been routinely voted best tasting room by local publications and is effectively the winery's reserve tasting room. It provides respite from the bustling, Mediterranean-style main tasting room and the somewhat unexceptional wines poured there. Among the best of the cheaper lineup are the fumé blanc and an unusual blend of sangiovese, cabernet sauvignon, and malbec called Siena.

FRICK WINERY

Proceeds from the sale of a '57 Chevy helped get Bill Frick started in the wine business in 1976 near Santa Cruz. He moved to this small hillside winery at the end of sleepy Walling Road at the far northern end of Dry Creek Valley in the late 1980s.

The six acres of estate vineyards at **Frick Winery** (23072 Walling Rd., off Canyon Rd. or Dutcher Creek Rd., Geyserville, 707/857-1980, www.frickwinery.com, noon-4:30pm Fri.-Sun., weekends only in winter, free tasting) are mainly planted to Rhône varietals, and owner Bill Frick is perhaps Dry Creek's most ardent Rhône Ranger. The 3,000 cases of wine produced each year include syrah, viognier, cinsault, and C-Squared, which is a blend of cinsault and carignane. More unusual still is the grenache blanc, a white version of this varietal that is rarely seen in California. Fittingly, the cottage tasting room is small, cozy, and doesn't accommodate large groups, meaning you will get a fun low-key tasting of some great French-style wines.

PEDRONCELLI WINERY

It no longer sells jug wines like it did up to the 1950s, but **Pedroncelli Winery** (1220 Canyon Rd., Geyserville, 707/857-3531 or 800/836-3894, www.pedroncelli.com, 10am-4:30pm daily, tasting $5) still produces some very approachable wines for the masses at the slightly ramshackle cluster of buildings on Canyon Road. None of the wines sell for more than $25 and most are under $15, making this a good place to buy a picnic wine or stock up with some everyday drinkers.

The winery has been a family affair since John Pedroncelli bought the rundown former Canota winery and 90 acres of vineyards in 1927. The 75,000-case production includes zinfandel, chardonnay, sangiovese, petite sirah, and cabernet sauvignon, all made in the style of robust, easy-drinking table wines. Nearly all the wines are sourced from Dry Creek Valley vineyards with one notable exception—a Russian River Valley pinot noir that's pretty good for its modest price.

Some more unusual wines include vintage port and a zinfandel rosé that is bone-dry compared to its distant cousin, the "white zin" found at supermarkets. Zinfandel is something of a specialty here, and the portfolio includes the Mother Clone zin, sourced from clones of Victorian-era vines.

In addition to the cheap wines, a bocce ball court, a nice picnic area, and regular exhibitions by local artists make this an entertaining place to visit.

FORCHINI VINEYARDS & WINERY

The Forchini family has been growing grapes in the Dry Creek and Russian River Valleys since the 1970s but only started making wines in the mid-1990s, and today makes only 3,000 cases of wine each year. As a result, the **Forchini Winery** (5141 Dry Creek Rd., Healdsburg, 707/431-8886, www.forchini.com, 11am-4:30pm Fri.-Sun., weekdays by appointment, tasting $10) has a charming homey character that makes you feel like a privileged guest.

The small tasting room is in the main house and features a sunny deck next to the cabernet vines lining the driveway. The portfolio includes a well-balanced Dry Creek cabernet sauvignon that is, unusually, blended with 10 percent carignane; the zinfandel, which is a typically intense Dry Creek style; and representing the Russian River vineyards, a big, rich chardonnay and a more reserved pinot noir. The cheap and cheerful Papa Nonno blend, made in the style of easy-drinking Tuscan table wine, is primarily zinfandel and makes a great picnic wine.

◖ RIDGE VINEYARDS

Not just the wines here but the entire building is organic. The tasting room at **Ridge Vineyards** (650 Lytton Springs Rd., Healdsburg, 707/433-7721, www.ridgewine.com, 11am-4pm daily, tasting $5-20) was constructed using only sustainable materials. The thick walls of the winery are made of rice-straw bales and a natural plaster made from the clay of the surrounding soil, both chosen for their superior insulating properties. Recycled lumber was used for the framing, flooring, and siding, and even the facing on the tasting room bar is made of pieces of old oak fermentation tanks. To cap it all off, 400 solar panels on the roof provide most of the winery's power. Contemporary in style and making full use of expansive canopied decks, the green ethos extends to the guest experience. Here, you taste wines while overlooking the vineyards, smelling the earth, and feeling the breeze.

Ridge is the king of zin, some years making more than 13 different versions that account for the majority of its 85,000-case annual production. Two-thirds of the zinfandel vineyards are in northern Sonoma, which makes the Lytton Springs outpost the company's Zinfandel Central, though it also makes chardonnay, syrah, petite sirah, grenache, and merlot. Even those who are not partial to zinfandel are likely to find at least a couple of wines to like here.

Ridge has another winery in the Santa Cruz Mountains that is more famous for its outstanding cabernet and chardonnay, and some of those wines can often be tasted here too with the pricey Single Vineyard/Monte Bello tasting option ($20). These are also featured as a part of the semi-private tour offered daily at 11am and 2pm by appointment. The experience lasts 90 minutes and costs $30 per person.

DRY CREEK VINEYARDS

Built in 1973 not far from Dry Creek itself, this ivy-clad winery was the first to be built in the valley since the repeal of Prohibition. Although it is by no means the oldest in the valley and is far more commercial than most of its neighbors, the **Dry Creek** winery (3770 Lambert Bridge Rd., Healdsburg, 707/433-1000 or 800/864-9463, www.drycreekvineyard.com, 10:30am-4:30pm daily, tasting $5-10) has, without a doubt, played an important role in transforming the valley from prune orchards to vineyards. What it lacks in homey charm it makes up for by producing some of the best white wines in the valley.

Unusual for the Dry Creek Valley, the flagship wine here is the fumé blanc, although zinfandels like the Heritage Clone are still well worth tasting. Together those two wines account for almost half the winery's annual production of 120,000 cases. A full range of other reds and whites are also made from grapes grown in the estate vineyards and throughout Sonoma, including cabernet sauvignon, chenin blanc, and a meritage blend. The picnic tables surrounded by lawn, flower gardens, and shading trees beg for a picnic, so grab a bottle of the bargain-priced Regatta white blend or chenin blanc and relax while planning the rest of your day.

◆ MICHEL-SCHLUMBERGER

In a beautiful mission-revival building surrounding a tranquil courtyard, **Michel-Schlumberger** (4155 Wine Creek Rd., off W. Dry Creek Rd., Healdsburg, 707/433-7427 or 800/447-3060, www.michelschlumberger. com, 11am-5pm daily, tasting $15-30) is tucked away up Wine Creek Canyon and surrounded by 100 acres of undulating benchland vineyards that create a multitude of different growing conditions, from the cool heights of

nearby Bradford Mountain down to the hotter canyon floor.

Unusually for the Dry Creek Valley, there is only one zinfandel in the wine portfolio here, but that's for good reason, according to the winemaker. Good zins come from old vines, he says, and Schlumberger, for the most part, has only young zinfandel vines. The cooler hillsides do, however, favor cabernet sauvignon, merlot, pinot blanc, chardonnay, and pinot noir. The cabernets, particularly the reserve, are outstanding illustrations that the Dry Creek Valley is good for growing more than just zinfandel. Some young-vine zinfandel does sometimes make it into the plush and popular Maison Rouge blend, however.

The estate tasting is a flight of five wines either in the tasting room, the terra-cotta tile terrace, or in the courtyard alongside the burbling pool. For a more extensive experience, but well worth it, take a tour of the estate followed by a seated tasting of the estate-grown wines. Tours are offered daily at 11am and 2pm and cost $30.

QUIVIRA VINEYARDS

Although the winery is named after a mythical place where Spanish explorers expected to find untold riches in the 1500s, there's nothing mythical about the qualities of the vineyard-designate zinfandels and the flavorful sauvignon blanc made by biodynamic **Quivira Vineyards** (4900 W. Dry Creek Rd., Healdsburg, 707/431-8333 or 800/292-8339, www.quivirawine.com, 11am-5pm daily, tasting $10).

Those wines are Quivira's specialties, but it also makes several Rhône-style wines, including a rosé, a syrah, a grenache, a mourvèdre, and a Goat Trek Vineyard cabernet. Quivira is also one of the few Sonoma wineries to have its vineyards certified biodynamic, and its green credentials were given a further boost when the winery installed its vast array of solar panels, providing all its electricity. You can learn more about the winery's commitment to sustainability on its appointment-only tours offered at 10am daily. On the other hand, the fruit of the grounds can be enjoyed at the tasting room, which also sells an assortment of estate honeys and preserves, or by grabbing a bottle of sauvignon blanc or rosé and planting yourself on one of its many picnic tables.

BELLA VINEYARDS

As its name suggests, **Bella Vineyards** (9711 W. Dry Creek Rd., Healdsburg, 707/473-9171 or 866/572-3552, www.bellawinery.com, 11am-4:30pm daily, tasting $10) is one of the prettiest wineries in the area, with a farm-like setting overlooking the valley. But the pristine caves with vines growing literally right above the entrance add a touch of class to the tasting experience. Tasting wines underneath a vineyard certainly is a cool summer diversion at this hot northern end of the valley.

Adding to the experience, of course, is the wine itself. Bella has been a rising star in the valley, and is particularly known as a producer of outstanding single-vineyard zinfandels, the best of which are sourced from old vines in each of Bella's three vineyards, including the robust and complex Lily Hill zinfandel from the vineyard around the winery. The winery also makes a rosé, a grenache, a couple of petite sirahs, and a syrah all from Sonoma County.

PRESTON VINEYARDS

Dry Creek's ubiquitous zinfandel falls way down the list of interesting wines at Lou Preston's idiosyncratic establishment. Homemade bread, organic vegetables, and olive oil get nearly equal attention as the wine, giving **Preston Vineyards** (9282 W. Dry Creek Rd., Healdsburg, 707/433-3372, www.prestonvineyards.com, 11am-4:30pm daily, tasting $5) a "back to the land" feel of the 1970s, when it was founded.

Inside the homespun tasting rooms where country farmhouse meets Victorian charm, you'll taste some organic wine from its small portfolio. Zinfandel is produced here, but the list is dominated by Rhône varietals, including a highly regarded petite sirah, syrah, viognier, and roussanne. Also worth trying are the spicy barbera, the grassy sauvignon blanc, and the rosé, a vin gris playfully called "Portugee Pink."

Along with the wine you can buy some organic vegetables grown on the farm, as well as olive oil and artisan bread from a commercial bakery on-site. The selection of locally produced foods here rivals that in some delis and makes this an ideal place to buy everything you need for an impromptu picnic next to the bocce courts outside in the company of the winery cats.

TIMBER CREST COLLECTIVE

The distinctive red barn up the hill next to Dry Creek Road marks the location of a collective winemaking facility, shared by some of the valley's best small wineries, **Timber Crest Farms** (4791 Dry Creek Rd., Healdsburg, 11am-4:30pm daily, tasting $10). The driveway is marked by a well-populated signpost next to the road. Four wineries make wines and have modest tasting rooms here—in some cases just a counter propped on barrels. Tasting is more about the wine and the unpretentious vibe than the surroundings. Indeed, the wineries are small enough that it's likely to be the winemakers themselves doing the pouring.

After decades of making wine for other valley wineries, Rick Hutchinson started his own **Amphora Winery** (707/431-7767, www.amphorawines.com) in 1997 and now makes nearly 20 different varietals, with the exception of one chardonnay. Most are vineyard-designate zinfandel, cabernet, carignane, malbec, and pinot noir. Pottery is Hutchinson's other passion, in particular the creation of the amphorae that inspired the winery's name and appear on the wine labels.

Another longtime Dry Creek producer, **Peterson Winery** (707/431-7568, www.petersonwinery.com, tasting 11am-4:30pm Fri.-Mon., by appointment Tues.-Wed.) makes small lots of about a dozen different wines. There are several very good and well-priced zinfandels, but it is some of the more unusual (and unusually named) blends that stand out here, including a powerful cabernet-syrah blend called Shinbone and a cheap and cheerful

Rhône blend called Zero Manipulation. You also can't go wrong with any of the single-vineyard wines (cabernet, syrah, and zinfandel) sourced from Fred Peterson's Bradford Mountain vineyard in the southwest corner of the valley.

The **Papapietro Perry Winery** (707/433-0422, www.papapietro-perry.com, tasting $10) was formed by two former San Francisco newspapermen, Ben Papapietro and Bruce Perry, in 1998 and has established quite a reputation for its more than half-dozen pinot noirs and zinfandels sourced from Dry Creek, Russian River, and Anderson Valley vineyards along with a more recent addition to the portfolio, a small amount of chardonnay. Although not all the vineyard- and clone-specific pinots are likely to be available to taste, there will still be a dizzying array of wines for any pinot or zin lover to try.

The fourth winery at Timber Crest is a relative newcomer to this area. **Kokomo Winery** (707/433-0200, www.kokomowines.com) is the brainchild of Eric Miller, originally from Kokomo, Indiana, who creates elegant, understated wines with the help of longtime local grower Randy Peters. The Dry Creek wines include zinfandel and sauvignon blanc. There are also a couple of pinot noirs, a chardonnay, and a malbec made using fruit from a vineyard to the south that straddles the Russian River Valley and Chalk Hill appellations.

DE LA MONTANYA WINERY

The single-lane Westside Road is dotted with checkerboard vineyards, ancient oaks dripping with Spanish moss, abandoned barns and handsome Victorians. But while feasting your eyes on this idyllic Wine Country panorama, be sure to keep them peeled for **De La Montanya Winery** (999 Forman Ln., Healdsburg, 707/433-3711, 11am-4:30pm daily, tasting $10). Owner Dennis De La Montanya has a palate for lesser-known varietals and an irreverent sense of humor. He built this winery on the strength of his wine club, tasting room, and award-winning wines. The winery produces 4,000 cases of small-batch,

handcrafted wines annually. Eighteen different wines, ranging in size from 1 to 12 barrels, are crafted from a broad spectrum of varietals. Signature wines include tempranillo, pinot noir, zinfandel, gewürztraminer, and a late-harvest botrytis white. The winery and tasting room, referred to as "The Barn," has a laid-back, welcoming vibe with cheeky, playful descriptions of the vintages. Outside is an outdoor kitchen, a garden picnic area with stunning views, and a bocce court. Dennis also takes pride in his wine labels, with the most popular being the "Pin Up" series. Provocative but tasteful photos of female wine club members harken back to World War II-style pinup poses.

ARMIDA

Come to the **Armida** (2201 Westside Rd., Healdsburg, 707/433-2222, www.armida.com, 11am-5pm daily, tasting $10) tasting room for the gorgeous scenery and the funky facilities, but stay for the wonderful wines. The driveway meanders up a Russian River hillside to a cluster of geodesic domes set amid lovely and sustainable landscaping. Bring a picnic to enjoy on the big deck overlooking the duck pond and the valley beyond. Before you get to eating, though, wander into the tasting room to check out some of the truly tasty Russian River red wines. You'll get your choice of smoky syrahs and jammy zinfandels. The flagship wine, Poizin, is well represented in the wines and logowear in the small gift shop that shares space with the tasting bar. Armida sells Poizin in a coffin-shaped box—ask nicely and they might open a bottle for you to taste (even if they don't, it's still worth buying).

SEGHESIO FAMILY VINEYARDS

One of the old Italian family wineries that helped define the northern Sonoma wine industry over the past hundred years is about a 20-minute walk (or 5-minute drive) from Healdsburg Plaza in a building dating from the 1890s. Although it is not surrounded by bucolic vineyards and fields, the ample gardens at **Seghesio** (700 Grove St., Healdsburg, 707/395-3629, www.seghesio.com, 10am-5pm daily, tasting $5) make it the best place to picnic and play a game of bocce within easy reach of the plaza.

Although the winery is now in a leafy residential area rather than farmland, it remains very much a family affair, run by the grandchildren of founder Edoardo Seghesio, who arrived in the region from Italy in 1886, planted his first vines in 1895, and established the winery in 1902. The wines are very much Italian as well, sourced from over 400 acres of vineyards throughout the Russian River, Alexander, and Dry Creek Valleys.

About half the winery's 80,000-case production is just one wine—the excellent and bargain-priced Sonoma County zinfandel. Even with so much made, however, it often sells out after receiving its almost-standard rave reviews in the press. At the opposite end of the zin scale are the limited-production and age-worthy San Lorenzo and one from the tiny Rockpile appellation at the northern end of the Dry Creek Valley. Sangiovese is the other dominant varietal here and an important component in Omaggio, a blend of cabernet and sangiovese that is Seghesio's version of a super-Tuscan. The limited-production Venom is sourced from the oldest sangiovese vines in the United States and named for the rattlesnakes that thrive in the hilltop vineyard.

The best way to experience the varied portfolio of wines here is with a wine and food pairing ($35) that is offered by appointment Friday-Sunday. Five wines are served with Cal-Ital appetizers like gorgonzola cannelloni with wild mushrooms and house-cured prosciutto at one of the winery's giant redwood-topped banquet tables.

WINERIES BY APPOINTMENT

Up a long driveway off West Dry Creek Road, just south of Wine Creek Road, is where the fourth generation of Rafanellis now makes its limited-production wines at the **A. Rafanelli Winery** (4685 W. Dry Creek Rd., 707/433-1385, http://arafanelliwinery.com, 10am-4pm daily, complimentary tasting). An intense zinfandel accounts for more than half the

11,000-case annual production, and the rest is cabernet and merlot sourced from the hillside vineyards. All the wines have attained an almost cultlike status, so the winery tends to attract those serious about their zins. The views from the vegetable garden next to the old redwood barn are also pretty spectacular, which along with the difficulty getting an appointment only adds to the slightly exclusive atmosphere.

There is more than the family's German heritage to the **Göpfrich Estate Vineyard and Winery** (7462 W. Dry Creek Rd., 707/433-1645, www.gopfrichwinery.com, noon-4:30pm Fri.-Sat., complimentary tasting). In addition to limited-production cabernet, zinfandel, and syrah wines from the Dry Creek estate, Göpfrich also sells limited quantities of fragrant, late-harvest German white wines including riesling, huxelrebe, and silvaner from its sister winery in the Rheinhessen region of Germany.

HEALDSBURG TASTING ROOMS

Being located at the junction of the three most important northern Sonoma appellations makes Healdsburg a good jumping-off point to visit them all. Westside Road heads down into the Russian River Valley, Dry Creek Road to its namesake's valley, and Healdsburg Avenue heads north into the Alexander Valley.

But it's just as easy to ditch the car and sample wines from those appellations and many more in the numerous downtown tasting rooms and wineries, all within walking distance from the plaza. There are more wineries represented here than most people can comfortably visit in a day, and more than in any other Wine Country town. In fact, there are well over 30. So many, in fact, that wineries are upping their ante with some outlandish style, unbelievable deals, and classy food pairing.

As of this printing, the most recent addition is Kendall-Jackson's **Partake by K-J** (241 Healdsburg Ave., 707/433-6000, http://partakebykj.com, 11am-9pm Sun.-Thurs., 11am-10pm Fri.-Sun.), which pairs flights wine with

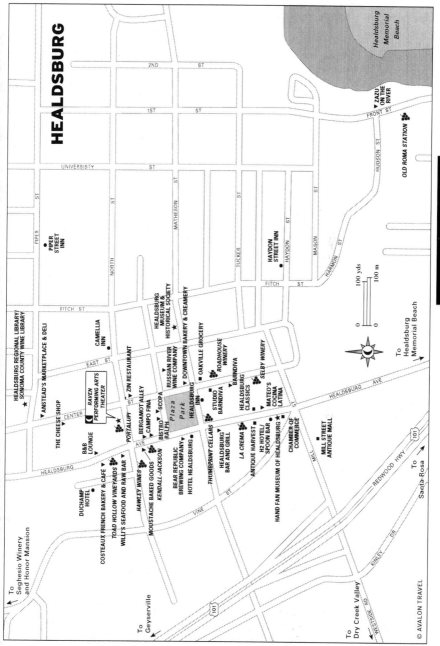

NORTHERN SONOMA

HEALDSBURG

Healdsburg Memorial Beach

2ND ST
1ST ST
FRONT ST
HUDSON ST
ZAZU ON THE RIVER
OLD ROMA STATION

UNIVERSISTY ST

PIPER ST
NORTH ST
MATHESON ST
TUCKER ST
MASON ST
HARMON ST

PIPER STREET INN

HAYDON STREET INN
HAYDON ST
FITCH ST

FITCH ST

HEALDSBURG REGIONAL LIBRARY/ SONOMA COUNTY WINE LIBRARY

ANSTEAD'S MARKETPLACE & DELI

CAMELLIA INN

HEALDSBURG MUSEUM & HISTORICAL SOCIETY

DOWNTOWN BAKERY & CREAMERY

OAKVILLE GROCERY

ROADHOUSE WINERY

BARNDIVA

SELBY WINERY

THE CHEESE SHOP

EAST ST

CENTER ST

RAVEN PERFORMING ARTS THEATER

ZIN RESTAURANT

PORTALUPI

BERGAMOT ALLEY

CAMPO FINA

SCOPA

BISTRO RALPH

RUSSIAN RIVER WINE COMPANY

Plaza Park

STUDIO BARNDIVA

HEALDSBURG INN

HEALDSBURG CLASSICS

MATEO'S COCINA LATINA

HEALDSBURG AVE

B&B LOUNGE

HAWLEY WINES

MOUSTACHE BAKED GOODS

KENDALL-JACKSON

BEAR REPUBLIC BREWING COMPANY

HOTEL HEALDSBURG

THUMBPRINT CELLARS

HEALDSBURG BAR AND GRILL

ANTIQUE HARVEST

LA CREMA

H2 HOTEL/ SPOON BAR

CHAMBER OF COMMERCE

MILL ST

MILL STREET ANTIQUE MALL

HEALDSBURG AVE

DUCHAMP HOTEL

COSTEAUX FRENCH BAKERY & CAFÉ

TOAD HOLLOW VINEYARDS

WILL'S SEAFOOD AND RAW BAR

VINE ST

HAND FAN MUSEUM OF HEALDSBURG

REDWOOD HWY

101

To Seghesio Winery and Honor Mansion

To Geyserville

To Dry Creek Valley

WESTSIDE RD

KINLEY DR

101

To Santa Rosa

To Healdsburg Memorial Beach

100 yds
100 m
0

© AVALON TRAVEL

classy small bites such as beef tartar, wine-braised turnips, and grape-skin flour pork buns in a sleek lounge setting. This new venture by the mammoth winemaker straddles the line between restaurant and tasting room. Regardless of what they offer, visiting these urban tasting rooms at least saves you from having to hop in and out of a hot car all day.

LA CREMA

One of the first tasting rooms you come to upon entering Healdsburg from the south is this fancy new outpost of a well-established Russian River Valley winery. **La Crema** (235 Healdsburg Ave., Healdsburg, 800/314-1762, www.lacrema.com, 10:30am-5:30pm daily, tasting $10-25) has long since been absorbed into the Kendall-Jackson wine empire and turns out huge volumes of sometimes mediocre wine, but still makes some nice examples of cool-climate pinot noir and chardonnay.

Look for the wines from the Russian River Valley, which tend to be better (and more expensive) than those from the larger Sonoma Coast region. La Crema also makes some nice pinot from other cool-climate appellations including Los Carneros and the Anderson Valley in Mendocino. The flagship wines are the limited-production pinot and chardonnay made under the Nine Barrel label, but they are only available to taste by appointment only, costing $25. But the real upshot to tasting here is the cool modern interior and the open-air bar that faces the street, adding a definite cosmopolitan flare.

THUMBPRINT CELLARS

Touting itself as a "micro-winery," **Thumbprint Cellars** (102 Matheson St., Healdsburg, 707/433-2393, www.thumbprintcellars.com, 11am-6pm daily, tasting $5-10) was started as a hobby for winemaker Scott Lindstrom-Dake in the late 1990s and has rapidly grown to become a member of the boutique brigade. It now makes more than 3,000 cases of mainly warmer-climate, fruit-forward wines from the Alexander and Dry Creek Valleys.

The small, relaxed tasting room has a vibe that's about as far from the corporate airs of Kendall-Jackson around the corner as you can get. Try the Threesome—a sexy blend of cabernet franc, cabernet sauvignon, and syrah—or any of the other lush red wines that include syrah, zinfandel, and cabernet sauvignon. The Russian River pinot noir is one of the few cooler-climate wines but just as approachable as the others. The winery has recently added several whites to its portfolio, which include viognier, a petit rosé, gewürztraminer, and Arousal, a blend of sauvignon blanc, semillon, and gewürztraminer. Food pairing is also available and features locally made cheese and charcuterie.

TOAD HOLLOW VINEYARDS

The toad in this hollow is actually owner Todd Williams, the half-brother of comedian Robin, who has sported the amphibious nickname since his youth. His winery, **Toad Hollow Vineyards** (409A Healdsburg Ave., Healdsburg, 707/431-8667, www.toadhollow.com, 11am-5pm Mon.-Fri., 10:30am-5:30pm Sat.-Sun., free tasting) is best known for its oak-free chardonnay, sourced from the 103 acres of estate vineyards, but it also makes estate pinot noir and merlot, a pinot noir rosé, and one or two unique (and uniquely named) wines, including the red blend called Erik's the Red, which is made from a staggering 15 different types of grape. The two sparkling wines are not local, however, but imported from France.

Many can be tasted free of charge at the gnarled redwood bar. And if the wines don't entertain, their colorful labels, painted by San Francisco artist Maureen Erickson, might. Serious wines sport a very conservative-looking toad, while the fun wines see the toad in party mood.

HAWLEY WINES

John Hawley, winemaker and proprietor of **Hawley Wines** (36 North St., Healdsburg, 707/473-9500, www.hawleywine.com, 11am-6pm daily, tasting $5) certainly knows how to make Sonoma wine, and lots of it. He started his winemaking career in the 1970s as a winemaker at the giant Clos du Bois and Kendall-Jackson wineries. In the mid-1990s he started making small quantities of wine under his own label, making less than a few hundred cases of nine or so different varietals sourced from a wide variety of northern Sonoma vineyards, including the family's own estate on Bradford Mountain in the Dry Creek Valley.

The tasting room, a block away from the square, is relaxed and warmed with carved wood, a bar made from old wine barrels, and the impressionist paintings of vineyards and other Northern California landscapes by its resident artist, Dana Hawley. Hawley's Russian River wines include pinot noir and chardonnay. Wines from the estate vineyard in the Dry Creek Valley include an acclaimed barrel-fermented viognier, a late-harvest zinfandel, an estate cabernet, and a merlot from the Bradford Mountain estate that usually sells out fast.

ROADHOUSE WINERY

Pinot noir may have developed a reputation for snootiness from the grape's devotees, but **Roadhouse Winery** (240 Center St., Healdsburg, 707/433-0433, www.roadhousewinery.com, noon-6pm Sun.-Thurs., 11am-7pm Fri.-Sat., tasting $10) is as unpretentious as it gets. Winemaker and proprietor Eric Hall began his career during the Bay Area's dot-com boom of the 1990s. Leaving the tech world behind, he discovered the Sonoma Coast and pinot noir. In 2010 he opened Roadhouse with a few friends and now makes less than 2,000 cases of his favorite wines.

At the tasting room, which is easygoing with lots of young wine lovers offering advice on where to eat while pouring wine, you'll get a chance to taste several pinots from Sonoma Mountain, the Sonoma Coast, and the Russian River Valley, many of which routinely score above 90 points from *Wine Enthusiast*. Because they are in Healdsburg, the winery also makes a Dry Creek zinfandel and Eric's Red Blend of zinfandel, syrah, petite sirah, cabernet, and pinot noir. Full bodied and fruit forward, this is a great wine to bring along to a casual dinner with friends.

SELBY WINERY

Down Center Street from Roadhouse and almost opposite the police department is the tiny tasting room of the **Selby Winery** (215 Center St., Healdsburg, 707/431-1288, www.selbywinery.com, 11am-5:30pm daily, tasting free or $5), which has its production facility in a nearby warehouse. The 10,000 cases of wine Selby makes each year come from vineyards all over Sonoma, with an emphasis on the nearby Russian River Valley, Alexander Valley, and Dry Creek Valley. The Russian River Valley chardonnay is perhaps the best wine here and one that regularly wins praise from the critics. The reserve chardonnay has even been served at the White House. Other wines include a Russian River pinot noir, a couple of nicely structured syrahs, including a dry syrah rosé, and some nice zinfandels, including a juicy port. Most of the red Bordeaux varietals are also in the winery's large portfolio, including a nice malbec from the nearby Chalk Hill appellation.

All can be tasted free in the relaxed and usually very quiet tasting room, where you're as likely to see a few locals hanging out as you are visitors. There's a nominal charge for trying the reserve wines.

KENDALL-JACKSON

The Healdsburg tasting room of **Kendall-Jackson** (337 Healdsburg Ave., Healdsburg, 707/433-7102, www.kj.com, 10am-5pm daily, tasting $5-20), the Sonoma wine titan, is a cavernous but chintzy place that offers tastes of some of its bewildering array of wines for $10, including not only Kendall-Jackson wines but also some from the numerous other wineries the company owns in California and Australia. Tasting the reasonably priced reserves and other high-end wines costs $20, while for $5 you can sample a flight of dessert wines. Each option comes with its own souvenir wineglass. While you may be tempted to pass on this corporate tasting room in favor of a more boutique winery down the road, the winery's website often offers a coupon that can be printed for a free tasting, making it potentially worth the stop.

PORTALUPI

If you take a survey of tasting room pourers' favorite Healdsburg tasting room (outside their own, of course), the answer invariably is **Portalupi** (107 North St., Healdsburg, 707/395-0960, www.portalupiwine.com, 11am-7pm daily, tasting $5-12). The winery was started in 2002 by husband and wife team Tim Borges and Jane Portalupi, who are both native Californians and veterans of the wine business. Along with their California roots, they also sought to incorporate their Italian heritages into their winery. In addition to the outstanding Russian River pinot noirs and zinfandel, their portfolio includes a port classically made from carignan, and a barbera from the Shenandoah Valley in Amador County, which has become their highly praised signature wine. A fun addition is the Vaso di Marina blend of pinot noir, zinfandel, and cabernet sauvignon. As a nod to her grandmother who used to make wine herself in her native village in Italy, the wine comes in a liter ($28) or half-gallon glass milk jug ($48). The sole white on the menu is the Bianco blend of sauvignon blanc, chardonnay, and muscat canelli.

The lush, inky quality of Portalupi's wines are perfectly matched by its sophisticated slate tasting room, accented and warmed by a deep purple sofa in the middle. Either Borges or Portalupi are usually on hand to pour flights of three ($5), six ($10), or eight ($12) wines, or by the glass ($8-15). Cheese and salami plates are also available ($15), and there is a small deli case offering local cheese and charcuturie and other snacks. Despite the tasting room's small size, this is a great place to hang out (or wait for a table at a nearby restaurant), particularly when the large glass doors are open, making it an indoor/outdoor space on a beautiful day or evening.

OLD ROMA STATION

A dozen small wineries have tasting rooms in the **Old Roma Station** (Front St. and Hudson St., Healdsburg, www.oldromastation.com), an old complex of warehouses on the southern edge of town right across from the Russian River, a pleasant 10-minute walk from the plaza. This was once home to the Roma Winery, a Victorian-era winery that shipped fortified wines by rail from its own station before the trains were halted by Prohibition. After finding various uses throughout the rest of the 20th century, the complex was renovated in 2004 and is once again home to wineries, often referred to by locals as the Front Street Wineries. Most offer tasting every day, but some are appointment-only, and a few are closed for a few days midweek. Whatever time you visit, however, you're sure to taste some unique wines from unique wineries, the most notable of which are listed below.

Dry Creek zinfandels and cabernets are the specialties of **Pezzi King Vineyards** (707/431-9388, www.pezziking.com, 11am-5pm daily, tasting $5). It makes a half-dozen zins, including several nice single-vineyard and old-vine versions sourced from the estate vineyard. The estate zinfandel and cabernet sauvignon are standouts, along with a nice Russian River Valley chardonnay.

Sapphire Hill Vineyards (707/431-1888, www.sapphirehill.com, 11am-4:30pm daily, tasting $5) produces several thousand cases of Russian River Valley chardonnay, syrah, pinot noir, and four single-vineyard zinfandels, including a late-harvest version. The winery also produces Cinque Gemma Red Cuvée, made from five Italian varietals meant to be a California chianti.

J. Keverson Winery (707/484-3097, www.jkeverson.com, 11am-4:30pm Thurs.-Mon., tasting $5) makes a couple of very good Dry Creek and Russian River zinfandels, but is also well known for its Carneros chardonnays. Also worth trying is a light and vibrant sangiovese from Mendocino. Food pairing is also available here by appointment. Five small-bite courses are paired with different vintages poured by the winemaker himself, with the food prepared by his wife. Larger groups are accommodated upstairs in one of the building's small rooms, but if you have a small party, expect to be seated in the downstairs tasting room.

The collective inside the collective is

Healdsburg

Hudson Street Wineries (707/433-2364, www.hudsonstreetwineries.com, 11am-5pm Mon. and Thurs.-Sat., noon-5pm Sun., tasting $5). Here, five wineries share the quaint tasting room. **Bluenose Wines** specializes in Dry Creek zinfandel, Sonoma County chardonnay, and syrah; from **Kelly & Young** come a Sonoma County sauvignon blanc and a Bordeaux-style rosé; **Maclaren** makes single-vineyard and blended Sonoma County syrahs; **Shippey Vineyards** also produces single-vineyard petite sirah and zinfandel along with their Midnight O Vineyard table wine blend; and from **Willowbrook** come two pinot noirs, one from Sonoma and the other from Marin. All five wineries produce less than 300 cases of each vintage, making them the boutiques of the boutiques.

SIGHTS

Healdsburg is one of the more appealing Wine Country towns, with the right mix of history, modernity, shops, and wine, and a population (11,000) that's large enough to prevent the town's economy from lurching too far in favor of wine tourism. There is still plenty of Wine Country paraphernalia here, however, and there are often-voiced concerns that the town is being "St. Helena-ized," but it remains decidedly less frenetic than that smaller Napa Valley town. This could be partly thanks to some of its active cultural counterweights, including the loose collective of local artists called Stark Raving Beautiful, who have the motto "Help Make Healdsburg Weird" and a desire to prevent the town from becoming a "bourgeois play-land."

The town has a history as storied as any other in the region. It was established in the mid-1800s by an enterprising former gold miner from Ohio, Harmon Heald, who eventually bought enough parcels of land to lay out the town around a Spanish-style plaza and sell plots to other businessmen. He bought the land from Captain Henry Fitch, who was granted most of the surrounding area by the Mexican government and whose name lives on in Fitch Mountain, the small hump at the bend in the Russian River just east of the town.

Healdsburg was incorporated in 1867 and boomed after the railroad arrived in 1871. Like many of the region's towns, it went through a slump brought on by the 1906 earthquake, the Great Depression, and Prohibition, but returned to prosperity after Prohibition, when the region's agriculture and wine industry took off.

The modest-looking **Healdsburg Museum & Historical Society** (221 Matheson St. at Fitch St., Healdsburg, 707/431-3325, www.healdsburgmuseum.org, 11am-4pm Wed.-Sun., free), a few blocks from the plaza, is a treasure trove of information and photos illustrating the town's Victorian heyday and its Native American roots. Serious history buffs can pore through oral histories, official records, and newspapers going back to the 1860s.

Ask for a pamphlet about historic homes and visit some of the many Victorian buildings around town. The library itself is in one of Healdsburg's most notable neoclassical buildings, and it is now home to the **Sonoma County Wine Library** (139 Piper St.,

Healdsburg Regional Library, Healdsburg, 707/433-3772, www.sonomalibrary.org/wine, 10am-6pm Tues. and Thurs.-Fri., 10am-8pm Wed., 10am-4pm Sat.), where a collection of over 5,000 books on wine, subscriptions to more than 80 wine periodicals, photos, prints, and wine labels await the amateur wine lover and serious oenophile alike. Among the 1,000 or so rare wine books, you'll find treatises on the history, business, and art of wine from as far back as 1512. The library is a perfect place for wine drinkers who want to take their habit or hobby to the next level. But if you want to access the library from the safety of your own laptop, the library does have an online resource, http://winefiles.org.

Thankfully, the **Healdsburg Plaza** is the perfect place to do that, as it is blanketed in wireless Internet and is of historical significance. The plaza was donated to the city by Harmon Heald in the 1850s, but nothing much was done with the patch of grass and oak trees until the 1870s, when it was cleared and fenced and the diagonal paths were laid out. Over the following decades features came and went with the fashions of the times—first a bell tower in the middle of the plaza, then a gazebo, and finally a bandstand. Most of the mature trees in the plaza today were planted between 1897 and 1900, including Canary date palms, orange and lemon trees, and a rare dawn redwood from China that is deciduous. The bandstand survived until 1960, when the modern plaza finally took shape, with a new fountain in its center and a new landscape design based around the mature trees. The last addition of note is the pavilion on the east side of the plaza, which was built in 1986 and resembles (in postmodernist style) the gazebo that had stood on the plaza a century earlier.

More history awaits you just off the square between the visitors center and the H2 Hotel. The tiny **Hand Fan Museum of Healdsburg** (219 Healdsburg Ave., Healdsburg, 707/431-2500, www.handfanmuseum.com, 11am-4pm Wed.-Sun.) seeks to tell the cultural histories of Europe, America, and Asia through the creation, decoration, and use of fans. It doesn't take long to view and enjoy both the permanent collection and seasonal exhibits at this fun little museum. You might be surprised to discover the level of artistry put into some of the fans here, be they paper or lace, antique or modern. And you'll learn a little bit about how fans were and are used in various societies (the 17th-19th-century courting practices and sexual invitations in some European countries included intricate movements of a lady's fan, directed at the gentleman of the hour).

ENTERTAINMENT

◖ Raven Performing Arts Theater

Hats off to Healdsburg's fiercely independent **Raven Performing Arts Theater** (115 North St., Healdsburg, 707/433-6335, www.raventheater.org) for keeping it real in the middle of Wine Country. The theater is owned by a performing arts cooperative, ensuring an eclectic mix of live performances, most of which revolve around music, from Broadway musicals to jazz, classical, and rock. Local artists feature as strongly as national and international acts, particularly in the occasional theater productions put on by local groups and ensembles. Check the website for a full calendar of events; general admission for a full-production show is roughly $26, with the curtain going up at 8pm.

Around the corner, the Raven has its own "multiplex." Well, sort of. The **Raven Film Center** (415 Center St., Healdsburg, 707/522-0330, www.srentertainmentgrp.com) has four movie theaters squeezed into this historic building (though one is about the size of an average living room), so there's usually a combination of mainstream, independent, and documentary films showing 3-5 times every day (entrance on Center St., admission $9.50, matinees $6.50). For a more unique Wine Country movie experience, opt for a Hollywood & Wine ticket, which costs an additional $9.50 for popcorn and wine.

Nightlife

A couple of local hangouts keep the bar scene in Healdsburg real too, staying open all day, every day until 2am. Both **John & Zeke's Bar & Grill** (111 Plaza St., Healdsburg, 707/433-3735) and the **B&B Lounge** (420 Healdsburg Ave., Healdsburg, 707/433-5960) have a no-nonsense attitude and grumpy bartenders, and they shun Wine Country frills for good old-fashioned barroom entertainment like jukeboxes, pool, and darts. The B&B is more popular with locals and slightly less of a dive.

For a beer and maybe some food, head over to the **Bear Republic Brewing Company** (345 Healdsburg Ave., Healdsburg, 707/433-2337, http://bearrepublic.com), where locals are known to grab a Racer 5 IPA and chill out after work. Beer, wine, and cocktails can be found down the street at the other pub in town, the **Healdsburg Bar and Grill** (245 Healdsburg Ave., Healdsburg, 707/433-3333, www.healdsburgbarandgrill.com). Here you'll find specialty drinks like the Hummingbird, which features St. Germaine; the Cucumber Collins made with Effen Cucumber Vodka and jalapeño and lime juice; and an assortment of "adult milkshakes" spiked with rum, Bailey's, or Jack Daniels. These all keep the large outside patio busy until the place closes at 9pm.

Cocktails are also king at the nearby **Spoonbar** (219 Healdsburg Ave., Healdsburg, 707/433-7222, http://spoonbar.com). The menu is equally long, inventive, and fun loving with such concoctions as Remember the Maine (rye whiskey and absinthe), Shark Week (cocoa-infused bourbon and walnut liquor), and the Burning Shrub (tequila, jalapeño, and grapefruit). Two large bars serve both diners and drinkers in the large dining room of the **H2 Hotel** (219 Healdsburg Ave., 707/922-5251, www.h2hotel.com, $275), which spills out onto the street when its floor-to-ceiling windows are opened on warm summer evenings.

A novel addition to the Healdsburg bar scene is actually a wine bar. The slim **Bergamot Alley** (328A Healdsburg Ave., Healdsburg, 707/433-8720, www.bergamotalley.com, 3pm-1am Mon.-Sat., 3pm-10pm Sun.) is all exposed brick, cool lighting, microbrews and European wines sold by the glass, and a turntable that plays full albums from start to finish

(i.e., no playlists here). There are small offerings to nibble on, like spiced popcorn and candied jalapeños. You are even invited to bring your own snacks, so long as they are not alcoholic beverages. Basically, Bergamot Alley has the vibe of the coolest basement hangout spot you can think of.

The best place to escape the Wine Country scene and nurse a cold beer at a small hole-in-the-wall bar is, ironically, right among the wineries of Dry Creek Valley. The **Dry Creek Bar** (3495 Dry Creek Rd., at Lambert Bridge Rd., Healdsburg, 707/433-4171, http://drycreekgeneralstore1881.com/Bar.html) at the Dry Creek General Store is open daily from 3pm. Grab a beer, sit outside, and watch the wine tasters drive by. Closing time varies and usually depends on how many people are left propping up the bar.

SHOPPING

Wine is about all you'll be buying in most of the Dry Creek Valley, except in Healdsburg, a town of boutiques and antiques. In fact, the town has gone so upscale that many residents jokingly call it "HealdsBevery Hills." Still, there are some old treasures and lots of cool shops for browsing.

The barnlike antiques cooperative **Healdsburg Classics** (226 Healdsburg Ave., Healdsburg, 707/433-4315, 10am-5pm daily) features the wares of more than 20 small dealers and is fun to rummage around in. There's another antiques cooperative a short distance away at the **Mill Street Antique Mall** (44 Mill St., just off Healdsburg Ave., Healdsburg, 707/433-8409, 11am-5pm daily). It boasts more than 20,000 square feet of floor space that is home to numerous local dealers and craftspeople.

Possibly the best place in town to buy a unique gift is **Studio Barndiva** (237 Center St., Healdsburg, 707/431-7404, www.studio-barndiva.com, 10am-5pm daily), a cavernous space in what used to be part of the town's opera house that is part studio and part housewares store. It is a spin-off of the **Barndiva** restaurant (231 Center St., Healdsburg, 707/431-0100, www.barndiva.com, lunch noon-2:30pm Wed.-Sat., dinner 5:30pm-9pm Wed.-Thurs. and Sun., 5:30pm-10pm Fri.-Sat., brunch 11am-2pm Sun., dinner entrées $12-40) next door, and it sells some of the same locally sourced glasses and dishes used at the restaurant. It's far from just a cynical marketing exercise for Barndiva, however, and has developed more of a showcase of weird and wonderful artistic creations from local and global artisans. Wine Country clichés are nowhere to be seen among the products, and prices of many of the unique creations are not as expensive as the hipper-than-thou atmosphere suggests.

Book lovers, music aficionados, epicureans, and home cooks alike will undoubtedly fall in love with **Levin & Company** (306 Center St., Healdsburg, 707/433-1118, 9am-9pm Mon.-Sat., 9am-6pm Sun.), an independent bookstore that has been around nearly 20 years. Inside, current fiction and nonfiction titles share shelf space with one of the best selections of culinary and wine books around. CDs of jazz, classical, and pop music can also be found

© ELIZABETH LINHART VENEMAN

Moustache Baked Goods

here. The only thing you need is a cup of coffee and a couple of hours.

Thankfully, this (coffee, at least) can be accommodated at **Moustache Baked Goods** (381 Healdsburg Ave., Healdsburg, 707/395-4111, www.moustachebakedgoods.com, 11am-7pm Mon.-Fri., 11am-8pm Sat.-Sun.), which pulls mean shots of Four Barrel espresso. You'll be tempted to pick up one of their handmade Oreo cookies, colorful macaroons, or devilishly delicious cupcakes displayed in the antique-looking display case. Advice? Do it. These sweets are worth the calories and the extra few dollars.

No Wine Country shopping trip would be complete without a stop in a well-heeled wine shop. In Healdsburg, the place to go is the **Russian River Wine Company** (132 Plaza St., Healdsburg, 707/433-0490, www.russianriverwineco.com, 8am-4pm Mon.-Fri.), which sells wine from all over the area, not just the Russian River, and specializes in smaller producers. Right next door is the cool, tranquil space of the **Healdsburg Center for the Arts** (130 Plaza St., Healdsburg, 707/431-1970, www.healdsburgcenterforthearts.com, 11am-5pm daily), which showcases varied, mainly contemporary art from its local-resident artists, one of whom will likely be staffing the front desk.

RECREATION
Lake Sonoma Recreation Area

When the Army Corps of Engineers completed the Warm Springs Dam at the northern end of Dry Creek Valley in 1983, the resulting lake not only made Dry Creek's name obsolete by providing a year-round source of water but also became one of the best regional recreation areas around.

Controversially, Lake Sonoma flooded some sacred sites of the Pomo people, now represented in a small exhibition in the **Milt Brandt Visitor Center** (3333 Skaggs Springs Rd., Geyserville, 707/433-5433, 8:30am-3:30pm Wed.-Sun.), right at the end of Dry Creek Road. Despite protests during the drawn-out planning stages in the 1970s, the flood control, water supply, and recreation advantages created by the dam won the day, and it was finally completed more than 20 years after first getting approval.

The 17,000 acres of hot oak-studded hills of the Lake Sonoma Recreation Area have more than 40 miles of trails for hikers, bikers, and riders, the region's best bass fishing, and plenty of open water (about 2,700 surface acres, to be precise) for swimming and boating. The main access points to the lake and trails are Stewarts Point Road, just south of the bridge; Rockpile Road, north of the bridge; and the grassy **Yorty Creek Recreation Area** (from S. Cloverdale Blvd., turn left on W. Brookside Rd., left on Foothill Rd., and right onto Hot Springs Rd.), which is on the eastern side of lake and is accessible from Cloverdale.

A couple of the easier and more accessible hiking trails start at the South Lake Trailhead (on Stewarts Point Rd. about 0.5 mile south from its junction with Skaggs Springs Rd., just before the marina turnoff). From there it's a quick jaunt up the hill to the **Overlook**, with great views of the lake. Or take the **South Lake Trail** for a longer hike, ducking in and out of groves of madrone and pine along the way. At about two miles, head right; it's then about 0.75 mile down to the Quicksilver Campground, where you can duck into the lake for a swim, if you came prepared. Alternatively, go left and stay on the South Lake Trail for as long as you want. Other trails start at another trailhead across the bridge off Rockpile Road. A trail map is available at the visitors center.

Mountain bikers will have to be content with just one loop on the **Half-a-Canoe Trail**, which starts at the No Name Flat Trailhead, about 1.5 miles north of the bridge on the left. The loop is about 4.5 miles of mostly fire road with a short section of single-track.

You might notice that it gets hotter as you drive up Dry Creek Valley. Temperatures around the lake regularly top 100°F in the summer, so take plenty of water, whatever you do (the lake water is not drinkable). Other natural hazards include the occasional rattlesnake, disease-carrying ticks, and poison oak. You might

be lucky enough to see the odd jackrabbit, a wild pig, or a rare peregrine falcon.

FISHING AND BOATING

The **Congressman Don Clausen Fish Hatchery** (behind the recreation area visitors center) was built to beef up the steelhead, chinook, and coho salmon populations in the Russian River and its tributaries and to mitigate some of the detrimental effects caused by construction of the Warm Springs and nearby Coyote Valley Dams. The main fishing draw on the lake is the healthy stock of largemouth bass, which love the submerged trees that were left in the Dry Creek arm of the lake when it was flooded. The bass record stands at just over 15 pounds, though most reportedly weigh less than 10 pounds. There are also smallmouth bass, catfish, crappies, sunfish, perch, and numerous other species, including some landlocked steelhead.

When the water is clearest, during the summer, sight fishing is possible in the shallower waters close to the shore, as is bank fishing, particularly at the Yorty Creek Recreation Area. The lake is primarily a boat-fishing lake, however, and boats can be rented at the **Lake Sonoma Marina** (100 Marina Dr., Healdsburg, 707/433-2200, $25-45/hour for fishing boats, depending on the season, $70-90/hour for larger powerboats), just off Stewarts Point Road about 0.5 mile south of Skaggs Springs Road.

There are three places to launch boats on Lake Sonoma—a trailer ramp at the Lake Sonoma Marina ($10 to launch), a big public ramp just across the bridge ($3), and a car-top launch area at Yorty Creek ($3). Check with a ranger for the boating rules. If fishing or high-octane boating doesn't appeal, canoes and kayaks can also be rented at the marina ($10-15/hour).

Unless you're fortunate to be camping at one of the hike-in or boat-in campsites, there are not many places with decent shoreline access for swimming on the lake. The only official swimming beach is at the Yorty Creek Recreation Area.

NORTHERN SONOMA

Healdsburg's Russian River

In Healdsburg, the Russian River provides a few water-related recreation opportunities. On the south side of town, just beyond the Old Roma Station complex and over the bridge, is **Memorial Beach,** a stretch of sandy and rocky shoreline along the river with a swimming area and concession for canoe rental. Parking at the beach costs $7, but the lot is often so crowded that a better option is to park on the other side of the bridge in a residential area and walk back to the beach. Alternatively, it's about a 15-minute walk from downtown Healdsburg.

During the summer (generally May-Oct.), canoes or kayaks can be rented at Memorial Beach from **River's Edge Kayak & Canoe Trips** (13840 Healdsburg Ave., Healdsburg, 707/433-7247, www.riversedgekayakandcanoe.com). Canoe prices are $75 for half a day, $90 for a full day. Kayaks are a bit cheaper at $45 for half and $55 for a full day, but double kayaks go for the same as canoes. The best aspect of renting a kayak or canoe for even a couple of hours is the access to more beaches. Paddle upstream under the railroad bridge toward the small hump of Fitch Mountain, and you'll find a whole host of little beaches and swimming holes. The public is allowed on all the beaches along the Russian River that fall below the winter high-water mark—basically every beach you see during the summer.

If you are more interested in joining a guided tour, another local outfit, **Russian River Adventures** (20 Healdsburg Ave., Healdsburg, 707/433-5599, www.rradventures.info, adults $50, children $25) offers guided paddles down a secluded section of the river in stable, sturdy inflatable canoes. Dogs, children, and even infants are welcome. The trip usually lasts 4-5 hours, with little white water and lots of serene shaded pools.

Golf

Touting itself as a Wine Country golf course, the **Tayman Park Golf Course** (927 S. Fitch Mountain Rd., Healdsburg, 707/433-4275, www.taymanparkgolfcourse.com) is actually in a Healdsburg residential area, a five-minute drive from downtown, but it does have some nice views west toward Dry Creek and the Russian River Valley. It's a 9-hole course that can also be played as an 18-hole par-68 course. Greens fees are $21-24 for 9 holes, depending on the time of the week, and $18-31 for 18 holes. Golf-cart rental starts at $7. Drive east on Matheson Street from Healdsburg Plaza; the road becomes Fitch Mountain Road and heads up the hill to the club.

ACCOMMODATIONS

Take one look at the expanses of vineyards and hills dotted with the occasional winery and it's clear that the Dry Creek Valley is not a part of the world that's chock-full of hotels. Pretty much every accommodation option is in the town of Healdsburg, where Victorian frills still dominate the scene, though some contemporary style has recently crept in. As would be expected in a premium Wine Country destination town, prices are not low, regardless of style.

Under $150

Few options exist for those on a budget other than chain hotels and motels. Cheaper lodging is available to the north in the Alexander Valley and south in the Russian River Valley, but the town of Healdsburg itself seems to work hard to retain its sense of exclusivity. One of the better chain lodging options is the **Dry Creek Inn** (198 Dry Creek Rd., Healdsburg, 707/433-0300, www.drycreekinn.com, $125), a Best Western property less than one mile from the plaza but perilously close to the freeway at the Dry Creek Road exit. Amenities that include free wireless Internet access, a large pool, and a free tasting coupon for Simi Winery make the stay a little more bearable.

$150-250

This could be classified as the Victorian frills price category, into which fall the many small family-owned inns and B&Bs in often historic houses. There might be some inflexibilities inherent to such small establishments (check whether smoking or pets are allowed, for example, and ask about the sometimes-strict cancellation policies), but the advantage is that the owners usually know the area like the backs of their hands and can offer great local insights and, of course, a great local breakfast.

One of the relative bargains in a crowded local field of frilly B&Bs is the **Camellia Inn** (211 North St., Healdsburg, 707/433-8182 or 800/727-8182, www.camelliainn.com, $225). Flowers abound on the walls and fabrics inside the elegant 1869 house and in the gardens, which contain more than 50 varieties of camellia, some planted by renowned horticulturist Luther Burbank, who was a friend of the original owners. Unusual for a small B&B, there is air-conditioning in all rooms as well as a small swimming pool. Four of the nine guest rooms have gas fireplaces. Wine shows up in the Victorian parlor most evenings, and you can chat with the innkeeper and winemaker himself, Ray Lewand.

There's a little more chintz on show at the ◖ **Haydon Street Inn** (321 Haydon St., Healdsburg, 707/433-5228 or 800/528-3703, www.haydon.com, $225), on a quiet residential street about a 10-minute walk from the plaza. The Queen Anne-style house was built in 1912 as a private residence and briefly used as a convent before becoming a B&B in the 1980s. The six rooms in the main house all have private baths, with the exception of the Blue Room, whose bathroom is across the hall. Two additional deluxe rooms are in a separate cottage on the manicured grounds and cost upward of $400 depending on the season.

Other standouts in the crowded Victorian B&B scene include six-room **Calderwood Inn** (25 W. Grant St., Healdsburg, 707/431-1110 or 800/600-5444, www.calderwoodinn.com, $250), not far from the Seghesio Family Winery. The Queen Anne Victorian boasts gardens that were laid out by famed horticulturist Luther Burbank and has a beautifully (and tastefully) restored interior, right down to the reproduction Victorian wallpaper. The spacious rooms all have garden views, and the Vineyard Suite with a full kitchen is a deal at $300 per night in the high season.

The town of Healdsburg might have a surplus of historic Victorian houses, but the ◖ **Madrona Manor** (1001 Westside Rd., Healdsburg, 707/433-4231 or 800/258-4003, www.madronamanor.com, $225-495), just outside the town at the southern end of the Dry Creek Valley appellation, puts them all in the shade. This enormous pile of Victorian opulence is the centerpiece of an eight-acre hilltop estate dating from the 1880s and is on the National Register of Historic Places. Not surprisingly, the Madrona Manor's movie-set looks make it a very popular wedding location, and they also attracted the attention of director Francis Ford Coppola, who bought the estate in 2006.

The elegantly furnished rooms and common areas contain plenty of genuine and reproduction antiques as well as most amenities, except for televisions, which is probably fine since no children under 12 can stay here anyway. Any bored adults can watch the fire burn or the sun set from the private decks of some of the 21 rooms and suites that are spread among five buildings. Room rates are not as high as the opulence suggests, with the cheapest rooms located in the Carriage House and manor house. But not to worry, many of these have a private deck and/or a fireplace. Once you move out to the Meadow Wood, Garden Cottage, and Schoolhouse Suites, the prices begin to climb as do the space and amenities. If the romantic setting, landscaped grounds, and swimming pool aren't enough to keep guests from ever leaving during their stay, then the manor's renowned restaurant might be. It serves the sumptuous breakfast included in the rate and a stylish, though pricey, dinner (on the big porch in the summer) with an outstanding wine list that leans heavily on the local appellations.

Over $250

In this price range, Victorian frills start to yield to more contemporary style, nowhere more so than at the **Hotel Healdsburg** (25 Matheson St., Healdsburg, 800/889-7188, www.hotel-healdsburg.com, $400), the centerpiece of the decidedly un-Victorian hunk of modern architecture that dominates the western side of the plaza. Strategically placed design elements and luxurious furnishings successfully soften the angular concrete minimalism of the interior, both in the rooms and the starkly minimalist lobby area. Such Manhattan style doesn't come cheap, however, even in sleepy Healdsburg. The smallest of the 49 rooms start at about $350, though they include the usual luxury amenities, including an iPod dock, a walk-in shower, and high-speed Internet. Add a tub and a few more square feet, and the rate jumps $100 more. All guests have access to the tranquil outdoor pool and small fitness room, while the minimally named **The Spa** offers a wide range of spa treatments and massages for $120 and up. Downstairs is the pricey and equally contemporary restaurant, the **Dry Creek Kitchen.**

A similar modern aesthetic at a lower price is offered by the hotel's new sister property just down the road, the **H2 Hotel** (219 Healdsburg Ave., 707/922-5251, www.h2hotel.com, $275). As seems to be the norm for trendy new hotels, the green credentials of the sleek new building are impeccable, from the undulating grass-covered "living" roof to the solar heating and water collection system and right down to the furniture in each room, made from reclaimed wood or sustainable bamboo. Still, it is hard to know what to make of the hotel's style with its rather institutional exterior dressed up in planks of hard wood and arty balconies for all 36 rooms. There is an impressive list of luxury features, from high-definition TVs to custom organic bathroom amenities. Complimentary bike rentals, a fireside lounge and bar, and the downstairs restaurant, **Spoonbar** (219 Healdsburg Ave., Healdsburg, 707/433-7222, http://spoonbar.com, noon-3:30pm and 5pm-9:30pm Sun.-Thurs., noon-3:30pm and 5pm-10pm Fri.-Sat., $23)—a destination in itself—all add to the package.

Slightly more reasonable rates but a slightly less contemporary feel can be found at the **Healdsburg Inn on the Plaza** (112 Matheson St., Healdsburg, 800/431-8663, www.healdsburginn.com, $295-450). The inn is part of the Four Sisters hotel chain, so comfort and a reasonable level of amenities are guaranteed. All rooms have bay windows or balconies, claw-foot or jetted spa bathtubs, and simple modern decor that blends with the original features of the Victorian building to create a sort of contemporary-lite character. Afternoon cookies and wine are usually on offer, and the inn will also lend you bikes, although being right on the plaza you might not need them.

Even more luxury, tranquility, and contemporary style can be found at the even more expensive **DuChamp Hotel** (421 Foss St., Healdsburg, 707/431-1300 or 800/431-9341, www.duchamphotel.com, $350-425), a short walk from the plaza. Where the Hotel Healdsburg sometimes feels like it's trying a bit too hard to be hip, the DuChamp feels effortlessly chic, from the low-key minimalism of the six pool- and creek-side villas. There's every luxury amenity you can imagine and a few you can't, such as a 50-foot lap pool, private terraces, and its private-label champagne (made by Iron Horse Vineyards). Private tastings can also be arranged at the nearby **DuChamp Estate Winery** (280 Chiquita Rd., 707/433-6665, www.duchampwinery.com, 10am-3pm daily by appointment, tasting $10), which makes only syrah.

A few Victorians offer some healthy competition to the high-end modern newcomers, not least the **Honor Mansion** (891 Grove St., Healdsburg, 707/433-4277 or 800/554-4667, www.honormansion.com, $240-400). At this gloriously indulgent establishment, the unusual antiques and period architectural features do the talking without an excess of applied frills, giving some rooms at the self-styled "resort inn" an almost artistic feel. The 13 rooms and suites don't come cheap, but do come with all amenities, including CD players and VCRs, as well as some fun features ranging from double-headed showers and ornate four-poster beds to private patios and giant fireplaces. There's even a two-story suite inside an old Victorian water tower. The three acres of verdant grounds contain a swimming pool, a koi pond, bocce and tennis courts, and a croquet lawn. The two- or three-course breakfast can be enjoyed out on the dining patio, weather permitting.

Camping

Lake Sonoma Recreation Area, at the northern end of Dry Creek Valley, is a tent-camping mecca, especially if you have a boat. There are more than 100 hike-in or boat-in primitive campsites along its 50 miles of shoreline, most of them on the Warm Springs arm of the lake. The most easily accessible on foot are the **Island View** or **Quicksilver Campgrounds,** though the heat and terrain make the 2.5-mile hikes to them fairly strenuous during the summer months.

Most of the campgrounds are small, with an average of about 10 tent sites. None have drinking water, but all have fire rings and chemical toilets. Apart from the usual wildlife warnings (look out for rattlesnakes, and ticks that carry Lyme disease), visitors should also keep an eye out for feral pigs, descendants of domestic pigs brought by early white settlers.

Also worth noting: Some campsites are located on lake areas designated for waterskiing, and the constant drone of powerboats and Jet Skis can spoil an otherwise idyllic scene. More peace and quiet can be found near parts of the lake designated as wake-free zones (marked on the free map available at the visitors center). Island View is the quieter of the two most accessible hike-in campgrounds.

Reservations cost $14 during the summer months (877/444-6777, www.recreation.org). Even with a reservation, all backcountry campers must first get a permit from the hard-to-miss **visitors center** (3333 Skaggs Springs Rd., Geyserville, 707/431-4533), which also has trail maps. A minimum two-night stay is required on weekends during the summer season, and on holiday weekends the minimum is three nights. If you are staying at Yorty Creek, you must still stop by the visitors center despite booking online. There you will pick up a parking pass as well as the gate code, which comes in handy after it is locked at 5pm.

For car campers, there's just one developed drive-in campground: **Liberty Glen** (877/444-6777, www.recreation.org). About a mile across the bridge from the visitors center, it has 95 sites for tents and RVs (no electrical hookups) that cost $16. Worth noting is that during the summer the gates to the site are closed to cars at 10pm, so don't plan on any late-night reveling.

FOOD

With Dry Creek largely devoid of shops and restaurants, it is left to Healdsburg to supply most of the food. In keeping with the town's breezy atmosphere, the culinary scene is also fairly relaxed. Restaurants generally never seem to be trying as hard as in some other Wine Country destination towns. There are a few exceptions, and well-known regional chefs have had their eye on the place for some time. Some big-name establishments have taken hold here, like Manzanita, with input from Bizou in San Francisco, but they lack the big-city attitude (and, reportedly, the polished big-city service). Dinner reservations, though usually not needed, are nearly always recommended, especially in summer.

Fine Dining

While nothing can replace the longtime favorite and Michelin-starred Cyrus, which closed at the end of 2012, ◖ **Spoonbar** (219 Healdsburg Ave., 707/433-7222, http://spoonbar.com, noon-3:30pm and 5pm-9:30pm Sun.-Thurs., noon-3:30pm and 5pm-10pm Fri.-Sat., $23) tries hard. The high-ceilinged, concrete, wood and glass dining room excels at minimalism. In fact, the warehouse-like dining room, which opens out to bustling Healdsburg Avenue, almost feels casual and even slightly cafeteria-like. But what comes out of the kitchen is a far cry from a high school lunch tray. Instead, servers carry out plates of slow-cooked pork belly, braised clams and mussels, and Cornish game hen roulade. Matching the sophisticated entrées, small plates of raw and cured fish, and snacks such as crispy rock shrimp and seeded granola is a wine list that ranges from local to European and a cocktail menu that masterfully combines fresh ingredients with boutique spirits. For such elegant food, the prices are particularly low, and the corkage fee is especially generous: free for any two bottles from the Dry Creek, Russian River, and Alexander Valleys, and $15 otherwise.

It's no surprise that almost half the wines available at **Zin Restaurant** (344 Center St., Healdsburg, 707/473-0946, www.zinrestaurant.com, lunch 11:30am-2pm Mon.-Fri., dinner from 5:30pm daily, dinner entrées $17-28) are zinfandels. More surprising is that chef Jeff Mall manages to match many of the dishes on the menu to one style of the wine or another, highlighting just how flexible the humble zinfandel grape really is. Of course, you don't need to be a zinfandel lover to enjoy the postindustrial interior, with its concrete walls and exposed beams, or the elegantly understated but exquisitely executed dishes made with seasonal local produce. Wines from all northern Sonoma regions are represented, and in addition to the reasonably priced main courses there are cheaper blue plate specials on many days of the week, depending on what's available down on the farm.

Bistro Ralph (109 Plaza St., Healdsburg, 707/433-1380, 11:30am-close Mon.-Sat., brunch 10am-3pm Sun., dinner entrées $15-29) is everything a cozy local bistro should be, with whitewashed brick walls, white-clothed tables, and giant plates of cheap fries. Owner Ralph Tingle kicked off Healdsburg's culinary resurgence with this bistro in the early 1990s, and it still serves sophisticated Cal-Ital food in a relaxed, if cramped, environment right across from the leafy plaza. Dinner can get pricey, but lunch remains a relative bargain.

The big red barn housing **Barndiva** (231 Center St., Healdsburg, 707/431-0100, www. barndiva.com, lunch noon-2:30pm Wed.-Sat., dinner 5:30pm-9pm Wed.-Thurs. and Sun., 5:30pm-10pm Fri.-Sat., brunch 11am-2pm Sun., dinner entrées $12-40) looks very Wine Country from the outside but inside is more Manhattan. This being a rural part of the world, the clientele doesn't quite match the contemporary interior, but it's still a fun and unusual scene. Like the best Wine Country restaurants, the food is French inspired but aims to reflect the *terroir* of the place. Ingredients are for the most part locally sourced and are made into such specialties as caramelized day boat scallops, bacon-wrapped pork tenderloin, and braised and roasted rabbit. The wine list is likewise largely local, with the occasional French and Italian vintages thrown in. Keeping up with the times (and its Manhattan vibe), Barndiva also has an impressive cocktail menu that in the parlance of the day is "retro-fresh."

Another newcomer to the small-plate phenomenon is **Willi's Seafood and Raw Bar** (403 Healdsburg Ave., Healdsburg, 707/433-9191, 11:30am-9pm Sun.-Thurs., 11:30am-10pm Fri.-Sat., small plates $8-13), a few blocks north of the plaza. This is a sister establishment to the popular Willi's Wine Bar (4404 Old Redwood Hwy., just south of River Rd., Santa Rosa, 707/526-3096, 11:30am-9:30pm Tues.-Thurs., 11:30am-10pm Fri.-Sat., 5pm-9:30pm Sun.-Mon., $7-15), just south of Healdsburg, and suffers from the same pleasant problem—there are just too many of the small plates of food to choose from. Most are under $10, so just try them all if you're peckish. There are also plenty of oysters, ceviche, and steamers to go around a group cocktail hour. This is also the place to experiment with food and wine pairing, particularly as most wines are available by the glass or half bottle. Although the decoration in the dining room is straight from Cuba, the inspiration for the food seems to come from all over the world.

If you want a Victorian setting for dinner, there is probably no better option than the restaurant at **Madrona Manor** (1001 Westside Rd., Healdsburg, 707/433-4321, 6pm-9pm Wed.-Sun.) just outside Healdsburg. Eating here is as much about the sumptuous five-room Victorian setting and candlelit table decorations as the food, though the very expensive and stylish modern cuisine gets rave reviews and has earned a Michelin star every year since 2008. The prix fixe menu is divided by themes such as crisp, smooth, meaty, and sweet and costs $91 for five courses. Wine pairing is an extra $68.

Casual Dining

Although Healdsburg may not be the fine dining destination of Yountville or St. Helena, its real strength lies in its mid-range restaurants that are casual, affordable, and excellent. All serve menus that are farm-to-table, and are executed with the skill of a seasoned chef.

Unpretentious and delicious Italian small plates, pizza, and pastas along with an energetic yet intimate vibe have made **Scopa** (109A Plaza St., Healdsburg, 707/433-5282, www.scopa-healdsburg.com, 5:30pm-10pm daily, $17) wildly popular since it was opened in 2008 by the former chef of Geyserville's award-winning Santi restaurant. Antipasti dishes like grilled calamari and Venetian-style sardines won't necessarily win awards for inventiveness but have won accolades for perfect execution and very reasonable prices. Main courses include pizzas, pastas, and simple meat dishes that exude the same rustic yet gourmet quality, and the wine list offers just as many regional Italian wines as northern Sonoma options. Being so popular makes securing one of the tables wedged into the long, narrow, industrial-looking space a challenge, however, so consider eating at the small bar instead.

Even more casual is Scopa's sister restaurant, **Campo Fina** (330 Healdsburg Ave., Healdsburg, 707/395-4640, www.campofina.com, 11:30am-10pm daily, $15), which serves everything from oysters on the half shell to antipasti plates to paninis to main courses like breaded pork loin. The small interior is cozy on a rainy afternoon, but the larger semi-covered patio is where you want to be. Bocce ball courts and the wood oven, from which come some of the best thin-crust pizzas in the Bay Area, compete for space with crowded tables of relaxed diners happy to stay put. Thankfully, the full bar keeps patrons' thirst quenched and the plentiful snack menu, reasonably full.

Making a departure from the en vogue Italian fare of Healdsburg is **Mateo's Cocina Latina** (214 Healdsburg Ave., Healdsburg, 707/433-1520, www.mateoscocinalatina.com, 11:30am-9pm Sun.-Tues. and Thurs., 11:30am-10:30pm Fri.-Sat., $12-23). Despite his seasoned pedigree at such Bay Area restaurants as Masa's and Dry Creek Kitchen, chef Mateo Granados began his solo career selling Yucatan tamales at the farmers markets. Soon he had a serious following, and eventually a restaurant where he still sells his signature tamales alongside other mouth-watering specialties such as slow-roasted suckling pig and mussels served with pork chorizo and a tomato-habanero sauce, all inspired from his childhood in the Yucatan. To wash down the spicy fare, Granados has put together a well-balanced drink menu of half a dozen microbrews, wines from the Russian and Dry Creek Valleys, and a whole host of tequila-inspired cocktails. True aficionados will swoon over the range of tequilas, reserve anejo tequilas, and mezcals available.

If you are craving a burger, then the place to go is the spacious **Healdsburg Bar & Grill** (245 Healdsburg Ave., Healdsburg, 707/433-3333, www.healdsburgbarandgrill.com, 11:30am-9pm daily, $8-12), with as many tables inside its saloon-style interior as outside on its shady patio. As its name and the giant outdoor barbecues suggest, this is paradise for lovers of big hunks of char-grilled meat, and they form the basis of the classic pub menu. There's a half-decent wine list and a wide variety of carefully crafted cocktails.

There's more saloon-style dining and food just around the corner at the **Bear Republic Brewing Company** (345 Healdsburg Ave., Healdsburg, 707/433-2337, www.bearrepublic.com, 11:30am-9pm Sun.-Thurs., 11:30am-9:30pm Fri.-Sat., $9-18), right behind the Hotel Healdsburg. The many microbrews are the main attraction, however, and can be enjoyed right in the shadow of stainless steel brewing tanks on the patio outside.

The southwest corner of Healdsburg's plaza is dominated by the bustling **Oakville Grocery** (124 Matheson St., Healdsburg, 707/433-3200, www.oakvillegrocery.com, 9:30am-5pm daily). Go there for deli food with that added Wine

Country flair (and price) to stock up for a picnic or to eat at one of the shaded tables on the large patio overlooking the plaza.

Adding some European flair to the deli scene is the **Costeaux French Bakery & Café** (417 Healdsburg Ave., Healdsburg, 707/433-1913, www.costeaux.com, 7am-4pm Mon.-Thurs., 7am-5pm Fri.-Sat., 7am-1pm Sun.). It sells the usual crusty bread and other bakery fare together with some tasty breakfasts and deli lunches that can be enjoyed on the big patio next to the sidewalk, a few blocks north of the plaza and considerably calmer than Oakville's. It also offers a light dinner and wine on Friday and Saturday evenings. Filling breakfasts and decadent pastries are the specialty of the **Downtown Bakery & Creamery** (308A Center St., Healdsburg, 707/431-2719, www. downtownbakery.net, 6am-5:30pm Mon.-Fri., 7:30am-5pm Sat., 7am-4pm Sun.), on the south side of the plaza.

During the summer, stake out a riverfront table at **Zazu on the River** (52 Front St., Healdsburg, 707/569-0171, www.zazurestaurant.com, 11:30am-6pm Fri.-Sun., summer only, $10), the Healdsburg outpost to the popular farm-to-table restaurant, Zazu, in Sebastopol. Here, the shack (and indeed it is a riverfront shack, although dressed up in shabby-chic) specializes in pork sandwiches, including an over-the-top BLT, a pulled pork, and a Black Pig salami sandwich. Vegetarians can also find something they might like with the grilled fontina sandwich that comes with apple cider slaw. Bocce ball courts and wines by the glass by the Davis Family Vineyards, which also shares the waterfront, make eating here a full afternoon activity.

Picnic Supplies

The **Oakville Grocery** (124 Matheson St., Healdsburg, 707/433-3200, 9:30am-5pm daily) is also picnic central, and it has just about everything, including wine, needed for either a gourmet alfresco feast or just some simple bread and cheese. Don't forget the sandwiches and bread available at the **Costeaux French Bakery & Café** (417 Healdsburg Ave., Healdsburg,

707/433-1913, www.costeaux.com, 7am-4pm Mon.-Thurs., 7am-5pm Fri.-Sat., 7am-1pm Sun.) and at the **Downtown Bakery & Creamery** (308A Center St., Healdsburg, 707/431-2719, www.downtownbakery.net, 6am-5:30pm Mon.-Fri., 7:30am-5pm Sat., 7am-4pm Sun.).

Artisanal cheeses from all over the world, together with bread and other potential picnic fare, is available nearby at **The Cheese Shop** (423 Center St., Healdsburg, 707/433-4998, www.sharpandnutty.com, 11am-6pm Mon.-Sat.). Also ask about cheese tastings and guest lectures by local cheese makers.

If you're heading up to the Alexander Valley or Dry Creek Valley, **Big John's Market** (1345 Healdsburg Ave., just north of W. Dry Creek Rd., Healdsburg, 707/433-7151, www.bigjohnsmarket.com, 7am-8pm daily), a bakery, deli, and grocery store all in one, is on the way.

Once in the Dry Creek Valley there's not many options, but one is the **Dry Creek General Store** (3495 Dry Creek Rd., Healdsburg, 707/433-4171, http://drycreek-generalstore1881.com, 6:30am-5:30pm Mon.-Sat., 7am-5:30pm Sun.), which has existed in some form or another since the 1880s and continues to supply modern-day picnickers and peckish winery employees with deli sandwiches and groceries. Another spot is **Preston Vineyards** (9282 W. Dry Creek Rd., Healdsburg, 707/433-3372, www.prestonvineyards.com, 11am-4:30pm daily), which sells artisan bread baked on-site and vegetables from the organic garden, along with other locally crafted picnic supplies.

Farmers Market

If you're after something really fresh, the **Healdsburg Farmers Market** is held 9am-noon Saturday mornings May-November in the parking lot of the Plaza Park (North St. and Vine St.), a few blocks west of the plaza itself. Those in the know say it's one of the best farmers markets in this part of Sonoma. On Wednesday evenings, 4pm-6:30pm June-October, the market sets up on the main plaza downtown.

INFORMATION AND SERVICES

As befitting such a desirable destination, the **Healdsburg Chamber of Commerce and Visitors Bureau** (217 Healdsburg Ave., Healdsburg, 707/433-6935, www.healdsburg.com, 9am-5pm Mon.-Fri., 9am-3pm Sat., 10am-2pm Sun.) is centrally located, just off U.S. Highway 101 when you come into town on Healdsburg Avenue. The friendly staff will be happy to load you up with maps, brochures, and helpful tips.

More comprehensive information about the wines and the winemakers of the Dry Creek Valley is available from the **Winegrowers of Dry Creek Valley** (707/433-3031, www.wdcv. com). The association does a sterling job of ensuring the area's wineries get national attention and organizes the sell-out Passport to Dry Creek Valley weekend event, a two-day party involving nearly all valley wineries on the last weekend in April.

For a bit of local flavor, the *Healdsburg Tribune* (www.sonomawest.com) is published every Thursday. If you need to mail a letter, the folks at the **post office** at 160 Foss Creek Circle will be happy to oblige. And for any aches and pains, the **Healdsburg District Hospital** (1375 University Ave., Healdsburg, 707/431-6300) has a 24-hour emergency room. But if all you want to do is grab some cash, there is a **Bank of American** at 502 Healdsburg Avenue, and a **Wells Fargo** at 999 Vine Street.

While cell phone reception is reliable in town, don't expect it to be once you start venturing onto Healdsburg's back roads. But unlike the rest of the region, getting online in Healdsburg is fairly easy. Most hotels and cafés offer access, for free or at a price, and the plaza has free Wi-Fi service set up by the city.

GETTING THERE AND AROUND
By Car

Healdsburg is an easy destination as it sits on U.S. Highway 101, 14 miles north of Santa Rosa. To reach downtown Healdsburg, take exit 503 (Central Healdsburg exit). From Guerneville just continue east on River Road. You'll pass through Forestville and Fulton before hitting 101, where you will turn north. If you're coming from Calistoga, continue north on Highway 128 for 17.4 miles. At Jimtown it will intersect with Alexander Valley Road. To go to Healdsburg, stay straight on Alexander Valley Road as Highway 128 turns right, heading north to Geyserville. After 3.3 miles, you'll turn left onto Healdsburg Avenue, which will take you into the heart of Healdsburg. Navigating the countryside couldn't be easier. The majority of wineries are either on Dry Creek Road or West Dry Creek Road; both run parallel to each other, straddling the creek. Making it even easier, Dry Creek Road runs through the heart of downtown Healdsburg.

By Bike

The Dry Creek Valley is great to navigate by bike. Many hotels now offer loaner bikes, but bikes can also be rented at **Wine Country Bikes** (61 Front St., Healdsburg, 866/922-4537, www. winecountrybikes.com, 9am-5pm daily). Road bikes, tandem bikes, and hybrids are available for $35-125 per day. Slightly cheaper rentals can be found at the Quonset hut that houses **Spoke Folk Cyclery** (201 Center St., Healdsburg, 707/433-7171, www.spokefolk.com, 10am-6pm Mon.-Fri., 10am-5pm Sat.-Sun.), where you can rent a bike for $50 per day.

Alexander Valley

Most people speeding north on the freeway might glimpse vineyards as they cruise past the Alexander Valley. Some might even stop to visit some of the valley's biggest wineries that are close to off-ramps. Finding the true character of this part of the Wine Country and many of its smaller wineries requires a little more time navigating Highway 128, however. The road runs from Geyserville through some rather alarming 90-degree bends and down into the rustic Chalk Hill and Knights Valley appellations. From there it's only a short drive to Calistoga at the northern end of the Napa Valley.

The 20-mile-long Alexander Valley stretches from Healdsburg in the south to the cow town of Cloverdale in the north. In between there is only one town of note: the hamlet of **Geyserville,** which for years has been destined to become the next big Wine Country resort town, only to stubbornly remain its old sleepy self, despite the recent additions of several tasting rooms and two excellent restaurants. Geyserville wasn't always so quiet. Back in the late 1800s the nearby geysers drew visitors from far and wide, and the resulting influx of money helped build the town's grand Victorian homes. Now the only signs of the area's underground hot water supply are the clouds of steam sometimes visible from the 19 geothermal plants in the hills east of Geyserville (an area known simply as The Geysers). The area is one of the world's largest geothermal energy sources.

As with many other parts of the Wine Country, this valley was once dominated by cattle pasture and fruit orchards. The cows still hold sway around **Cloverdale** and farther north, where dairies are still more common than wineries, but the vineyards are spreading. Cloverdale marks the end of Northern California's most famous wine regions and

Alexander Valley has a rustic charm.

the beginning of the new frontier of winemaking in Mendocino County, Hopland, and the Anderson Valley, only short drives away.

The Wines

The **Alexander Valley** is the northernmost appellation in Sonoma and also one of the hottest, despite the fact that the Russian River floodplain is wide enough to allow some of the more persistent fog to creep this far north on summer nights. Summer temperatures in Geyserville can often be 10 degrees higher than in Healdsburg just a few miles south. Cloverdale is hotter still.

With the ripening power of the sun and heat, together with the rich alluvial soils deposited by the Russian River over millions of years, it's relatively easy to guess what style of wine can be made here—big and opulent. Indeed, Alexander Valley cabernets have a softness and suppleness that they attain in few other places. There was good reason why the cabernet specialist Silver Oak Cellars chose this valley in 1993 for its first vineyard and winery outside the Napa Valley. Sometimes the wines can get a little too soft and undistinguished. In general, however, Alexander Valley cabernets are characterized by soft tannins and lush fruit with hints of dark chocolate, making them perhaps the easiest drinking in California, if not necessarily the most complex or long-lived. Other varietals grown here include chardonnay, which ripens easily to make rich and flavorful wines, along with merlot, zinfandel, and increasing quantities of syrah and sangiovese. The appellation expanded in 1990 to include the vineyards creeping up the hillsides, particularly on the eastern side of the valley where the mountains climb to more than 2,500 feet. As growers experiment with the cooler hillside vineyards, subtler styles of wine are being created than the blockbusters from the fertile, sun-drenched valley floor.

At the southern end of Alexander Valley, east of Santa Rosa, is the **Chalk Hill** appellation, which derives its name from soils that contain chalk-like volcanic ash, similar to those at the northern end of the Napa Valley. It's directly in the path of the cooler Russian River Valley air and is mostly contained within the easternmost part of the Russian River appellation. The few wineries here are perhaps best known for some tangy chardonnays.

Sandwiched between the eastern parts of Chalk Hill and Alexander Valley, with the border of Napa County to the west, is the **Knights Valley** appellation, a primarily grape-growing region with just a couple of small wineries. Millions of years ago the Russian River ran down the Alexander Valley, through Knights Valley, and into the Napa Valley, depositing gravelly soils ideal for growing grapes. Knights Valley soils are also part volcanic, deposited during the volcanic eruptions that eventually changed the course of the river westward to its present-day path past Healdsburg and Guerneville to the ocean. Completely shielded from the cool ocean air, Knights Valley is the hottest of Sonoma's appellations, providing ideal conditions for sauvignon blanc and cabernet sauvignon. Look for the Knights Valley appellation in the wines from Napa Valley's Beringer Vineyards, which owns about half the vineyards here.

WINERIES

From the north end of the valley at the historic Asti winery, home of the Italian-Swiss Colony (no longer open to the public), the Alexander Valley stretches southeast, past Healdsburg, down to the Chalk Hill Road. Most major wineries are on Geyserville Avenue, which runs parallel to the freeway between Healdsburg and Cloverdale, and on Highway 128, which runs southeast from Geyserville.

PASTORI

One of the northernmost wineries open to the public is also one of the quirkiest and among the smallest in the valley. The primitive, cinder-block tasting room of **Pastori** (23189 Geyserville Ave., Cloverdale, 707/857-3418, open whenever there's someone there, usually 9am-5pm daily, free tasting), squeezed into one of the old warehouses at the side of the road,

CALIFORNIA'S LITTLE PIEDMONT

It is not by chance or climate alone that there is a preponderance of Italian names among the wineries of the Dry Creek and Alexander Valleys. In the 1880s an Italian immigrant named **Andrea Sbarboro,** a financier by trade, had the bright idea of starting a sort of grape-growing cooperative, or colony, to provide worthwhile work and lodging to the many other Italians arriving by the boatload in San Francisco.

He and his financial backers, including several Swiss businessmen, bought about 1,500 acres of land just south of Cloverdale and called the place Asti, after the town in the Piedmont region of Italy that was (and still is) famous for its wines. The Italian-Swiss Agricultural Colony, later shortened to Italian-Swiss Colony, was born.

The idea was that workers recruited to work there contributed a small portion of their salary each month in exchange for food and lodging, and to buy shares in the venture, thus making some money for Sbarboro and giving workers a sense of ownership. Things didn't go quite to plan. Workers were suspicious of Sbarboro's financial intentions and didn't want to share the risk. The falling price of grapes soon meant the colony had to build its own winery to remain viable. But the colony and its winery eventually became a huge success. By the turn of the 20th

century it was both profitable and said to be the biggest producer of table wine in California. By 1910 it was making more than 14 million gallons of wine per year.

Early generations of many local wine families came to work at the colony. Edoardo and Angela Seghesio met there, and Ed went on to create the Seghesio Family Vineyards in the early 1900s, for example. Ferrari, Martini, and Rossi are other Italian names once associated with the colony that have been influential in the local wine world over the last century. Pietro Rossi was Sbarboro's first winemaker, and the Rossi family bought the winery during Prohibition, keeping it alive as the Asti Grape Products Company before reentering the commercial wine business after repeal. It was eventually sold in the 1940s, and in the 1960s the historic winery became the second most visited attraction in California after Disneyland. After changing hands a few more times it was finally bought by Fosters Wine Estates in 1988.

The old winery at Asti has been well preserved, even after Fosters invested in new winemaking equipment for its Souverain and Cellar No. 8 brands that are made there today. The winery was briefly opened for tours and tastings in 2009, but sadly, it shut its doors once more to the public in 2012.

---

is a throwback to the old days of winemaking when locals would come and fill up their jugs for a couple of bucks.

Frank Pastori is one of Sonoma's old-timers, and his family has been making wine here since the early 1900s. If the tasting room is open at all (it seems to have no regular hours), he's likely to be the only one there and will happily spin yarns about the good old days of winemaking and perhaps try to convince you that white wine is "not real wine." He offers good old prices for his zinfandel wine and port, and jug wines (bring your own jug). Don't expect much more than basic table wines, but do expect an unusual Wine Country experience.

SILVER OAK CELLARS

On just the other side of the freeway from Pastori is a temple for red-wine lovers, the Sonoma outpost of **Silver Oak Cellars** (24625 Chianti Rd., Geyserville, 707/942-7082, www. silveroak.com, 10am-5pm Mon.-Sat., 11am-5pm Sun., tasting $10), which makes just one wine—cabernet sauvignon. If you like cabernet, you'll undoubtedly like Silver Oak's powerful, velvety version that some say has an unusual aroma from being aged for years in only American oak barrels. You might not like the price, however.

The Alexander Valley cabernet is $70 per bottle, and the Napa version made at the

Oakville winery is over $100. Both facilities have legions of die-hard fans that line up each year to buy the new release, despite its ready availability, a testament to the loyalty of the Silver Oak crowd and the quality of the wine. Some less adoring fans, however, think this cult status makes the wines more expensive than they perhaps deserve to be. Not surprisingly, there's a $10 tasting fee, although you can keep the glass. Another option for $10 is to take the tour offered weekdays only at 1pm, which culminates in a tasting of both Silver Oak wines and a Napa Valley merlot from sister winery **Twomey** (1183 Dunaweal Ln., Calistoga, 707/942-2489, www.twomey.com, 10am-5pm Mon.-Sat., 11am-5pm Sun, tasting $10)—but no free glass. You might also be able to taste the more moderately priced port that's only available at the winery.

GEYSER PEAK WINERY

Just down Chianti Road from Silver Oak is the giant ivy-clad home of one of the region's biggest wineries. **Geyser Peak Winery** (22281 Chianti Rd., Geyserville, 707/857-2500 or 800/255-9463, www.geyserpeakwinery.com, 10am-5pm daily, tasting $10-15) turns out hundreds of thousands of cases of mediocre wines and a few very good ones.

There has been a winery on the site since 1880, but the Geyser Peak name dates from 1911. Today, a dizzying selection of wines makes up the 350,000-case production, including cabernet, merlot, zinfandel, shiraz, sauvignon blanc, and chardonnay, nearly all available as regular, reserve, and vineyard-designate wines. Expect to see more than two dozen wines on the tasting list. The cheaper wines in particular can be a good value, but the winery is perhaps best known for its concentrated Alexander Valley cabernets and red blends that compared well with some of the best in the valley.

The giant tasting room is big enough to cope with the vast number of wines and crowds but has an understandably corporate vibe, and you won't necessarily learn much about the wines from the inexperienced staff. Five of the lower-end wines can be tasted for $10, while four of the better single-vineyard wines can be tried upstairs in the more relaxing reserve tasting room overlooking the barrel room for $15. Friday-Sunday, $5 more gets you a tour of the historic cellars, while for another $15 you can pair your reserve flight with cheese. Without the tour, cheese pairing costs $25, and all are appointment only.

FRANCIS FORD COPPOLA WINERY

You have to give "Francis," as he is known by all the staff here, credit; he isn't trying to bill the **Francis Ford Coppola Winery** (300 Via Archimedes, Geyserville, 707/857-1400, www.franciscoppolawinery.com, 11am-6pm daily, tasting $10-15) something it is not. Called a "Wine Wonderland," the winery has a concierge desk, restaurant, full bar, a gift store selling a surprisingly wide variety of tableware, bocce ball, and a pool, complete with *cabines* to rent for the day and a poolside café. In fact, only the acres of grapevines surrounding the buildings indicate that this is a winery, that and the tasting bar, but even that is housed inside a museum of memorabilia of Coppola's different films. Still, flights are cheap, and even complimentary for a taste of two less expensive table wines, which is another reason to give Francis some credit.

It may be easy to deride the winery's theme park-like atmosphere. When asked why a *pool,* the young woman at the front desk happily replied that Francis wanted his next winery to be a place where the whole family could spend the day and have fun. It seems hard to argue his intention, particularly as the quality of what is here is fairly high and not outrageously priced. The restaurant, **Rustic** (11am-9pm, $20), serves a mash-up of high-quality food from ribs to Neapolitan-style pizzas to specialties like lamb Marrakesh. Seating is either on the back veranda, which overlooks the quiet of the valley or inside the high-beamed dining room. Nearby, the tasting room/Coppola museum pours flights and glasses of Coppola's mid-range wines. You won't find his more elegant, handcrafted Inglenook wines here, but

NORTHERN SONOMA

© ELIZABETH LINHART VENEMAN

cabines at Francis Ford Coppola Winery

something perfect for a picnic or a casual dinner back home. And for those who want something stiffer for their Wine Country getaway, a backlit bar shakes, stirs, and serves well-made cocktails.

If you do have squirrelly kids in tow, or simply want to soak in the Alexander Valley rays, you can jump in the pool or relax on chaise lounges nearby. The **pool** is open 11am-6pm daily in the summer and Friday-Sunday in the fall and spring. Passes cost $20 for adults and $10 for children. *Cabines* (pronounced kab-eens) with private showers and a place to keep your clothes are available for rent. The hefty price ($125/day) does include four pool passes, use of four towels and chaise lounges, and four flights of wine. For something other than alcohol, the **Poolside Café** serves panini, salads, and gelato, delivered right to your lounge chair. So, no outside food, please.

Coppola may be trying to move his Napa Valley operation further into the territory of fine wine and historical significance when he rebranded Rubicon Inglenook, but the new Francis Ford Coppola makes no bones about it: This is the place for guilt-free family fun, even if the wines themselves take a backseat.

TRENTADUE WINERY

In keeping with the Tuscan heritage of the founding family, **Trentadue Winery** (19170 Geyserville Ave., Geyserville, 707/433-3104 or 888/332-3032, www.trentadue.com, 10am-5pm daily, tasting $10-15) was one of the first wineries in this region to grow sangiovese grapes and now produces a cluster of sangiovese-based wines. The flagship La Storia Cuvée 32 wine (*trentadue* is Italian for the number 32) is a super-Tuscan style blend of sangiovese, merlot, and cabernet. By contrast, zinfandel dominates the Old Patch Red blend, named for a 100-year-old block of zinfandel vines, which is very affordable at under $15.

Trentadue also makes some of the best-value wines in the valley. The limited-production La Storia wines regularly score over 90 points in the press yet start at well under $30. The cheaper Trentadue wines are rarely over $20.

Many of the wines are produced in small lots, however, so they sell out quickly. About one-fifth of the winery's 20,000-case production is merlot, but sauvignon blanc, viognier, zinfandel, cabernet, petite sirah, and a sparkling wine are also made here. To take in the beautiful estate, book a seat on the gondola tour offered every day by appointment ($20). This is a particular treat during harvest time.

SIMI WINERY

Brothers Pietro and Giuseppe Simi came from Tuscany in the 1860s and set themselves up as winemakers and traders in San Francisco before moving to the current site of **Simi Winery** (16275 Healdsburg Ave., Healdsburg, 800/746-4880, www.simiwinery.com, 10am-5pm daily, tasting $10), just north of Healdsburg, in 1881. In its heyday, the winery boasted Sonoma's first public tasting room—a 25,000-gallon redwood tank set up at the side of the road. It was evidently a roaring success, but the current tasting room is a more modern affair inside the historic stone cellar building, which dates from the late 1800s.

The winery is best known for its chardonnay, sourced from the Russian River Valley, and its cabernets, from the Alexander Valley, both of which garner consistently good reviews. Other wines in the portfolio include sauvignon blanc, pinot noir, and merlot sourced from a variety of vineyards in Sonoma County. Tastings are $10, and for the same price you can also get an informative tour of the gardens, which include a stand of redwood trees planted by Isabelle Simi. Tours followed by a tasting are offered twice daily at 11am and 2pm.

STRYKER SONOMA WINERY

The name is appropriate considering the new **Stryker Sonoma Winery** (5110 Hwy. 128, Geyserville, 707/433-1944 or 800/433-1944, www.strykersonoma.com, 10:30am-5pm daily, tasting $10-20) is housed in one of the most striking buildings in the Alexander Valley, a contemporary glass, wood, and concrete structure that won an architectural award when it was completed in 2002. The huge glass-walled tasting room overlooks 26 acres of estate vineyards, from which are made cabernet, merlot, zinfandel, semillon, and chardonnay plus some interesting blends.

The cabernets are the standouts and range from the intense version from the Monte Rosso vineyard high in the Mayacamas Mountains farther south to the plush estate version, which is a fine example of an Alexander Valley cab. There are also other cabernets from the Knights Valley and Dry Creek Valley. Many are only available in the tasting room. Also worth trying are the Alexander zinfandels and one of the more unusual reds, the inky and pungent petit verdot, which is normally used as a blending grape in Bordeaux-style wines. The portfolio of whites is tiny, by contrast, but includes a couple of nice Russian River chardonnays and a chardonnay-semillon blend with an enticing mix of citrus and tropical fruit flavors.

ROBERT YOUNG ESTATE WINERY

Chardonnay dominates among the 14 varietals grown on the 320 acres of Alexander Valley vineyards owned by the **Robert Young Winery** (4960 Red Winery Rd., Geyserville, 707/4331-4811, www.ryew.com, 10am-4:30pm daily, tasting $10), and a rich, full-bodied version of this varietal is what the winery is best known for. In fact, there is a Robert Young clone of the chardonnay grape. Much of the rest of the estate is planted with merlot and cabernet, both of which go into the flagship Scion blend.

The Young family first settled this part of the world in 1858, but it was Robert Young who planted grapes here in the 1960s, slowly transforming what had been prune orchards and grazing land into hundreds of acres of vineyards, planting the very first cabernet sauvignon vines in the valley in 1963, and chardonnay in 1967. Robert died in 2009 at the ripe old age of 91, but there are still plenty of other Youngs who call the beautiful estate home, including Fred Young, who established the winemaking operations, and Jim Young, who is the vineyard manager.

MEDLOCK AMES

Make sure to get detailed directions to **Medlock Ames** (13414 Chalk Hill Rd., Healdsburg, 707/431-8845, www.medlockames.com, 10am-4:30pm daily, tasting $15), about a mile off the Chalk Hill Road down what seems like an endless dirt driveway. Take a wrong turn and you might end up in a neighbor's driveway. Take the right turn and you'll find the striking stone and steel winery building surrounded by manicured lawns, organic vineyards, and perhaps some stray wildlife. Medlock Ames was started by two 30-something friends, Ames Morrison and Chris Medlock James, who had money to invest and a passion for the Wine Country lifestyle. The winery now makes limited-production merlot, cabernet, and chardonnay from the 55 acres of organic vineyard.

Tasting four current-release wines is $10, but for $20 you can jump up to the library wine tasting, which is likely to include a vertical cabernet tasting. Food pairing is also available for $20 and includes a cheese and charcuterie plate plus some specialty inspired by the bounty of the organic gardens outside. If you are inspired to tour the ranch with its variety of vineyards and gardens, make an appointment; it costs $35.

WHITE OAK

At **White Oak** (7505 Hwy. 128, Healdsburg, 707/433-8429, www.whiteoakwinery.com, 10am-5pm daily, tasting $5), you'll find a wonderful combination of whimsy and wine. This Spanish mission-inspired winery complex is surrounded by green gardens dotted with fun sculptures. Beyond the gardens, estate vineyards grow grapes for Old Vine zinfandels and other fine wines. Go inside to taste some of those wines—the tasting list is small but prestigious. While white-wine drinkers enjoy the sauvignon blanc and chardonnay, big reds are the specialty of the house. Cabernet sauvignon and zinfandel lovers flock to White Oak for the fabulous regular releases and occasional special library selections. Tours at White Oak give participants a special look at wine tasting,

describing and illustrating the various components that make up a wine's fragrance.

◖ ALEXANDER VALLEY VINEYARDS

Alexander Valley Vineyards (8644 Hwy. 128, Healdsburg, 707/433-7209 or 800/888-7209, www.avvwine.com, 10am-5pm daily, free tasting) shares the name of the historic valley for good reason. In the 1960s the founders of the winery bought a large chunk of the original homestead once owned by Cyrus Alexander, the mountain man who became a ranch manager and finally a landowner credited with planting the valley's first vineyards in 1846.

Whether Alexander ever made wine from those grapes is not known, but today's vineyards provide the grapes for cabernet, merlot, chardonnay, and zinfandel that are made into two decadent blends, Temptation Zin and Redemption Zin. Other varietals include chardonnay, pinot noir, sangiovese, syrah, and viognier, together with some interesting red blends, including the flagship wine called Cyrus, a Bordeaux-style wine honoring the winery's namesake. While the wine routinely gets rave reviews, a 2008 vintage magnum sold for a record-breaking $215,000 at a Texas wine auction in 2013.

Historic sites pepper the current estate, including a wooden schoolhouse built by Alexander in 1853 and the Alexander family gravesite up the hill behind the winery. Educational tours of the expansive wine caves are available daily at 11am and 2pm and are complimentary. If you are just dying to pay something, private tours and tastings are by appointment and cost $10, and a cheese pairing tasting is available at 11am and 4pm daily April-August. Reservations must be made 24 hours in advance for the $25 pairing.

FIELD STONE WINERY

Built from stones unearthed during construction in 1977, the small **Field Stone Winery** (10075 Hwy. 128, Healdsburg, 707/433-7266 or 800/544-7273, www.fieldstonewinery.com, 10am-5pm daily, tasting $10), cut into a dusty valley hillside, was one of the first of a wave

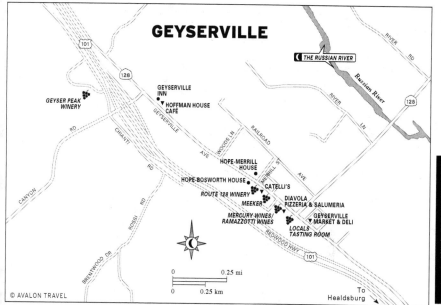

NORTHERN SONOMA

of modern underground wineries built in the Wine Country. Grapes from the 50 acres of estate vineyards, together with some from the Russian River Valley and Mendocino, go into the 10,000 cases of wine made each year. Reds include cabernet, merlot, sangiovese, and the winery's signature, petite sirah. Whites include a limited-production viognier, sauvignon blanc, chardonnay, and gewürztraminer. Some of the proceeds from the sale of the Convivio line of lower-priced wines are donated to a local clinic serving farm workers.

Oak trees shade two small picnic areas outside the small tasting room, sometimes shared with the local wild turkeys, and staff might be willing to take you on an impromptu tour if it's not too busy.

Geyserville Tasting Rooms

There isn't much of a downtown Geyserville; in fact, "downtown" means one historic block at the intersection of Geyserville Avenue and Highway 128. Nevertheless, the cozy spot is worth the short detour off the highway, as

seven wineries now fill the 19th-century buildings. An added bonus: The tasting rooms stay open later than almost anywhere else in Wine Country, making them a great end of the day destination.

MEEKER

The first to arrive, **Meeker** (21035 Geyserville Ave., Geyserville, 707/431-2148, www.meeker-wine.com, 10:30am-6pm, tasting $5) is known for its big reds, which is often code here for strong tannins with heavy fruit on the nose thrown together with unusual bits of white pepper, cola, coffee, and vanilla. For the modest fee, you'll taste what they have on hand, which is generally five wines that include zinfandel, cabernet, a Bordeaux blend, petite sirah, and merlot. While it is evident that proprietor Charley Meeker has his hand in everything related to winemaking, including selecting the grapes and creating (or resurrecting in the case of his Fossil blend) new Bordeaux-style blends, this is most (at least visibly) evident in the Winemaker's Handprint Merlot, in which every bottle is covered in painted hand prints of, you guessed it, Charley Meeker.

There is no doubt that the winery has a certain bombastic quality to it. Perhaps it comes from Charley's time as president of Metro-Goldwyn-Mayer in Los Angeles during the 1990s, or the winery's upstart early days in the mid-1980s when it was pouring wine, including one that was in *Wine Spectator*'s "100 Best Wines of the World," in a tipi. Yes, its first tasting room was a 40-foot-tall authentic Sioux tipi. Today, Meeker makes about 16,000 cases per year from grapes grown in Sonoma and Napa, and the tasting room has graduated to the historic 1903 Geyserville Bank. If you love big reds, make Meeker a stop on your way through the Alexander Valley, and even if you don't, it is worth it just to experience Charley's outsized approach to wine.

MERCURY WINES/RAMAZZOTTI WINES

For wines that don't take themselves quite so seriously, swing by the joint tasting room of **Mercury and Ramazzotti Wines** (21015 Geyserville Ave., Geyserville, 11am-6pm daily). Both wineries were started during the 2000s and have a wide selection of Alexander Valley whites and reds. **Mercury Wines** (707/857-9870, www.mercurywine.com, tasting $5) was started by winemaker Brad Beard, an Arizona native, and is named for the quicksilver mining history of the area. Its label and vibe, however, is pure pop-culture. The two standout wines are the Messenger, a cabernet blend, and the Heavy Metal, a petit verdot. Both are made in the European tradition, co-fermented, with big heavy fruit exemplifying the best big reds of the Alexander Valley. But Mercury is also a great place to taste. Beard's brother, Grady, is usually behind the counter and always up for some fun. If you are in the valley in March, be sure to stop by during Barrel Tasting when the back patio is open and Mercury's hotdog cart is dishing dogs to go with its wine. Either way, you'll be met at the door with lots of big dog kisses from the resident black lab. His name? Freddy, Freddy Mercury, of course!

While Beard may be a transplant from Phoenix, the **Ramazzotti** (707/814-0016, www.ramazzottiwines.com, tasting $5-10) clan grew up in the Alexander Valley and are second-generation Italian Americans, touching the Italian heritage of the area. You can see it reflected in the wines they make. While there is the standard chardonnay, cabernet franc, and grenache, there are also Italian varietals such as barberra and sangiovese, as well as unique Tuscan blends. All of their wines are co-fermented, giving the wines a particular depth and complexity of flavor. Neither winery sells bottles for more than $55, and most prices hover around the $30 mark; both wineries make less than 1,000 cases a year.

ROUTE 128 WINERY

At the far north end of "downtown" tucked to the side of Gigi's Antiques is the unassuming **Route 128 Winery** (21079 Geyserville Ave., Geyserville, 707/696-0004, www.route128winery.com, 11am-5pm Fri.-Sun., tasting $5). Here you'll also be greeted by a big black lab (this one's name is Ralph), and you'll taste wines that are unfiltered and co-fermented. There are fewer offerings here, as this winery is a "hobby gone awry," as owner and winemaker Pete Opatz likes to say. Opatz and his wife, Lorna, have been in the wine business for 30 years. Actually, Pete keeps his day job working in the Napa Valley, while Lorna runs the business side of the winery full time. She is the one likely to be pouring your wine during the three days the tasting room is open. The winery makes just 450 cases per year of viognier, zinfandel, syrah, and a couple of blends. The High-Five is a particular standout, but sells out quickly as only one barrel is made. Another unusual bottle is the Sweet Sarah, a syrah blend (with chardonnay concentrate) that is both sweet but with enough tannins to remind you that you are drinking a full-bodied red.

LOCALS TASTING ROOM

Meeker may be the first winery to set up shop on Geyserville Avenue, but **Locals Tasting Room** (Geyserville Ave. at Hwy. 128, Geyserville, 707/857-4900, www.tastelocalwine.com,

11am-6pm daily, free tasting) is the first wine cooperative in the state, and one of the few tasting rooms to offer complimentary tasting. This is because, with 60 or more wines open at any time, owner Carolyn Lewis says, people usually will find something they want to take home. And with good reason. Most of the wines sit at $20-40 and hail from northern Sonoma's boutique wineries. It is a broad mix of wineries representing wines from as far south as the Central Coast up to Mendocino and most points between. Local also has its own wine club incorporating most of the wineries represented here, making it one of the more varied and worthwhile clubs to join.

They include the Russian River region's **Eric Ross** winery as well as several small Dry Creek Valley producers that include **Peterson Winery, Arbios,** and **Praxis,** the Mendocino syrah specialist **Saracina,** and **Gunfighter,** which makes single-vineyard Dry Creek cabernet and zinfandel. The 2010 Eberle zinfandel is one of the stylish tasting room's most popular, as it best represents the region's signature varietal, complete with heavy, jammy fruit.

Wineries by Appointment
LANCASTER ESTATE
You might miss the turnoff from Highway 128 to Chalk Hill Road, but you won't miss the striking modern gates of the **Lancaster Estate** (15001 Chalk Hill Rd., Healdsburg, 707/433-8178, www.lancaster-estate.com, 10am-3pm Mon.-Sat. fall-spring, 10am-3pm daily in summer, tour and tasting $25). This small but exclusive maker of cabernet sauvignon offers a tour of the vineyards, state-of-the-art winemaking facility, and caves before retiring to what seems like a private salon for tastings of the Bordeaux-style red wines, which range from the limited-production Nicole's Red blend to the flagship Lancaster Estate cabernet.

JORDAN VINEYARD ESTATE
While Judy Jordan focuses on bubbly and pinot noir at the J Winery in the Russian River appellation, father Tom crafts rich fruit-forward cabernet sauvignon and crisp chardonnay at the château-style **Jordan Vineyard Estate** (1474 Alexander Valley Rd., Healdsburg, 707/431-5250 or 800/654-1213, www.jordanwinery.com, 11am-3pm daily in summer, 11am-3pm Mon.-Sat. fall-spring, by appointment, tasting $20, tour and tasting $30).

The beautifully manicured estate is perhaps the most picturesque winery setting in the valley and is best appreciated on the hour-long tour that culminates in a tasting of wines and the estate olive oil together with some tasty morsels of food. Cabernet lovers might want to opt for the library tasting, which includes current releases of red and white wines along with several older vintages of the estate cabernet sauvignon, accompanied by a cheese plate.

SIGHTS
The modest **Cloverdale Historical Museum** (215 N. Cloverdale Blvd., Cloverdale, 707/894-2067, www.cloverdalehistory.org, 10am-4pm Thurs. and Sat., 10am-2pm Fri., noon-4pm Sun., free) is actually the meticulously restored Gothic revival-style Gould-Shaw Victorian house and headquarters for the nonprofit Cloverdale Historical Society. The house itself is one of the oldest dwellings still standing in Cloverdale, and almost everything in it, from the iron crib to the pump organ, is from the same era, donated or borrowed from other historic homes in the area. It also houses the society's research center, with archives going back to the late 1800s, and you can pick up a guide for a short walking tour of some of the other historic Victorian homes in the town.

ENTERTAINMENT
If you can ignore the ugly concrete scar it creates halfway up the otherwise unspoiled hillside, the **River Rock Casino** (3250 Hwy. 128, Geyserville, 707/857-2777, www.riverrock-casino.com, open 24 hours) provides one of the more unusual entertainment opportunities in the county. That is, if you call winning or losing money entertainment. The casino is jointly owned by a Nevada gaming company and the Dry Creek Band of the Pomo Indian tribe. (The Pomo tribe's 85-acre Dry Creek

Rancheria, on which the casino is built, is a far cry from the vast territory of mountains and valleys in the region they used to call home.) The casino has sweeping sunset views over the vineyards of the Alexander Valley, as well as the usual array of modern amenities to help visitors part with their money, including restaurants, bars, 1,600 slot machines, and 16 tables. It's also easy to find—the entrance is right off Highway 128 about three miles south of the bridge over the river, just past the red barn on the left.

RECREATION

Some of the best outdoor pursuits can be found in the neighboring Dry Creek and Russian River Valleys, but the Alexander Valley and Chalk Hill areas do have their own unique possibilities. Although most opportunities to float on the river are focused south of Healdsburg, the stretch of Russian River between Cloverdale and Healdsburg is long, straight, and probably one of the easiest to navigate. It's also a pretty route through the vineyards.

River's Edge Kayak & Canoe Trips (13840 Healdsburg Ave., Healdsburg, 707/433-7247, www.riversedgekayakandcanoe.com, Apr.-Oct. only), at the bridge in Healdsburg, offers a couple of self-guided trips starting from either the top of the valley near Asti or halfway down and floating downstream to the beach in Healdsburg or beyond. There are a few rough patches of water but nothing worse than feeble Class I rapids. Later in the summer it will probably be a totally smooth float downstream. The full-day trips are 11-15 miles, which usually takes 4-6 hours and gives plenty of time for stopping at swimming holes along the way. The shorter trips are about half that. In all cases the price includes the rental of the kayak ($45-55/day) or canoe ($75-90/day) and a free shuttle ride upriver to start the adventure. Double kayaks are the same price as canoes.

Safari West

Cruising around the Alexander Valley in a rental car might not exactly bring to mind the savannas of Africa, unless you happen upon this little animal oasis of cheetahs, zebras, and giraffes that happily laze away in the sun just over the hill from many of Chalk Hill's wineries. The Chalk Hill appellation is the unlikely setting for the 400-acre **Safari West** wildlife preserve (3115 Porter Creek Rd., Santa Rosa, 707/579-2551 or 800/616-2695, www.safari-west.com, adults $68-80, children 3-12 $32, ages 1-2 $15), home to a wide variety of endangered species from around the world, including many from central Africa. Whether the weather in Africa is similar to northern Sonoma is somewhat irrelevant considering the apparent happiness of the animals. This is not a zoo or safari in the regular sense of the word, however. Instead, it started out in the late 1980s as a private ranch and preserve dedicated to saving endangered species from around the world. Humans were only admitted in 1993.

Seeing the magnificent beasts requires a reservation for one of the three-hour tours that set off three times a day (twice a day in winter) in a customized old jeep. The more adventurous might consider sleeping overnight in one of the luxurious tent cabins ($200-315 for two people, each extra guest $25) or cottages ($350 for two people). Lunch and dinner are available at the on-site café; wine is served, but antelope steaks are not. Because it's a working preserve, visitors get easy access to the wildlife experts who work there and who are happy to reel off fascinating facts about the animals. This little corner of wild Africa in Sonoma also provides a welcome escape from the wilds of Wine Country tourism.

ACCOMMODATIONS

The Alexander Valley has more places to stay than its rural setting and tiny towns might suggest. Most of the B&Bs are clustered up at the far northern end of the valley in the quiet cow town of Cloverdale, but there are a few worthwhile places to consider around Geyserville to the south.

Under $100

With all the B&Bs in the valley costing well over $100, it is once again left to the motels to accommodate those with tight budgets or an aversion to Victorian inns. The biggest concentration of motels (all totally unexceptional) in this area is just off the freeway on Cloverdale Boulevard (take the Citrus Fair Dr. exit) and includes the **Cloverdale Oaks Inn** (123 S. Cloverdale Blvd., 707/894-2404) and the **Best Western** (324 S. Cloverdale Blvd., 707/894-7500).

$100-200

At the lowest end of the price range is the conveniently located **Geyserville Inn** (21714 Geyserville Ave., Geyserville, 707/857-4343 or 877/857-4343, www.geyservilleinn.com, $140), a modern two-floor building resembling an upscale motel at the northern edge of Geyserville. Request an east-facing room to get a view of the vineyards and mountains rather than the freeway, which is a little too close for comfort. The larger (and more expensive) of the 38 rooms have a fireplace and many have a balcony or patio. Next door is the homey **Hoffman House Café** (21712 Geyserville Ave., Geyserville, 707/857-3264, 8am-2pm Mon.-Fri., 7:30am-2pm Sat.-Sun., $10), which serves breakfast and lunch every day.

Driving through Geyserville, it's easy to miss two bargain B&Bs among the homes along the main road, but slow down and the historic elegance of the two Victorian-style **C Hope Inns** (21253 Geyserville Ave., Geyserville, 707/857-3356 or 800/825-4233, www.hope-inns.com) becomes more obvious. The richly decorated interiors were restored in painstaking detail by the Hope family in the 1980s, and they put many of the historic Healdsburg B&Bs to shame.

There are eight guest rooms ($150-290) in the **Hope-Merrill House,** an 1870 Eastlake-style Victorian that features silk-screened wallpapers, coffered ceilings, and original woodwork. This is where the dining room (where breakfast is served), pool, and registration desk are located. Across the street is the Queen Anne-style **Hope-Bosworth House,** which has four guest rooms ($150-200) featuring the more restrained furnishings of

that period. Only one room, the sumptuous Sterling Suite in the Hope-Merrill House, has a television, though others have some features that more than compensate, from fireplaces and chaise longues to whirlpool and claw-foot tubs. Free wireless Internet access was recently added.

The huge brick fireplace in the lobby of the **Old Crocker Inn** (1126 Old Crocker Inn Rd., Cloverdale, 707/894-4000 or 800/716-2007, www.oldcrockerinn.com, $165-245), just south of Cloverdale, gives a hint of the Wild West roots of this charming lodge. It was built in the early 20th century by railway magnate Charles Crocker, founder of the Central Pacific Railroad, as a grand summer house, and the current owners have re-created the rustic character that it must originally have had—an odd blend of the Wild West and Victoriana. The biggest guest room is the namesake Crocker room, which has a massive mahogany four-poster bed, while the other four guest rooms in the main lodge building are named after Crocker's railroad partners. There are also five small cottages, two of them able to comfortably sleep four people. All the rooms have old and modern features alike, including claw-foot tubs, gas fireplaces, TVs, and Internet access. The peaceful five-acre property also has an outdoor pool and feels like it's far from the madding crowds of the Wine Country. The complimentary gourmet breakfast is served in the lodge's spacious dining room.

Camping

The valley's main campground is the **Cloverdale KOA Wine Country Campground** (1166 Asti Ridge Rd., across the River Rd. bridge from Geyserville Ave., 707/894-3337, www.winecountrykoa.com), next to the hamlet of Asti. It might be part of the KOA chain, but it is a clean, easily accessible, and family-friendly option when the sites at nearby Lake Sonoma in the Dry Creek Valley are full. It also has a well-stocked fishing pond, bicycles for rent, and a big swimming pool.

There are 47 tent sites that cost from $48, and over 100 RV sites from $55. Reserve at

800/368-4558 or www.winecountrykoa.com. The rustic little one- and two-room **Kamping Kabins** ($72-90) might also be an alternative if the local B&Bs are full, though you have to supply your own bedding. Better still are the so-called **Lodges** dotted around the hillside. Each is like a luxury mini cabin with one bedroom plus a futon sofa, a full kitchen, and a barbeque outside (but no linens or towels). They cost $190-260 and will comfortably sleep four with no extra charge.

Those with an aversion to developed campsites would do better to head 20 minutes west to **Lake Sonoma** in the Dry Creek Valley, where there are dozens of more primitive campsites, including many hike-in or boat-in sites.

FOOD
Geyserville
While most people head to Healdsburg after a day of tasting in the Alexander Valley, tiny Geyserville is increasingly becoming a secret dining destination. That may seem odd,

Catelli's is an excellent restaurant in Geyserville.

especially as there are only three restaurants in town, but they are all excellent.

ITALIAN
For a long time the renowned Taverna Santi was the heart of Geyserville's restaurant scene. **Catelli's** (21047 Geyserville Ave., Geyserville, 707/857-3471, www.mycatellis.com, 11:30am-8pm Tues.-Thurs., 11:30am-9pm Fri., noon-9pm Sat., noon-8pm Sun., $15-32) was originally opened in 1936, and now it has been reclaimed by the next generation of Catellis and rechristened under their name. It only so happens that one member of this next generation happens to be a celebrity chef who has appeared on *Iron Chef* and *Oprah*. Steering the restaurant back to her family's roots, but with an added dedication to healthy local food, Domenica Catelli and her brother, Nick, have created an earthy, high-quality Italian eatery. Homey sides like fries get a touch of truffle oil, and meatball sliders are made with local organic beef. There are plenty of pasta dishes, and entrées are happily geared toward sophisticated comfort food.

Just a few doors down from Catelli's is **Diavola** restaurant (21021 Geyserville Ave., Geyserville, 707/814-0111, www.diavolapizzeria.com, 11:30am-9pm daily, $14-25), which also dishes up seasonal Italian-inspired food served in a rustic and historic brick-walled building. However, here the action is centered around the wood-burning oven, which produces amazing thin-crust pizzas. And then there is the chef's true passion: butchering and curing meat, skills he developed during his seven-year-long apprenticeship in Italy. That is why you'll find traditional dishes accented with items such as crispy pork belly or pork cheek. If you can't decide between these two stellar Italian restaurants, Diavola is the only one open for lunch, which means you can fill up on one of their lunch sandwiches, like the tender and flavorful Philly cheese steak, venture out, taste some wine, and finish the evening at Catelli's.

BREAKFAST
For breakfast, the place to go (in fact the only place), is the **Hoffman House Café** (21712

Geyserville Ave., Geyserville, 707/857-3264, 8am-2pm Mon.-Fri., 7:30am-2pm Sat.-Sun., $10), a little farther north on Geyserville Avenue. While it may be the only place to get a plate of eggs, fortunately everything on the menu is great. Hearty plates of crab cake omelets, vanilla French toast, and breakfast burritos pair perfectly with the sunny wrap-around porch of the Craftsman-style building. If you are too late for breakfast, try one of the Grown-Up Grilled Cheese sandwiches or the truffle mac and cheese (winter only), or simply go for the burger. Either way, you can't go wrong. Besides, there is plenty of espresso, mimosas, or Bloody Marys to wash anything down.

PICNIC SUPPLIES

It may not look like much, but the **Geyserville Market & Deli** (21010 Geyserville Ave., 707/431-7090, 9am-5pm daily) has just about everything you need for snacks or a picnic lunch in Alexander Valley. The deli has a great assortment of local cheeses, plus freshly made sandwiches that are well below the $10 mark. Boxed lunches are also available as are local wines, many of which you can't find outside the area. Across the street, you can also pick up supplies at **Diavola** (21021 Geyserville Ave., Geyserville, 707/814-0111, www.diavolapizzeria.com, 11:30am-9pm daily). Just inside the door is a deli case full of the house-made sausages, pork belly along with a half a dozen different sauces. While many of these may not be best for a picnic without a barbecue present, the containers of pickled white anchovies, marinated olives, roasted peppers, and even the guinea ham terrine certainly would be.

The premier spot to go, in fact *the* place to make a detour for, is the bright yellow and green **Jimtown Store** (6706 Hwy. 128 at Alexander Valley Rd., Healdsburg, 707/433-1212, 7:30am-5pm daily in summer, check website for winter hours), with its bright red vintage pickup truck parked outside. It's a valley fixture and seems to sell a bit of everything, including its own label wine. The boxed lunches alone are worth a detour and include a fat gourmet baguette sandwich, cookies, salad, and fruit, all for less than $14.

FARMERS MARKET

Despite its location in the heart of farming country, **Geyserville's Farmers Market** runs only on the last Thursday of the month 5pm-8pm June-October at the parking lot of the Geyserville Inn at 21714 Geyserville Avenue.

Cloverdale

The hard-working farm town of Cloverdale may not be quite the culinary destination of Healdsburg or even Geyserville, but you can certainly find a decent burger, plate of barbecue, or even a filling burrito along North Cloverdale Boulevard in the heart of town. Still, a couple of standouts have arrived recently.

CAFÉS

Plank Coffee (227 N. Cloverdale Blvd., Cloverdale, 707/894-6187, 6am-6pm Mon.-Sat., 7am-5pm Sun.) adds a touch of style to the 1950s vibe of downtown Cloverdale. With vintage red leather-clad chairs, a heavy brushed-metal communal table, and tons and tons of wood in all shapes, colors, and finishes everywhere else, Plank earns its name. The coffee, however, is how it gets its reputation. Locally roasted Flying Goat Coffee is pulled for espresso drinks and French-pressed into pots perfect to share and sip alongside pastries freshly baked in the back. If you are not a coffee lover, the café makes its own chai and seasonal Italian sodas. Either way, a seat at one of the beautiful tables made from reclaimed wood or beneath a bright red umbrella at one of the sidewalk tables is the perfect place to watch the business of a small unpretentious town go by.

THAI

101 Thai Way (1198 S. Cloverdale Blvd., Cloverdale, 707/894-9999, www.101thaiway.com, 11:30am-9pm daily, $11-17) has been luring locals from Healdsburg and beyond to its unappealing location in a tiny strip mall off the freeway. But once you take your first bite of food, you'll see why. The fairly standard Thai menu (soups, curries, and noodle dishes) is executed with tons of fresh vegetables and bright spices. A local favorite is the Spicy Seafood Sizzling in which an assortment of shellfish is sautéed with pumpkin, chili paste, and basil. Another is the pan-fried Drunken Noodles with egg, tomato, and bell pepper. Ironic, don't you think?

FARMERS MARKET
Things are a little more festive at the **Cloverdale farmers market**. On Friday evenings 5:30pm-9pm June-September, Cloverdale Boulevard between 1st and 2nd Streets is closed off. More than 50 vendors show up as does, it seems, every resident in town.

INFORMATION AND SERVICES
More information about the history and businesses of Cloverdale and Geyserville can be obtained from their respective chambers of commerce. The **Geyserville Chamber of Commerce** (707/857-3745, www.geyservillecc.com) is not open to the public but has an excellent website. The **Cloverdale Chamber of Commerce** (126 N. Cloverdale Blvd., Cloverdale, 707/894-4470, www.cloverdale.net) is next to city hall. It has maps, guides, and discount vouchers for anyone planning to explore northern Sonoma and Mendocino wineries. Another resource for the area's wines together with a comprehensive winery map can be found on the **Alexander Valley Winegrowers Association** website (www.alexandervalley.org).

GETTING THERE AND AROUND
Geyserville is located where Highway 128 meets U.S. Highway 101. It is 25 miles north of Calistoga, and 8 and 21 miles north of Healdsburg and Santa Rosa, respectively. Cloverdale is only another 10 miles farther north. Like the Dry Creek Valley, the Alexander Valley is fairly easy to navigate. Most of the wineries are located just off Highway 128, which travels all the way to Calistoga, or off Geyserville Avenue, which hugs U.S. Highway 101 to Alexander Valley Road, eventually becoming Healdsburg Avenue.

www.moon.com

DESTINATIONS | ACTIVITIES | BLOGS | MAPS | BOOKS

MOON.COM is ready to help plan your next trip! Filled with fresh trip ideas and strategies, author interviews, informative travel blogs, a detailed map library, and descriptions of all the Moon guidebooks, Moon.com is all you need to get out and explore the world—or even places in your own backyard. While at Moon.com, sign up for our monthly e-newsletter for updates on new releases, travel tips, and expert advice from our on-the-go Moon authors. As always, when you travel with Moon, expect an experience that is uncommon and truly unique.

KEEP UP WITH MOON ON FACEBOOK AND TWITTER
JOIN THE MOON PHOTO GROUP ON FLICKR

MAP SYMBOLS

Expressway	Highlight	Airfield	Golf Course
Primary Road	City/Town	Airport	Parking Area
Secondary Road	State Capital	Mountain	Archaeological Site
Unpaved Road	National Capital	Unique Natural Feature	Church
Trail	Point of Interest		Gas Station
Ferry	Accommodation	Waterfall	Glacier
Railroad	Restaurant/Bar	Park	Mangrove
Pedestrian Walkway	Other Location	Trailhead	Reef
Stairs	Campground	Skiing Area	Swamp

CONVERSION TABLES

°C = (°F - 32) / 1.8
°F = (°C x 1.8) + 32
1 inch = 2.54 centimeters (cm)
1 foot = 0.304 meters (m)
1 yard = 0.914 meters
1 mile = 1.6093 kilometers (km)
1 km = 0.6214 miles
1 fathom = 1.8288 m
1 chain = 20.1168 m
1 furlong = 201.168 m
1 acre = 0.4047 hectares
1 sq km = 100 hectares
1 sq mile = 2.59 square km
1 ounce = 28.35 grams
1 pound = 0.4536 kilograms
1 short ton = 0.90718 metric ton
1 short ton = 2,000 pounds
1 long ton = 1.016 metric tons
1 long ton = 2,240 pounds
1 metric ton = 1,000 kilograms
1 quart = 0.94635 liters
1 US gallon = 3.7854 liters
1 Imperial gallon = 4.5459 liters
1 nautical mile = 1.852 km

MOON SPOTLIGHT SONOMA VALLEY

Avalon Travel
a member of the Perseus Books Group
1700 Fourth Street
Berkeley, CA 94710, USA
www.moon.com

Editors: Erin Raber, Sabrina Young
Series Manager: Kathryn Ettinger
Copy Editor: Ann Seifert
Production and Graphics Coordinator: Darren Alessi
Cover Designer: Darren Alessi
Map Editor: Albert Angulo
Cartographers: Stephanie Poulain, Brian Shotwell,
 Kat Bennett

ISBN-13: 978-1-59880-678-6

Text © 2013 by Avalon Travel.
Maps © 2013 by Avalon Travel.
All rights reserved.

Some photos and illustrations are used by permission
 and are the property of the original copyright
 owners.

Front cover photo: Sonoma Vineyard
6287534 © Ron Kacmarcik | istockphoto.com
Title page photo: © Teodora George/123rf.com

Printed in the United States

All recommendations, including those for sights,
activities, hotels, restaurants, and shops, are based
on each author's individual judgment. We do not
accept payment for inclusion in our travel guides,
and our authors don't accept free goods or services
in exchange for positive coverage.

KEEPING CURRENT

If you have a favorite gem you'd like to see included in the next edition, or see anything
that needs updating, clarification, or correction, please drop us a line. Send your com-
ments via email to feedback@moon.com, or use the address above.

ABOUT THE AUTHOR

© GERRIT VENEMAN

Elizabeth Linhart Veneman

Elizabeth Linhart Veneman has always viewed growing up in Northern California as both a blessing and curse. There is so much to see, do, and experience all within a short drive – from broad sequoias in the Sierra to ancient lava beds north of Mount Shasta, from creaky Gold Rush towns to the pampering Wine Country – that she began to wonder why anyone would ever leave.

Elizabeth was eventually lured out of the Golden State to Alaska's far north, where she traveled the Inside Passage, baked bread under the midnight sun in Denali National Park, and chronicled the state's burgeoning sustainable agriculture for *Alaska Magazine*. These adventures culminated in penning *InsightGuides: Alaska*.

But Elizabeth knew her California roots were too deep to stay away for long. Raised in Carmel, where her great-great grandmother opened the town's first restaurant (a soup kitchen with dirt floors!) at the turn of the 20th century, she will always call California home. So she returned and devoted herself to writing about the state she loves most. Her work has included *SmartGuide: San Francisco* and *InsightGuides: San Francisco*. She also reports on food and sustainable agriculture for local publications.

Elizabeth currently lives with her family in San Francisco.